Letters to Amanda

Marion Hill Fitzpatrick, twenty-five years-old. Circa 1860.
Photographic Reproduction by Rene Victor Bidez, Fayetteville, Georgia.

Letters to Amanda

The Civil War Letters of Marion Hill Fitzpatrick, Army of Northern Virginia

Edited by
Jeffrey C. Lowe and Sam Hodges

Mercer University Press
Macon, Georgia

©1998 Mercer University Press
6316 Peake Road
Macon, Georgia 31210
All rights reserved
0-86554-591-X
MUP/H444

Second Printing May 1999

∞ The paper used in this publication meets the minimum
requirements of the American National Standard for
Information Sciences—Permanence of Paper for Printed
Library Materials, ANSI Z39.48–1984.

Endleaves: detail from map carried by
M. H. Fitzpatrick during the war.

Library of Congress Cataloging-in-Publication Data
Fitzpatrick, Marion Hill, d. 1865
Letters to Amanda: the Civil War letters of Marion Hill Fitzpatrick, Army of
Northern Virginia / edited by Jeffrey C. Lowe and Sam Hodges. — 1st ed.
p. cm.
Includes bibliographical references and index.
ISBN 0-86554-591-X (alk. paper)
1. Fitzpatrick, Marion Hill, d. 1865—Correspondence. 2. Confederate States of
America. Army. Georgia Infantry Regiment, 45th. 3. Soldiers—Georgia—
Crawford County—Correspondence. 4. United States—History—Civil War,
1861-1865—Personal narratives, Confederate. 5. Georgia—History—Civil War,
1861-1865—Personal narratives. 6. United Staes—History—Civil War, 1861-
1865—Regimental histories. 7. Georgia—History—Civil War, 1861-1865—
Regimental histories. 8 Crawford County (Ga.)—Biography. I. Lowe, Jeffrey C. II.
Hodges, Sam. III. Title.
E559.5 45th. F58 1998
973.7'82—dc21
[b]
98-36817
CIP

Table of Contents

Foreword

Marion Hill Fitzpatrick and his wife Amanda White Fitzpatrick experienced the full brunt of the Civil War. He fought with the 45th Georgia Infantry in the Army of Northern Virginia from the Seven Days through the fall of Richmond, while she struggled, together with their young son, to cope with hardship and separation on the family's farm in Georgia. His letters to her provide an excellent window on the life of the common soldier in Robert E. Lee's army, illuminating the detail of camp life, the hardships of active campaigning, and the brutality and harsh consequences of battle. Because Fitzpatrick responded to many of Amanda's comments in her part of their correspondence, his letters also reveal a good deal about the Confederate home front. "Many a soldier can now realize the value of women's work," he wrote in the spring of 1863 after cataloging the many tasks she carried out, "that thought but little or nothing about it before the war commenced."

Anyone interested in the topics of Confederate morale or national sentiment will find these letters especially enlightening. Fitzpatrick sustained wounds at Glendale on June 30, 1862, and at Fredericksburg on December 13, 1862. He wrote often about insufficient clothing, poor footwear, and scanty rations. He expressed anguish at his inability to assist Amanda as she labored to manage the family and farm. More than once he read passages in her letters urging him to bend every effort to come home. Over the course of about three years in the army, he received just two furloughs. In short, Fitzpatrick endured much that could have eroded his commitment to fight on for Confederate victory and independence. Yet he maintained a high degree of national loyalty and consistently urged Amanda to do the same. In a typical passage, written just before the battle of Chancellorsville, he told her to "expect hard times" but added that "we must bear up under them with fortitude and be willing to suffer almost anything, to gain our liberty." A few days after Chancellorsville he noted that soldiers who skulked during the battle had been put on trial. "So help me God . . . ," he stated, "my bones will bleech the hills of Virginia before they shall have me up for that." As late as January 7, 1865, he refused to acknowledge that defeat was certain. Things looked dark, he conceded, and many Confederates desponded. But if "croakers would but consider a moment the consequences of subjugation," he insisted, "they would certainly talk different."

How pervasive was sentiment such as Fitzpatrick's? It is impossible to know with certainty. He claimed in his letter of January 7, 1865, that "a large number" of his comrades had "resolved to die rather than submit to Yankee rule, and never, never give it up." Whatever the number of soldiers and civilians in the Confederacy who shared this attitude, Fitzpatrick's letters should give pause to those who argue that most white southerners began to lose faith in their cause after the summer of 1863.

Apart from their value in chronicling a common soldier's activities and attitudes during three tumultuous years, these letters offer memorable vignettes of events and famous personalities. Fitzpatrick commented about the Seven Days, Second Manassas, Fredericksburg, Chancellorsville, the Overland campaign, and Petersburg. He described feeling in the ranks toward Robert E. Lee, Stonewall Jackson, and other leaders. He left no doubt of the central role religion played in the lives of countless mid-19th-century Americans, as well as the inestimable importance of home and family. In short, this excellent testimony does more than help us, at a distance of more than a century and a third, understand the day-to-day process by which soldiers went about the business of living and campaigning. It also illuminates the broader context of the world in which the Fitzpatricks and millions of other Civil War-era Americans lived. Happily available in a fully annotated edition for the first time, these letters will reward in ample measure those who traverse the war alongside Sergeant Major Fitzpatrick.

Gary W. Gallagher
Charlottesville, Virginia
July 1998

Introduction

The stakes could hardly have been higher for Marion Hill Fitzpatrick when he left Crawford County, Georgia, in May 1862 to join the Confederate Army in Virginia. He had a wife of eighteen, a son of under one year, a widowed mother, a farm, and a store.

Letters became crucial. They were the sole way, apart from the occasional furloughed soldier going to or from Central Georgia, of staying in touch with home. Fitzpatrick wrote to let his family know he was alive, and to make sure they were. He wrote to influence the operation of the farm and the rearing of his son. Through letters he requested of his wife, Amanda, important foodstuffs and essential clothing. He used letters to reassure and sympathize with her, knowing his absence had profoundly increased her load. Letters also gave Fitzpatrick an occasion—perhaps an excuse—to reflect on what he was experiencing, thinking and feeling as he persevered in a war that was at once the great adventure and tragedy of his life.

For all these reasons—and probably also because he liked to write, and knew he was good at it—Fitzpatrick wrote home nearly every chance he had. He wrote even when it meant begging paper and turning polk berries into ink. "The boys sometimes laugh at me for writing home so often," he wrote Amanda on January 5, 1863, "but I think I know best about that."

Readers should know that we, the two editors of this edition of *Letters to Amanda*, are great-great grandsons of Fitzpatrick. We are not out to burnish our academic reputations—we don't have any—but rather to join in a family tradition of sharing our ancestor's valuable epistolary witness to the Civil War. That war continues to provoke emotional argument, and these letters, like every other pertinent document, will be seized on as evidence by those of hardened opinion. But we believe open-minded, empathetic readers are likely to fall under the letters' spell, and to conclude with us that Marion Hill Fitzpatrick rose to the occasion of the Civil War, both as soldier and as correspondent.

At age twenty-seven, Fitzpatrick joined the 45th Georgia Volunteer Infantry Regiment, Company K, an assembly of several dozen young men, almost all of them from Crawford County. He stayed with that outfit until the end. He began as private and regular infantryman but soon volunteered to be a skirmisher. As the war progressed, he was appointed sergeant major and assigned to the regimental staff. He fought at the Seven Days Battles, Second Manassas, Fredericksburg,

Chancellorsville, the Wilderness, Spottsylvania, Hanover Junction, Second Cold Harbor, and Petersburg. He was hospitalized several times, both for illnesses and gunshot wounds. The Confederate Congress honored him, of all the members of his company, for valor at the Battle of Chancellorsville.

He must have written hundreds of letters while away at war. Exactly one hundred from him to his wife Amanda have survived. Few if any Confederate soldiers of middle class background are represented by so extensive, accessible, and moving a collection. That the letters are to a single intimate correspondent, covering so much of the war, distinguishes them further.

Because we are family, and cannot help ourselves, let us put forward additional specific reasons for why these letters deserve to be read. First, Fitzpatrick's letters constitute a remarkable text from which to understand the daily life of a Confederate soldier. They could serve as a reenactor's handbook or an appendix to Bell Wiley's *The Life of Johnny Reb*, so full are they of detail about the struggle to stay fed, clothed, sheltered, and whole. The letters include a handful of vivid battle descriptions. They are at least as good about life in camp, on the march, in the hospital, on return from furlough. Fitzpatrick seems to have had and written about nearly every war experience except that of prisoner. But he captured one. "I took a prisoner about dark, a great big strapping fellow weighing about 200 lbs.," he wrote to Amanda on September 2, 1862. "I marched him in with some little pride."

Less directly, but no less importantly, Fitzpatrick's letters illuminate the experience of women back home. The Civil War brought about a role reversal in his marriage and no doubt in the marriages of many thousands of other soldiers. Fitzpatrick joins the Confederate army, probably dreaming of battlefield glory, and immediately finds himself assigned to nurse a dying friend and fellow company member. Later, his cooking and sewing skills improve to the point that he makes extra money baking pies and patching uniforms. Meanwhile, Amanda is overseeing the planting and harvesting of crops, and the slaughtering of hogs. Her centrality is not lost on Fitzpatrick. "You must be the man and woman both now you know," he wrote her on December 16, 1863.

Along with what they say about hard experience, Fitzpatrick's letters bear witness to the beliefs, values, and attitudes of the Southern soldier. This second claim is trickier. Fitzpatrick was no Confederate Everyman. But given that he stayed in for the duration, earned promotions and special assignments, enjoyed a wide range of friendships within and without his regiment, and rarely used his letters to criticize a fellow soldier, commanding officer or political leader, it is safe to assume that he was no rebel within the Rebel army, but rather reflected mainstream views.

Certainly his letters can be studied for what they say about religious faith among Confederates, and how that grew in intensity as prospects for victory declined. They point to what must have been a commonly felt tension between the desire to conduct oneself honorably and the desire to survive. Fitzpatrick was preoccupied with honor and manhood.

The letters also challenge the notion that rank-and-file Confederates considered this a "rich man's war and poor man's fight." Indeed, they are notable for their lack of cynicism, and for their impatience with anyone who isn't conforming in the interest of victory.

Fitzpatrick's letters suggest that for the common solider the Confederate cause embraced, but was not confined to, preservation of slavery. Fitzpatrick came from a small slave-holding family and from a region where slavery undergirded the agricultural economy. If slavery troubled his very large Christian conscience, the evidence is not in these letters. They include numerous references to race relations, all either taking for granted or defending Old South ways, occasionally in language even his most favorably-disposed reader will find harsh.

But the letters also are insistent on the Southern states' right to control their destiny. This theme—complete with the use of the word "liberty"—comes up time and again. It could be argued that this is just a covering rhetoric, but a common soldier like Fitzpatrick, writing uncensored to an intimate like Amanda, would have had no need for propaganda. He seems truly to have believed that military action to prevent secession was a monstrous Northern wrong.

It is worth noting that Fitzpatrick joins the debate about whether slaves should be armed and enlisted in his army. In a late letter to Amanda, he agrees they should be. Presumably he knew that the deal, at least as conceived by Robert E. Lee, was freedom in exchange for military service. Fitzpatrick would have accepted that. Southern independence was a large and controlling goal for him and many thousands like him. "I have no distant dream of ever giving up," he wrote Amanda on January 1, 1865. "Yankees may kill me but will never subjugate me."

The third and best reason to read these letters stands apart from what they say about the Confederate experience and mind. It is that the letters are, quite simply, a pleasure to read. There's a gathering tenderness to them. Fitzpatrick often calls Amanda "Cout," and he almost always refers to their son Henry as "my darling boy" or, even more winningly, "my noble boy." The letters could shame many a published novel for what they offer in character, atmosphere, incident, and suspense. Certainly Fitzpatrick will pass most readers' test as protagonist. He goes through so much, and with such resilience of spirit, that one becomes invested in his fate. And he could write! From time to time he puffed up into artificial lyricism, but almost always he composed a clear, straightforward prose that beautifully reveals him and his situation.

His best lines stick:

"I have changed much in my feelings. The bombs and balls excite me but little and a battlefield strewed with dead and wounded is an everyday consequence." . . . "None but those that have been to Richmond can know how mean a place it is or how glad a man is to get away from there." . . . "I think and highly hope that this war will end this year, and Oh then what a happy time we will have. No need of writing then but we can talk and talk again, and my boy can talk to me and I will never tire of listening to him and he will want to go with me everywhere I go, and I will be certain to let him go if there is any possible chance."

That voice—that man—compels and rewards a reader's attention.

———————————

Marion Hill Fitzpatrick was born on March 15, 1835, in Macon County, Georgia, south and west of the important Central Georgia city of Macon. He was the eighth of nine surviving children of Alexander Fitzpatrick (1791-1849) and Nancy Hill Fitzpatrick (1795-1875). The last three—Alex, Marion Hill, and James G. or "Doc"—were close in age and maintained a close relationship through the Civil War. Marion Hill almost certainly got his first name from Francis Marion, the Revolutionary War hero. But friends and family called him "Hill."

Of his mother's family we know discouragingly little. Drawing from family histories and the few available records, we can say with some confidence that Nancy Hill Fitzpatrick's parents, James and Elizabeth Hill, came to Greene County, Georgia, from Mecklenburg County, Virginia, in the late 18th century. They died in Greene County when Nancy and her younger sister Elizabeth were young. Greene County records suggest a William Hubbard stepped in as guardian. But further information about him, or about Nancy's life until she married, has proved elusive.

The Fitzpatricks are better documented, having arrived in Virginia from Ireland early in the 18th century and pushed on to Georgia a generation later. They could claim modest distinction as early white settlers of Greene and Morgan Counties, in the central eastern part of the state. Benjamin Fitzpatrick (1745-1821), Alexander's father and Hill's grandfather, joined the Revolutionary Army. Morgan County records suggest he became a significant land and slave owner, and he is credited with helping found the little Morgan County town of Buckhead, on the west side of the Oconee River. A more famous "Benjamin Fitzpatrick," part of the extended family, moved to Alabama and became an antebellum governor and US Senator of that state.

Alexander Fitzpatrick and Nancy Hill married in Morgan County on Feb. 27, 1813. They soon moved south and west to Macon County, and had children. Fitzpatrick followed his father's lead in acquiring land and slaves. At least once a "fortunate drawer" in the state's land lotteries, he owned, according to the 1838 Macon County tax digest, almost 2,000 acres in three Georgia counties, and fourteen slaves.

The family moved to nearby Crawford County in 1843, when Alexander Fitzpatrick traded for 607 1/2 acres there. His fortunes appear to have remained good through 1845, when the Crawford County tax digest has him owning about 1,500 acres in five Georgia counties, and twelve slaves.

But something happened. Perhaps he had crop failures, or overextended in buying land, or both. But in September 1846 he sold two-thirds of the Crawford County acreage. Two years later he took out a security deed for $178 on the rest of it. He had apparently sold most or all of the land he owned in other counties to cover debts. Alexander Fitzpatrick died in 1849, and his estate records speak sympathetically but pointedly of a "reversal in fortune." The 1850 Census finds Nancy Hill Fitzpatrick living on the greatly-reduced Crawford County farm with teenage sons Alex, Hill, and Doc, and four slaves.

These days Crawford County consists in large measure of loblolly pine plantations owned by remote paper companies. But before the Civil War, and well into the 20th century, farm yielded to farm. The Fitzpatricks lived in the northwest or piedmont part of Crawford, just above the geographical "fall line," on rolling clay land that was neither the worst nor best in the county for growing the principal cash crop: cotton. Their community, one of many that dotted Crawford County, was called Hickory Grove.

Two documents helped us understand better antebellum Crawford County. The first was written by Thomas Marshall Green, currently a lawyer in Roberta, the county's largest town. He wrote his 1978 senior thesis at Harvard College on Crawford's history and politics from 1822 to 1861, with particular emphasis on small slaveholders like the Fitzpatricks. We also were fortunate to obtain a copy of an unpublished diary kept from 1861 to 1863 by Benjamin Thomas Smisson, a Crawford Countian who served with Fitzpatrick in Company K of the 45th Georgia.

Smisson's diary (a subject-in-waiting for historians) makes clear the intensely agricultural character of the county before the war. His brief, almost telegraphic, entries speak to the specific tasks required for growing cotton, corn, sweet potatoes, wheat, and other crops. They suggest understandable concern about rainfall and the weather generally. Smisson's seemingly relentless field work is broken mainly by hunting, fishing, church-going (he attends different local primitive Baptist churches, on a schedule which suggests each had services once a month), and in winter by attendance at occasional "frolics" and plays.

Green's paper adds complexity to the portrait of this apparently static agricultural community. According to Green, many people passed through Crawford on their way to even more frontier-like country in the west, and some, disappointed, came back through on the heavily trafficked main roads. Railroads were expanding rapidly through Central Georgia, with Macon connected to the cotton port of Savannah by 1843. Both Macon and nearby Columbus were rising textile manufacturing centers.

The sectional conflicts that would bring about the Civil War certainly reverberated in Crawford County. As both the Green paper and Smisson diary note, Crawford had its runaway slaves and rumors of insurrection. Leading men of the county—both large and small slave-owners—participated fully in the tortured politics that led to secession. Smisson's diary, in between such entries as "pulled fodder" and "went to mill," dispassionately records musterings, political meetings and Confederate volunteers heading off to war.

Before the Civil War, Crawford County was an agrarian community in flux and under stress. And it was Marion Hill Fitzpatrick's world as a teenage boy and young man. As to specific episodes of his early life, we are almost empty-handed. Nor can we say how much of a shadow was cast by his father's "reversal in fortune." We can assume that a boy in his situation, even with slaves about, would have learned farming, hunting, fishing, and other self-sufficiency skills. Beyond that, the best we can do is speculate about influences. Family, church, and education would have to rank high.

As his letters attest, Fitzpatrick remained close not only to his mother and two nearest-in-age brothers, but also to other siblings, aunts, uncles, and cousins. An uncle, Bennett Fitzpatrick, lived in Crawford County with his wife and their children. Other relatives lived in neighboring counties. A particular favorite was Louisa Greene, the "Lou" of these letters who was in fact Marion Hill Fitzpatrick's niece, but only three years his junior.

The Fitzpatricks were dedicated church-goers, and references to Elim Baptist Church abound in the letters. Elim, a Missionary Baptist church located near the Fitzpatrick farm, had both slave-owners and slaves among its members. Nancy Hill Fitzpatrick is listed in church minutes as having joined in 1843, the year the family moved to the county. Husband Alexander is not listed in the minutes, but is buried in the church graveyard. Brothers Alex and Hill would, as young men, serve Elim as church clerks and as delegates to Missionary Baptist association meetings.

Exactly where Hill Fitzpatrick got his sturdy formal education, we cannot say. A handful of private schools existed in Crawford County before the war. Very probably he attended one or more of them. Certainly the importance of education in the Fitzpatrick family is unmistakable. An early Morgan County record lists Alexander Fitzpatrick as trustee of a private school. His estate records show he owned both a bookcase and a "lot" of books. Hill's older brother, Benjamin, left Georgia for a school-teaching job in Mississippi well before the Civil War. Their brother Alex appears to have been a teacher in Knoxville, the Crawford County seat, as late as 1860. A Crawford County cousin, Emily Fitzpatrick, taught school.

Hill did too, possibly in Crawford County, definitely in Texas. For most of our time researching these letters, we assumed provincially that he had never been out of Georgia before joining the Confederate Army. But then, casting about on the Internet, we found a reference to a Marion Hill Fitzpatrick having taught school in Cass County, Texas, in 1856. A friend who grew up in northeast Texas put us in touch with Charles A. Steger, a Cass County historian, who further astonished us by saying he had a dictionary and logbook of Fitzpatrick's. The latter showed that in 1856 he spent about two weeks traveling west on horseback. Fastidiously recording expenditures for tolls and forage, he took the "Texas Road" through west Georgia, Alabama, Mississippi, and Louisiana, arriving finally in northeast Texas. There he taught school in the town of Linden, near the farm of his older sister Sarah Fitzpatrick Law, who had migrated from Georgia with her husband, Henry, in 1853. Going off to war was Hill Fitzpatrick's second big adventure. Texas came first.

Fitzpatrick returned to Crawford County in 1858, and must have begun at once to court his neighbor and fellow church member, young Amanda Elizabeth White. She was the fourth of nine children born to Alley Rowe White and William Benjamin White, Sr. The Whites were prosperous, owning 525 acres and nineteen slaves. They lived near the Fitzpatricks in Hickory Grove, and were early members of Elim Missionary Baptist.

In one of his Civil War letters to Amanda, Hill Fitzpatrick reminds her that she rejected his first offer of marriage. Age might have been the reason. She was just sixteen when they did marry, on February 26, 1860. Fitzpatrick was a hoary twenty-five.

A close reading of *Letters to Amanda* suggests they occupied a house very near his mother's, in Hickory Grove. They probably lived on her land. Along with farming, and possibly teaching school, Fitzpatrick operated some kind of business. Family legend calls it a store. He and Amanda remained active in Elim Baptist, and he joined the nearby Masonic Lodge, as did brother Alex.

On June 28, 1861, Amanda gave birth to a son, Henry Thomas Fitzpatrick. The birth came six months after Georgia seceded, and two months after Confederates fired on Fort Sumter.

Fitzpatrick waited almost another year to join the Confederate Army. His younger and unattached brother, Doc, left first, enlisting in the 27th Georgia Volunteer Infantry Regiment, Company C, on September 10, 1861. The Smisson diary records the leaving of other individuals and units, often to fanfare.

One can easily imagine the pressures Hill Fitzpatrick faced, both to go and to stay. He was a depended-upon husband and father. But he was also a Southern patriot and the grandson of a Revolutionary soldier. The threat of conscription may have forced his hand. He chose, about the time the conscription bill became law, to join the 45th Georgia Volunteer Infantry. Company K—the Ray Guards, they called themselves—appears to have left Crawford County in early April 1862. Fitzpatrick lingered a few more days, then with Smisson and a handful of others traveled by rail from Macon to Virginia. It was in Richmond, before he formally enlisted at nearby Camp Anderson, that he wrote the first of the surviving letters to Amanda.

For more than a century, Fitzpatrick's letters went unread except by a few family members in Central Georgia. Then in 1975, Mansel Hammock—a grandson of the soldier, and our great uncle—fulfilled a long dream of seeing them published. Ably assisted by family members Reba Bush (who transcribed from the originals) and Raymond Rigdon (who helped with editing and printing), Hammock brought out his own plain, soft-cover volume called *Letters to Amanda*. The first edition, just 300 copies, sold out.

Rigdon did a re-printing of one-hundred copies in 1982, three years after Hammock's death. These all sold too. The letters remained out of print for ten years until yet another descendant, Henry Vaughan McCrea, published his own historical-biographical-novel account of

Fitzpatrick, *Red Dirt and Isinglass*, with the letters included as an appendix.

These home-made efforts—labors of love, all—were the little bit of help Fitzpatrick's letters needed. Our first indication that they had taken root came a few years back at a Civil War reenactment. One of us had gone as spectator, and during a break struck up a conversation with a gray-clad participant. Mention was made of *Letters to Amanda*. The reenactor brightened, volunteering that he and everyone in his outfit had read and loved it. They had passed around a single, dog-eared photo-copy.

Following this intriguing bit of intelligence, the other of us noticed that Ernest Furgurson's *Chancellorsville 1863* quoted from Fitzpatrick's eyewitness account of the battle. That was the first we'd heard of one of the letters surfacing in a bona fide history book. Feeling a bit caught off guard, we began to check around at libraries and bookstores. We found that John Hennessey's *Return to Bull Run* also quoted from a Fitzpatrick letter. Other discoveries followed. To date, we have counted nine recent books, by such noted authors as Stephen Sears and Gary Gallagher, that draw on Fitzpatrick.

It was pleasing to learn that individual Fitzpatrick letters were serving Civil War history. But we knew they carried far more power read one after the other. That was how they made a claim beyond utility—a claim for a place in Civil War literature.

We began to consider whether it might be our time to do right by our ancestor's letters. We had been college students when they were first published. Now we had cleared forty and settled into occupations (pastor and reporter) that involved research, writing, and editing. We certainly had less of an excuse not to act than had Mansel Hammock, a farmer and businessman, back in the 1970s. Moreover, our faith in the letters as valuable and captivating increased with each re-reading. Doing right by them, we concluded, meant getting them back into print as a collection, preferably with a university press, definitely with their first-ever footnotes, identifying (to the extent possible) obscure references and providing sufficient military context for the general reader.

That is what we have tried to do with this new edition of *Letters to Amanda*.

Acknowledgments

Though we have taken the lead in preparing this edition, we have had been backed up and sometimes pushed forward by many good people.

Our spouses, Ann Lowe and Kit Lively, listened with patience as we jabbered on about every incremental research development. They also gave good advice on editorial considerations. Our mothers, Marion Hodges and Frances Lowe, were a constant source of encouragement. Marion Hodges also turned up important family history documents and artifacts, and put us in touch with family members we had not known well.

No one in the family has been anything other than supportive. At the risk of omitting someone, we list the following family members and close friends as having provided specific help of one kind or another: Raymond Rigdon, Hartford Green, Hill Hammock, Jane Brooks, Jan Lowe, Vally Sharpe, June Kosciuszco, Bill Hodges, Carl Hodges, Amanda Hodges, Julie Hodges, Polly Hodges, Martha Lowe, and Henry Vaughan McCrea.

In Crawford County and environs, we were very lucky to get to know David Lee, Thomas Green, Bobby Stokes, and Constance Fleeman. They helped us understand local history, geography, agriculture and family connections.

The late Robert G. Jordan, Jr., of Memphis, transcribed and edited the fascinating diary of his great-grandfather, Benjamin T. Smisson, who was in the 45th Georgia, Company K, with Marion Hill Fitzpatrick. Robert Jordan's son, Alfred Jordan, kindly made available to us a copy of the edited Smisson diary.

Charles Steger of Atlanta, Texas, was an invaluable source on Fitzpatrick's time as a schoolteacher in northeast Texas. Without his research and writing, we would never have known that Fitzpatrick had ventured from Georgia before the war.

Much of our research was conducted at the Georgia Department of Archives and History in Atlanta. We wish to thank the staff there, particularly Elizabeth Knowlton. Charlotte Ray, retired director, also provided key research suggestions.

Other experts who helped us include: William Reynolds of Southwestern Baptist Theological Seminary in Fort Worth, Texas; Art Bergeron, historian at Pamplin Park in Petersburg, Virginia; Frederick Schmidt, archivist at Montpelier in Orange County, Virginia; Martha Wilson of Historic Jonesboro, in Jonesboro, Georgia; Fred Anderson, director of the Virginia Baptist Historical Society in Richmond; John

Coski, historian of the Museum of the Confederacy in Richmond; Myers Brown, assistant military curator of the Atlanta History Center; Susan Broome, director of special collections at the Mercer University Main Library; Joan Clemens, archivist at the Pitts Theological Library of Emory University in Atlanta; Pat Taylor, cemeteries administrator for the city of Richmond; and the excellent staff of the genealogical room in the Washington Memorial Library in Macon, Georgia.

Further assistance came from the Clopton Family Association, Lee Nelson, Clint Johnson, Evelyn Pulliam Blackwood, Charles Smith, Carlton Ethridge, Mark Thomas, Linda Murphy, Rob Gavin, Catherine Jennings, Scott Hudgins, Terry Ford, Damon Fowler, and Ruby Love. Marc Jolley, of Mercer University Press, has been an enthusiastic and accessible editor.

Finally, we wish to acknowledge our employers, the First Baptist Church of Riverdale and the *Mobile Register*, for indulging our somewhat divided attention for the last year and a half.

THE FITZPATRICK FAMILY

Marion Hill Fitzpatrick—The letter writer. Farmer, teacher, businessman. Known to family and friends as "Hill." At age twenty-seven, he leaves Crawford County, Georgia, and joins the Confederate Army in Virginia. He enlists in the 45th Georgia Volunteer Infantry, Company K, which consists almost entirely of young men from Crawford County.

Amanda White Fitzpatrick—Wife of Hill, and the recipient of the letters published here. She is eighteen, and recently a mother, when her husband goes off to war. Hill's unusual but obviously affectionate nickname for her is "Cout," which he sometimes spells "Coot."

Henry Thomas Fitzpatrick—Son of Hill and Amanda White Fitzpatrick. He is under one year old when his father enlists in the Confederate Army. The "darling boy" and "noble boy" of these letters.

Nancy Hill Fitzpatrick—Hill's "Ma." A widow for eleven years when the war begins, she lives on a farm near Hill and Amanda's in Crawford County.

Alexander or "Alex" Fitzpatrick—Hill's brother, older by two years. A school teacher and Mason. He joins a Confederate home guard unit.

James G. or "Doc" Fitzpatrick—Hill's younger brother, who joins the 27th Georgia Volunteer Infantry in September 1861.

Various other Fitzpatricks, as well as members of Amanda's family, figure in these letters. So do Hill's friends and fellow soldiers. They will be identified in footnotes accompanying the text.

A Note About the Text and Footnotes

Most of the Fitzpatrick letters are in the Georgia Department of Archives and History in Atlanta. Those originals in private hands are available on microfilm at the state archives.

Our basic method in preparing the text for this edition was to compare the original letters with Reba Bush's transcription of the mid-1970s. We have differed with her on some points, but not many. She became a heroine to us as we discovered how much work that transcription required, and how well she did the work.

Her task, and ours, was made easier by Fitzpatrick's generally beautiful handwriting. Where there is a hole or tear in an original letter, or where the ink or pencil has faded into illegibility, we have so designated with a _____. Where it has been absolutely necessary for clarity, we have added words and punctuation. Brackets enclose these few additions.

We have retained Fitzpatrick's grammar, spelling, punctuation, and his abbreviations. His abbreviation of "et cetera," we have rendered "&c," to mimic better his actual mark.

Our footnotes are meant to provide military context, explain unfamiliar terms, and identify people mentioned in the letters.

Here we must pay tribute to Lillian Henderson's *Roster of the Confederate Soldiers of Georgia, 1861-1865*. This remarkable six-volume work summarizes the military careers of soldiers in sixty-six Georgia infantry regiments. It was first published from 1955 to 1962, and re-published in 1994 by the Georgia Division of the United Daughters of the Confederacy. Unless otherwise credited, our footnotes about the men who served with Fitzpatrick come from Henderson.

Identifying civilians has been a harder trick. Some mysteries remain about both the civilians and soldiers mentioned in *Letters to Amanda*, but these we leave to another, better generation of family historians.

Crawford County, Georgia

Elim Settlement, home of Hill and
Amanda Fitzpatrick, was west of
Knoxville, the county seat.

Amanda White Fitzpatrick with son Henry
and daughter Marion. Circa 1870.
Photo of tintype by Rene Victor Bidez, Fayetteville, Georgia

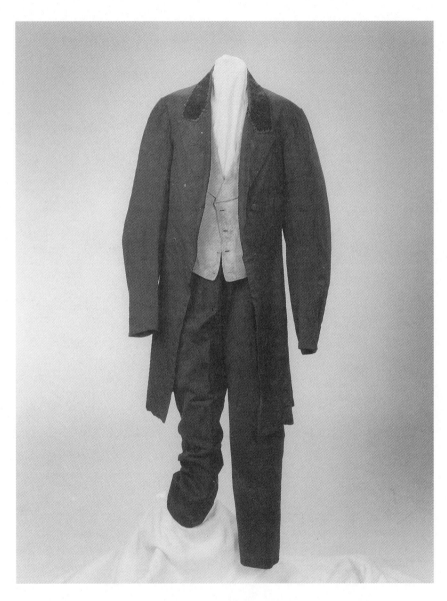

Suit worn by Hill Fitzpatrick when he and Amanda White
married on February 26, 1860.
Photo: Rene Victor Bidez, Fayetteville, Georgia

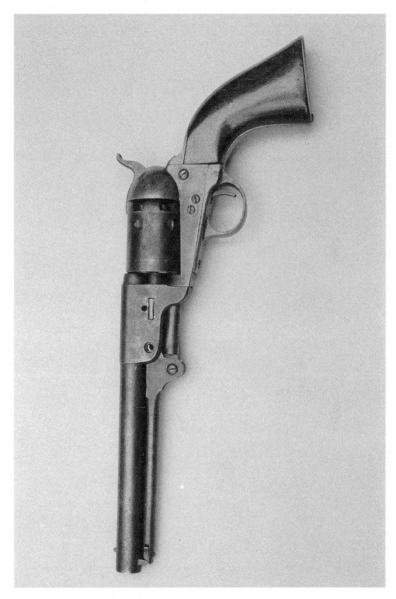

Confederate-made pistol given by Hill Fitzpatrick
to Amanda during his last furlough in
January-February, 1865.
Photo: Polly Hodges, Holly Hills, Florida.

Travel Passes sent by Hill Fitzpatrick to Amanda
in his letter dated April 30, 1863.
Photo: Rene Victor Bidez, Fayetteville, Georgia

Letters
1862

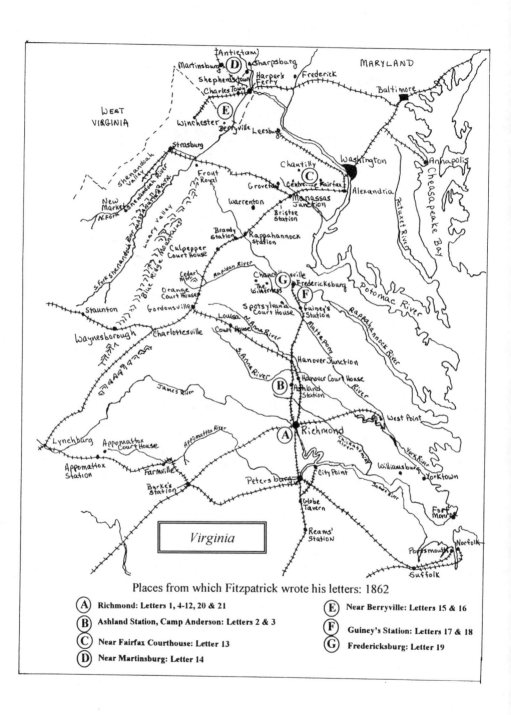

Places from which Fitzpatrick wrote his letters: 1862

Richmond, Va. (*Letter Number 1*)
May 8th, 1862

My Dear Wife,

We have arrived safely here. I am well, but very much fatigued. We got here tonight at dark and Mr. Gibson[1] got a room for us upstairs in a Hotel where I am now sitting writing on my knee. I merely write to let you know I am well knowing that you are looking anxiously for a letter from me. Tomorrow I will find Doc if I can and if I get the chance will add a P S to this. I understand the Ray Guards[2] are about 40 miles from here near Fredericksburg.

There are 11 of us, Henry Gibson, J. Webb, T. Smisson, T. Hammock, Spillers, Culbreath, Jack Wilder, Henry Sanders, Moses Colvin, Bill Johnson and myself.[3] They are all well. Johnson lost all of his clothes at Reynolds.[4] We did not leave Macon at the time I wrote you we would in the letter I sent you by the Dr. We left at 9 o'clock Tuesday night. Rumor says they had a severe fight near Yorktown Monday.[5] Our loss 500 killed and wounded. We took 900 prisoners from them. Their loss in killed and wounded not known. I will write you a long letter when I get to camp.

Be cheerful and do the best you can. May God bless you and my darling boy.[6] Kiss him for me.

Your husband,
M.H. Fitzpatrick

May 9th

P. S. I have just returned from the Hospital. Doc, Jim Wilson and John Murchison[7] left about an hour before I got there for Lynchburg,

---

[1] Aurelius W. Gibson was elected captain of Co. K and mustered into service on March 4, 1862.

[2] Co. K was first called the "Ray Guards." With the rest of the 45th Georgia, they were at Camp Anderson, near Guinea's Station, Va.

[3] Probably recruits for Co. K who traveled together to Richmond. Thomas Smisson, "Tip" Hammock (Aurelius H.), John S. Spillers, Jack Wilder (Andrew J.), Henry Sanders (actually "Saunders"), and Moses F. Colvin will be mentioned several times in these letters.

[4] A town in Taylor County, Ga., adjacent to Crawford County.

[5] The Battle of Williamsburg occurred May 5, 1862, as the Confederate Army was slowly withdrawing up the Virginia peninsula in the face of George McClellan's Army of the Potomac.

[6] MHF and Amanda's infant son, Henry.

Va. so I did not get to see Doc at last. I was sorry for it as I came so near seeing him. They are sending all the convalacent soldiers to the Hospital at Lynchburg. They said that Doc was nearly well and could go all over town.

They are fighting all around here and the people are badly scared for fear the Yankees will take this place. We will leave here tomorrow morning about 40 miles from here on the road to Fredericksburg. I slept sound last night, eat a good warm breakfast and feel about as well as I ever did in my life.

MHF

2 PS Just as I was closing John Murchison sliped in. He did not go with Doc and Jim Wilson. He says they are going to a much better place than this. He say Doc looked very well and is doing finely but Jim Wilson was quite feeble but was improving. After John came we went to another Hospital and found several Crawford boys among whom were Lee McMichael. Poor fellow he cried like a child when I spoke to him. He has the Typhoyd Fever and is very sick. He is in the Wynder Hospital. I saw Mr. Wallace there also. He is not sick much. He has the Diareah, also Bud Wilder and Simon Johnson. Bud is dangerously sick. I fear he has the typhoid fever. Mr. Wallace said he would try to get a discharge for Lee.[8] I will close. May God bless you.

Your Husband,
M.H. Fitzpatrick

2❧

---

[7] James Martin Wilson and John C. Murchison were from Crawford County and served with Doc in Co. C, 27th Ga. Infantry.

[8] Lee McMichael was Leroy B. McMichael, a private in Co. C, 27th Ga. He was admitted to General Hospital in Richmond on May 7, 1862. "Mr. Wallace" was William S. Wallace, captain of Co. E, 45th Ga., from Taylor County and an attorney in civilian life. "Bud Wilder" was one of the four Wilders in Co. K. Simon Johnson was a private in Co. C., 27th Ga.

Camp Anderson, Va. (*Letter Number 2*)
May 11th, 1862

My Dear Wife,

We arrived safely here yesterday evening. I am well and getting on finely. I never enjoyed better health in my life. I have not even taken a cold. I wrote you a long letter in Richmond which I suppose you have received before now, or at least before you get this.

We are in half mile of Guiness Station 12 miles South of Fredericksburg. This is a beautiful place. It is Oak and Hickory and is slightly rolling. The Yankees are as thick as hops about here. Our force here is about 30,000. It is said this regiment will be ordered back to Richmond soon. We were examined by a surgeon yesterday evening and mustered into Service.[9] The recruits will draw tents and equipment soon.

Jim Webb and I are staying in a tent with Jim Drue[10], at this time there [are] only four of us in the tent and we fare finely. I am well pleased so far. We get flour and bacon a plenty and have some of the best biscuits now out. They are going out on inspection now and I will close till they come back as I want to see them.

The inspection is closed and I will now resume my letter. There is a good deal of sickness in the company. They have lost three men but Hatcher and Ross[11] are not dead as reported back there. All of the recruits are complaining of cold. Jim Webb is complaining considerably.

Our forces have vacuated Yorktown and are preparing for a heavy fight near Richmond. I hear so many reports that I do not know whether any are true or not. You will be in the dark if you do not get the letter I wrote in Richmond. I wrote all about Doc and Jim Wilson, for fear you do not get it. I will say again that Doc and Jim left for Lynchburg an hour before I got there. Doc was getting well, and so was Jim, but Jim has had a hard time of it. We had a quick trip from Macon to Richmond. The cars were crowded all the way. I have seen a great deal since I left home. The scenery as we approached Richmond was

---

[9] Henderson's *Roster* states that MHF was 5th sergeant of Co. K when he enlisted. In his Compiled Service Record he is listed either a private or a sergeant. He appears to have been paid as a private.

[10] James D. Drew was a private in Co. K and is mentioned frequently in these letters.

[11] Probably 1st Sgt. G.A.L. Hatcher and Pvt. Jonathan E. Ross. Apparently both men became ill when the 45th Ga. was at Camp Mason, near Goldsboro, N.C., from March 17-22, 1862. Ross died in Goldsboro on May 30, 1862. Hatcher regained his health and rejoined Co. K in Virginia.

grand indeed. It was just at dusk.[12] We were in open cars and the railroad bridge was about two hundred feet from the water. I have enjoyed some hearty laughs since I left home. Bill Johnson has kept us alive all the time with his droll sayings. The land in Va. is excellent but some of them run the rows right up and down the hill. The trees are just buding out here, and people are just planting corn. We have had fine weather so far. It is not cold much here now. It is about like the first days of March in Gia.[13]

Today is Sunday. There will be preaching this evening. I will have to tax you with the postage. The boys say the rascals here will tare the postage stamps off the letters, which, of course prevents the letters from going.

Direct your letter to Guiness Station, Va, care of Capt. Gibson, Company K, 45 Regiment Gia. Vol. Tell all of them to write to me soon. You must not be low spirited atall but pray for me. Kiss my darling boy for me. Write soon and write me a long letter. May God bless you.

Your husband,
M.H. Fitzpatrick

ॐ

Ashland, Va.[14] (*Letter Number 3*)
May 26th, 1862

My Dear Wife,

Through the kind Providence of God I am permitted to write to you again. I am well an alive and am not yet a prisoner but within the last 48 hours have been through enough to make me almost anything but the two first and only lacked five minutes of being the last mentioned.

I wrote to Mr. White[15] last Friday night and wrote him that we had orders to march the next day at 11 o'clock. Jim Webb and Stiles Taylor[16] were too sick to go and somebody had to be detailed to nurse them. I packed my knapsack and prepared to go, with the Regiment but they both plead pitifully for me to stay with them. I consented and was

---

[12] According to the Thomas Smisson diary, the recruits left Macon at 9 p.m. on May 6, 1862. Traveling through Augusta, Ga., Kingville and Wilmington, N.C., they passed through Weldon, Va., at noon on May 8, then through Petersburg at 3 p.m. and arrived in Richmond about dark (Diary of Benjamin Thomas Smisson, unpublished manuscript: entries for May 6-May 9, 1862).

[13] Georgia.

[14] About twelve miles north of Richmond.

[15] William B. White, Sr., Amanda's father.

[16] Private, Co. K.

detailed for that purpose. It was raining and they were to be moved to a house as soon as it held up, but it did not hold up till pretty late in the evening. There were 7 of the Regiment left there sick and three nurses with Dr. Harwood[17] to supervise the whole. The others had been sent to a house previous. Late in the evening we were going to prepare to move them when we received a dispatch to carry them to the railroad at once as the last train would leave there in a short time. Harwood told me to double quick and get a wagon. I picked it up nicely for a half mile and found a negroe going to mill. I pressed[18] the wagon and carried Jim and Stiles to the depot.

["]On quick, men, this is the last train["] was sounded from one end of the car to the other. There were a good many ambulances on the cars but they were crowded with sick already. I had to put Jim and Stiles on some tents partly under a wagon with their heads and shoulders exposed to the open air. In a few minutes we rolled away. It was very cold. What the well much less the sick suffered that night I will not attempt to describe. We were detained a great deal burning the Railroad bridges behind us &c.[19] We got here the next evening and pressed an empty post office and put our sick in it. The hospitals are overflowing and there is no chance to get them in. The consequence of all this is sad indeed. Jim Webb, I fear, is now dieing and there is 9 chances to one against Stiles Taylor. Jim Webb had the measles broke out on him when he started and of course they went in again. We have poured down stimulants almost incessantly but have failed to bring them out. He has not been rational since we started with him. He is raving at times and I had to take his knife from him to keep him from hurting himself or some of us. I moved Stiles to a private house yesterday, by hard work I got a little room, but he uses his own bed clothes. He has the Pneumonia. I have got straw mattresses for them to lie on and they are fixed up tolerably comfortable. I thought I would get Jim in a private house but I could get no room but this and it would injure Taylor to crowd him in here and he is just as well fixed or better where he is than he would be here. I commenced this letter yesterday and have written by piece meals. Jim Webb is gradually sinking yet. I will write to his wife as soon as he dies. I deeply sympathize with her.

We have drawed rations for five days and hire it cooked. The ladies here are very kind to us. Our Regiment is somewhere near here, but I do not know how long they will stay. I am anxious to get with them

---

17 Probably Pvt. B.A. Harwood, Co. K. Henderson, *Roster*, says of Harwood: "Left to nurse sick Apr. 1862. Discharged, disability, July 10, 1862."

18 "Pressed" as in "impressed," meaning to take.

19 MHF's mark for "et cetera."

again. I have just given you an outline and will leave the rest for you to imagine. I have stood it all without being sick yet. I feel and know that prayers have been offered up for me at home. If I had not found the negroe going to mill, ere this, I would have been in the hands of our foes unless I had run off and left the sick and so help me God, I would have died with them first. We suffered with hunger as we came[,] the sick especially. Oh Amanda may you never feel the keen pangs of hunger. I gave 50 cts for a commonsized tin cup full of soup with 3 or 4 little pieces of chicken in it for Jim and Stiles. When I carried it in the cars, one poor fellow saw it and asked his nurse for God's sake, to get him a piece of chicken, he was so hungry. His nurse told him that he had tried his best and could find none. (It was a mere accident that I got it.) The poor soldier then closed his eyes and fell back on his seat seemingly in utter despair. As soon as Jim and Styles were done eating, I took a piece of cracker with a little chicken and gave it to him. I never before saw such an expression of gratitude as he gave.

When we got through fixing the sick the night after we got here I was tired down, in the true sense of the word, but I got some sleep that night and felt tolerably well the next morning. We have to sit up with Jim Webb every night now but we take it turn about. I got a young soldier to stay in here with Stiles last night. It is harder on me having them separated, but I do the best I can. I heard from our Regiment today. They were eight miles from here and were drawn up in a line of battle and were 1 1/2 miles from the Yankees. Some of the people here are scared badly, for they think if our forces are not victorious we will be taken prisoners or have to run again but I hope for better things. Oh how I wish I was with my company but it may be all for the best.

I have tried to talk to Jim Webb about his family and business but I can get him to say but little about it. He always recollects Fannie[20] when I speak to him of her, but he soon runs off on some other subject. I will close, give my respects to all enquiring friends. Direct your letter to Richmond, and it will be forwarded to the Regiment at any point in Va. I have received no letters yet but am anxiously waiting. Be cheerful and kiss my boy for me. Remember me in your prayers. May God bless you.

Your husband,
M.H. Fitzpatrick

---

[20] "Fannie" refers to Jim Webb's wife, Frances. The Census of 1860 shows they had a small daughter.

∂❧

3 1/2 Miles North of Richmond *(Letter Number 4)*
May 30th, 1862

Dear Amanda,

I will drop you a line this morning to let you know that I am still alive and that I am tolerably well. We marched from Ashland here, and got here yesterday evening nearly worn out. I have lost the most of my things. I now have but one pair of pants, one blanket, 2 pr. drawers, 2 shirts. I could not carry them. It was very hot a part of the time and a great many have lost all. I wrote you a long letter in Ashland. Our Regiment was called out and formed a line of battle several times but did not get a fire. That night they retreated to Ashland and the next morning I was ordered to join them and came on with them here. Stiles Taylor was left in the care of Dr. Harwood and I suppose is in Richmond now. I want you to send me a pair of britches if you can but nothing else till we get stationed. I have got my overcoat yet, our tents were put on the cars and started to Richmond. I am very tired now is all that is the matter with me. May God bless you. Good-by. I have received no letters yet.

Your husband,
M.H. Fitzpatrick

∂❧

3 1/2 Miles North of Richmond *(Letter Number 5)*
June 1st, 1862

Dear Amanda,

I received your kind letter of May 20th night before last and was more than glad to hear from you but sorry to hear that you and little Henry were not well. I hope you have both got well before this time.

I feel fortunate this morning. I got a good night's sleep last night. We got some straw and made a half tent with one blanket and slept oh, so sweet. It rained, thundered and lightened all night, night before last. I was on Guard but we were taken off and told to do the best we could, which was bad enough.

Jim Webb died the next morning after I wrote to you in Ashland. I wrote to his wife as soon as he died. A letter came here to him from Fannie the morning after we got here, but poor fellow he was not here to read it. We have been here three nights. I wrote you a short letter the morning after we got here. They were fighting below Richmond all day yesterday. We could hear the firing distinctly and expected every minute to be called out and go into it, but we are here yet. I have heard nothing direct from the fight. I am pretty certain the 27th Gia. was in it and I am anxious to hear from them.[21]

I was sorry you did not get the letter I wrote in Richmond, but I suppose some of you saw Gilman and he told you all about it.

The battle has opened again this morning. Canon are firing rapidly right at this time. We are still in rediness and willing to do the best we can. They are about 6 or 7 miles from here now.

I wrote you about losing my clothes and wrote you to send me a pair of britches, but I do not want you to trouble about it now. If I had them I could not carry them and travel like we have to. When we get settled again, you can send them if there is a chance there will be some arrangements made to get clothes after awhile. I expect that half the Regiment is in the same fix I am and some a great deal worse, but still there is no grumbling. I heard from our sick boys yesterday. They are all in Richmond. Stiles Taylor is very low. Bill Johnson is also very bad off. He has lost the use of one of his legs. Tom Rickerson is also there very sick. I have got no ink and scarcely any paper. I would like to give you a full description of our trials, but I could not do the subject justice if I were to try, and [if] I did you would not believe it. I am glad Henry[22] is getting on well with the farm. I would write to him if I had the chance or paper. Tell him to write me a long letter about the farm, &c. right away. May God bless you and my boy.

Your husband,
M.H. Fitzpatrick

---

21 MHF refers to the Battle of Seven Pines, where portions of the Confederate Army of Virginia, under Gen. Joseph E. Johnston, attacked two Federal corps that were south of the Chickahominy River. The 27th Ga. was part of the only successful Confederate assault in a very mismanaged battle. Johnston was wounded, prompting his replacement by Gen. Robert E. Lee.

22 Henry C. White, one of Amanda's younger brothers, was helping on the Fitzpatrick farm.

❧

2 Miles Northeast Richmond *(Letter Number 6)*
June 9th, 1862

Dear Amanda,

Knowing that you would like to hear from me often during these exciting times I concluded to write to you again today. I wrote to Mother day before yesterday about being sick and being moved to some out houses. I am still here at the house but am nearly well except weakness, and I am gaining my strength very fast. The worst trouble I have is eating too much that is not suitable for a sick man. I have the appetite of a wolf now. I will guard against it all I can though.

I wrote to Doc yesterday. From what I can learn the 27th Gia. is about three miles below here. I will try in a day or two if we stay here to get to go to see him and Georgie[23] and all the boys. Rass Hicks is dead and Jack McCrary[24] started yesterday to carry him home. If he does not leave to come back before you get this, send me one shirt and a plain pair of britches if you get the chance. The reason I want a shirt is that I saved the two checkered shirts and they are wearing out already. I saved them because they were the coolest and lightest and it was very warm when we were on the retreat. Do not have a long tail to the shirt, it makes it warmer in marching.

I heard this morning that Nels and George Williams[25] were both killed in the late battle but I cannot vouch for the truth of it. We have had quite a calm for several days except a few bombs which sounds like the deep low growl of the Lion before he springs upon his prey. We are getting nearer and nearer together. We can see the devils plain now. There is a bridge close to our Regiment which we keep well guarded. The Yankees are working at nights in the swamps on the other side of the river but we do not know what they are doing. It is a very small river, but is full now and has been for some time. It is about three miles from here to the late battle ground.

---

[23] Amanda's brother, George W. White, private, Co. C, 27th Ga.
[24] "Rass Hicks" was Erastus W. Hicks, 4th corporal of Co. K. He died of disease at Richmond, June 8, 1862, at age eighteen. McCrary was Jackson J. McCrary, 5th sergeant, Co. K.
[25] Thomas Nelson ("Nels") Williams and George W. Williams were brothers serving in Co. C, 27th Ga. Both were killed at the Battle of Seven Pines.

We have pretty weather now, which makes the soldiers heart pound with gratitude. I was fearful the battle would come off here while I was sick but I hope I will be able now to take a hand. You must not be atall uneasy about me, but trust in God and if I fall I will fall like a man and leave no stigma on my darling boy. I was sorry to hear that he had fallen away but I hope he is entirely well now. I am glad to hear that he can go up stairs and shu out the hens and that he knows my type.[26] Bless his sweet little soul I hope he can run every where on his little patters now and can talk right plain. Tell him his Pa wants to see him bad enough and that he must be a little man. You must get him a knife as soon as he can use one.

I have got Jim Webb's knife and am saving it for Fannie if I ever get back. I have been sorry ever since that I did not send Fannie some of Jim's hair, but we had to retreat rapidly from the place soon after he died and there was so much confusion and excitement that I did not think of it. He would have been sent home so say the Capt. and Colonel if it had not been under such circumstances. There were two letters received yesterday for Jim. One from his mother and the other from Fannie. It made me feel sad indeed to see them. I suppose they have heard of his death before this time. I wrote to Fannie soon after he died. I wrote her all about him as near as I could but tell her if there is any other particular about him that she wants to know to let me know it and I will explain it to her if it is in my power. You must go to see her and do all you can for her.

Tip Hammock is a little sick this morning, but I hope he will soon get over it. I went to the camp this morning and staid a good while. Tip was so kind to me when I was sick. I shall never forget him. You must go to see his mother and tell her Tip is one of the best boys that ever lived.

I was fortunate enough this morning to borrow this piece of paper and I also sent to Richmond for a Dollars worth of paper and a pack of envelopes. Some of the boys here get a sheet of paper and an envelope sent to them in the same letter that is written to them. I was going to ask you to play the same game but I reckon that I will get some now.

If you do not get to send those pants and shirt do not be atall uneasy. I have a plenty to do me at present and only wanted you to send them because I thought there might be a opportunity.

You spoke of trying to weave. I know you have a hard time and I deeply sympathize with you, but you must try to do the best you can every way and be cheerful all the time. I know you are sad at times but

---

[26] "Type" as in tintype or ambrotype, early forms of photographs.

you must not form a habit of being sad. I am glad you have a good garden. You and Henry must write more particulars about the farm, &c the next time. I have seen many farms going to waste and many handsome dwellings deserted. On the wall of a dwelling not far from here is a beautiful poem written by a soldier in regard to the deserted mansion, our country &c. If I get the chance I am going to draw it off and send it to the Southern Recorder[27] for publication.

Well I have written you a long letter of something, if you can ever read it. I will write to you or some of you there again soon. I wrote a long letter to Pap[28] just before we left Guineas and am looking for an answer to it. Be sure to write often. Pray for me.

Your husband,
M. H. Fitzpatrick

പ

Near Richmond, Va. *(Letter Number 7)*
June 16th, 1862

Dear Amanda,

I received yours of June 4th four or five days ago and was truly glad to hear from you again and to know that all were well. I was nearly well as I thought when I received your letter but the next day I was taken again with the diareah and sick stomach. I would throw up and then turn nearly blind and be so weak I could hardly move. I did not have the bloody flux the last time but an immense quantity of bile and from this I believe it was for my good for I now feel clearer and easier than I have for a long time. I have just eat breakfast and feel like a new man. We are still here in the overseer's house. There are two men from our Company detailed to draw our rations and wait on us. Before they made that arrangement we had to buy nearly all we got, and we would get so hungry that when we could get it we would eat too much. We now fare better without spending any money. The men here were very kind to me when I was so sick. I can never repay the gratitude I owe to

---

[27] A newspaper published in Milledgeville, Ga.
[28] Probably Amanda's father, William B. White, Sr.

them. I can walk all about now and am determined to take better care of myself this time.

I got a letter from Doc yesterday. He was not well but was with his Regiment. He gave out before he got to the battleground,[29] but the shots bombs balls and shell fell thick and fast around him. He said he did not have a cent of passable money. I sent him 10 Dollars of the twenty that Alex sent to him. I sent it in a letter. I hated to risk the whole twenty and I would have been nearly flat myself. Our Regiment will draw in a day or two, but the recruits are not included this time, but they say we will get our bounty and all before long. We have no fight here yet, but I do not know how soon it may come. Tip Hammock is well. He is detailed to throw up breastworks and I do not get to see him often.

I am so glad that you have a fine garden and so many chickens. It makes my mouth water to think of them. I learn from a few lines that Henry[30] sent in your letter that he had given up the business. It is just as I expected. I am sorry on your account but you must brave up. You must cultivate a strong nerve and a cool and determined resolution. What I mean by a strong nerve is not to fear man, woman or the Devil, and what I mean by a cool and determined resolution is to make a cool calculation on your business and when you have decided, carry it out or burst. For the want of these qualities, men and women fail in business. I long to be with you, but it cannot be so now, and I thank God your condition is no worse. I have seen women and children here driven from their homes and such suffering as I cannot describe.

I am glad to hear that Pa's boy can almost walk and talk. You must write me how many teeth he has and all about him. Tell him Pa is coming home after he whips the Yankees, and is going to bring him a knife and some candy. Tell Thornt[31] to make him a little wagon of nights and odd times[32] and tell him to stay down there with you of nights, and if he don't keep things straight, darn him, I will half kill him when I get back. If I was only there a few days I would straighten things, but I must serve my Country now.

Be kind, Amanda, and obliging to all. I find that one kind word or deed will often accomplish great things, by so acting you will never

---

[29] Battle of Seven Pines.

[30] Henry White, one of Amanda's younger brothers, mentioned in Letter 5 as helping on the Fitzpatrick farm. The "business" referred to here may have been the farm or even a store.

[31] Thornton or "Thornt" was a slave owned by Nancy Fitzpatrick. In the appraisal of Alexander Fitzpatrick's property after his death in 1849, there were four slaves listed, including Thornton.

[32] Meaning in his spare time.

lack for friends. Do not be uneasy about me. I will write to you often. Doc is about 3 miles from here. He said he would come to see me if he could. Write soon. May God bless you.

Your husband,
M. H. Fitzpatrick

ॐ

Near Richmond (*Letter Number 8*)
June 20th, 1862

Dear Amanda,

Having the chance to send this by hand as far as Ft. Valley,[33] I thought I would write again although I have very recently written to you and Alex both. I reckon you get tired paying postage if you get all the letters I write, but it is a great pleasure to me to write home. And you cannot tell how eagerly I watch for the mail every morning. I have no room for grumbling, but I often feel sad when there is no letter for me.

I am happy to say to you that I feel almost as well as I ever did in my life this morning, but not as strong altogether. I expect this will get to you before either of the letters that I have recently written. I wrote Alex that I was going back to camp that evening, but the Surgeon soon came and sent off all except our company.

There are two rooms to this house and I moved to the other end where there were no measels and got with a decent crowd. I am now faring better than I have been in a long time. The Surgeon says I must regain my strength fully before I go to Camp unless we get too badly crowded here. I have not heard from Doc since I wrote you last. They had a heavy skirmish down where he is day before yesterday just before night, but his Regiment was not engaged from what I can learn, at least there were no casualties in it. Our Regiment was thrown into a line of battle yesterday, but it proved to be a false alarm. It was thought the enemy were crossing the bridge near us. All is quiet this morning, but nobody can tell what will soon turn up.

I know you were very uneasy about me when you heard of the battle near here, and I know that you are still uneasy about my being

---

[33] A town near Crawford County.

sick and the approaching battle. But you must keep as quiet as possible and hope strongly for the best.

It is strange that you received my Ashland letter and the one I wrote the 30th May at the same time. I wrote to you the 2nd June in reply to the first letter you wrote me and it should have reached home by the time, or soon after Alex wrote, to know if I was in the fight.

We may not have a fight here in a long while yet, but things apparently indicate an engagement. There is much sickness in our Regiment, but we have beautiful weather now and I hope the general health will improve rapidly now.

Hand the enclosed note to Alex. It is merely [an] answer to a simple question. I do not care for your seeing it but do not want everybody to see it. I wrote to him in regard to it but fearing that the letter might be miscarried, I enclose this also.

I have been looking for a letter from Lou[34] for some time. She wrote some in Mother's letter, but said she would write again soon. I do not wait for answers but write to first one and then the other of you. Of course I intend for all of you to hear from the same letter. I want you to take time and just write me every thing you can think of. Write me all about how little Henry does[,] what sort of capers he cuts, and whether he ever gets mad and cries or not. Be gentle with him. Do not teaze or fret or deceive him, nor let anybody else do it no matter who it is, or how grossly you have to insult them. I saw a certain young man rumple up his hair one day to fret him. It made me mad, it was in my own house and he soon quit and I said nothing to him, but if it was to be done again I should act quite differently. I have learned to stand up for my rights since I joined the army without regard to any man's feelings when necessary.

I do not wish to excite vain hopes in you but, I confidently believe that we will have peace soon. At least it is the general opinion of the intelligent class, and their logic I think, at least plausible. Among many reasons I will give one. Lincoln promised Europe cotton when they opened our ports. Lincoln took New Orleans, Europe waits, but gets no cotton. They have commenced bombing heavily below here. It has just opened. They may fight yet today, but they bomb everyday.

---

[34] Lou was Nancy Louisa Greene, MHF's niece, but only three years his junior. Lou, daughter of MHF's older sister Amanda and Burwell Greene, Jr., lived in Macon County but seems to have spent considerable time on the Fitzpatrick farms in Crawford. She was close both to MHF and his mother and is mentioned frequently in these letters.

I will close. Just then some of the boys saw a bomb burst. I ran out and saw the smoke. They are about a mile below, but this is sign of an immediate battle. May God bless you.

Your husband,
M. Hill Fitzpatrick

੨✿

Near Richmond, Va. (*Letter Number 9*)
July 1st, 1862

Dear Amanda,

Through the providence of God I am alive yet, but I am slightly wounded just above my left breast. I was struck with a spent ball or one that had struck another object and glanced, it went through my cartridge box belt and partly through my coat collar and bruised the bone, but did not break the skin. It is pretty sore but is getting better fast. I could fight now if I could carry my cartridge box but it is right where the belt works. I got wounded about dark last night which is _____ battle I have been into. I am staying at a temporary established hospital about 1/2 mile from the battleground.

We marched nearly all day yesterday and went into the fight at dark.[35] We soon came within 50 yds. of a Regiment which we thought were friends. While the subject was being discussed among our officers some of our men shouted three cheers for Jefferson Davis. They then poured a deadly fire in our ranks, never in my life did balls fly so thick around me. We returned the fire. I fired two rounds and just as I was going to fire again, the ball struck me. It stuned me but I raised and found myself by the side of Lieu. McCrary. He took _____ told me to fall back. I went half mile lay _____ till this morning. I thought at first the wound was much worse than it was. One

---

[35] This paragraph describes the 45th Ga.'s part in the June 30, 1862 Battle of Frayser's Farm (Glendale). This was the third of the Seven Days Battles that together forced McClellan's Army of the Potomac from Richmond. The 45th was brigaded with the 14th Ga., the 35th Ga., the 49th Ga., and the 2nd La. Battalion under Brig. Gen. Joseph A. Anderson, in A. P. Hill's Division. Anderson's Brigade was Hill's last reserve when they were ordered down the Long Bridge Road around 8:30 p.m. to widen a breach in the Federal line. The confused fighting described in this paragraph ended the Battle of Frayser's Farm. See Stephen W. Sears, *To the Gates of Richmond: The Peninsula Campaign* (Houghton Mifflin: New York, 1992), for an excellent account of the Seven Days Battles.

of our Company is killed, John Sandafor. John Wilder slightly wounded in the arm, Captain Gibson slightly wounded. We went in with 25 rank and file and came out with 8 unhurt, one or two are missing, _____ come in yet. Col. Hardeman is seriously wounded, Lieu. Simons got wounded in the first battle.[36]

We are on the South Side of the Chickahomany now, not very far from the James River. The other two fights were on the other side of the Chickahomany. We were held in reserve in the first fight but were exposed to the fire. Our Regiment was the first to charge their battery in the second fight but was repulsed with severe loss. I fired 7 rounds there and came through unscratched. Our Regiment lost 53 wounded and 9 killed there. We then fell back and was not called into the fight again. Our loss yesterday evening was immense but I do not know the amount. Our Regiment held their ground, drove the enemy back, and slept on the battle field last night. We have whipped the enemy every time yet but our loss has been tremendous.[37]

Tip Hammock was left at our camp night before last. He was tired out. I have stood the tramp finely and my general health is good now. I just have to write on scraps of paper, one piece I picked up in a Yankee camp.[38] I lost my overcoat and blanket. I got another blanket but lost it in the fight last night. I picked up another before I stopped and slept on it last night. I have it yet. I will give the particulars more full the first chance I get. I shall go to my regiment in a day or two if my shoulder keeps mending. I think we will have peace soon and then I will come home and tell you about my ups and downs. Write soon.

Your husband,
M.H. Fitzpatrick

---

[36] John W. Sandifer was killed at the Battle of Frayser's Farm and Capt. Gibson of Co. K was wounded there. "Col. Hardeman" was Thomas Hardeman, Jr. of the 45th Ga., and "Lieu. Simons" was Lt. Col. Thomas J. Simmons, who was wounded at the Battle of Gaines' Mill on June 27, 1862.

[37] The "first fight" was the Battle of Mechanicsville, or Beaver Dam Creek, on May 26, 1862, when A.P. Hill rashly threw much of his division against a heavily fortified Federal line behind the creek. The "second fight" was the Battle of Gaines' Mill, June 27, where Hill again threw his division against a very strong Federal position taken behind Boatswain's Swamp, near New Cold Harbor. Hill's Division lost heavily as they attacked the Federal line of Fitz John Porter's V Army Corps. The Confederate victory at Gaines' Mill finally occurred when sixteen brigades from D.H. Hill's, Longstreet's and Jackson's Divisions crushed Porter's lines. See Sears, *To the Gates of Richmond*, 200-209, 222-242.

[38] This letter was written on a part of the Federal "Surgeon's Morning Report," dated June 10th, 1861.

꙳

Near Richmond, Virginia *(Letter Number 10)*
July 23rd, 1862

Dear Amanda,

I have just received yours of July 12th and have the chance to send an answer to it right back by one eyed Lewis Mobly.[39] I sent off a letter to Mother yesterday morning, by old man Ford,[40] in which I told all about my late sickness, and should not write again so soon if it was not for the chance of sending it by hand. I am still improving and now hope that I will soon be well again. I have a severe blister on my side which is troubling me very much to cure up. I have a looseness in my bowels which I suppose is the best for me now and occasionally difficulty of breathing caused by pain in the breast. I am still staying here at the house and I fare finely in both eating and sleeping now. I can now walk to camp which is not far, and eat with the boys there when it is not too warm. Before I could walk about, I had to depend upon the Hospital nurses for something to eat which was just the same as starving, but luckily I had a little money and could buy what I wanted here. I have now made arrangements to have it sent to me from Camp when I do not go after it. The boy that cooks for me is the best cook I almost ever saw. I went down to dinner today and met up with Lewis Mobbly. I was glad to see him, we had a long chatt. I did not find out at last what his business was. He said he just came to see what in the hell we were all doing here.

Well, Coot, I have been writing a good deal about clothes, but I have now come to one shirt and one pr. drawers, having lost my knapsack, which I explained in Mother's letter. A few days ago they sent around for all that wanted clothes to make a requisition. I put down for 1 shirt and pr. drawers, not knowing what you would send me by McCrary,[41] but after I received what you sent and received a letter from Alex stating that he could not get my shirts off, I enlarged my requisition considerably, but it was too late to get it in, but if I get the first

---

[39] Probably Pvt. Lewis Mobley, Co. E, 6th Ga. Infantry, the first company raised from Crawford County. Tip Hammock and several other Co. K men served in this company during the early months of the War.
[40] Identity unknown to editors.
[41] 5th Sgt Jackson J. McCrary, Co. K.

requisition I can make out very well and I will also try to buy some if I get the chance. I suppose John Wilder[42] will bring my things, but if you can't get them off do not be uneasy, I reckon Providence will provide some way.

I learn from Mobly that Mr. White is in Richmond, but fear he will not get to come to see me. I have not heard from George, only that he was wounded in two places and the wounds was not considered fatal.[43]

I am glad to learn that my boy can walk but you do not say a word about his talking. You must tell me all about what he says and what sort of capers he cuts and be sure to make him some britches right away with pockets in them if you have not already done it, and get him a knife.

I am glad to hear that you have such a good garden, and that you have just had a good rain. I received your letter of June 22nd a day or two ago. It is strange it was so long coming.

In that letter I was grieved to learn that you were very low spirited, but I hope you have gotten over that before now, and above all things I would not grieve about Henry's[44] quitting you, for to be candid I think he acted very wrong. He wrote me expressly that he wanted Alex to come back from Macon and take charge of the business so that he could quit and go to school. I see no use then of his making such a fuss because Alex done it, and another thing he promised me to stay there for $15.00 per month. He staid one month and charged $16.00. You would have had to paid a portion of his wages. Alex is charging nothing for his services. These are plain facts .

Well Coot you must cheer up and write to me often. I long to be with you to help you to eat vegetables and chickens, but it cannot be so yet, but I hope it will soon.

Your husband,
M. H. Fitzpatrick

ൟ

---

[42] Pvt. John A. Wilder, Co. K.

[43] Amanda's father apparently traveled to Richmond to care for George White, one of Amanda's brothers, who was wounded in both legs during the Seven Days Battles.

[44] Henry White, another of Amanda's brothers, who was mentioned in the June 16, 1862 letter as failing to fulfill his commitment to help Amanda in the family business. Henry was only seventeen years of age. From May 27 to November 16, 1861, he had been a private in Co. E, 6th Ga. He later enlisted in Company C, 27th Ga.

Near Richmond, Va. *(Letter Number 11)*
Aug. 1st, 1862

Dear Amanda,

I was surprised day before yesterday to receive a letter from you dated July 1st. I do not know where it could have been all this time as I have received and answered letters from you of a much later date. However, I was glad to get it and to hear that you were getting on so well making dresses, bonnets &c. I wrote to Alex a day or two ago in regard to my being here and the moving of the Reg. The whole Division is gone now I believe. They have been moving for several days. Our Regiment did not get off till yesterday. I understand they have gone up about Gordonville to join Old Stonewall, but do not know how true it is.[45]

I am improving fast now and hope to be able to rejoin my Reg. in a short time. I am at the Brigade hospital now about a mile from the old camps. We have flies[46] to stay under and draw a plenty to eat. There are 11 of our company here. There are 5 in my crowd and one of them has a negroe which is a great help to us. There are about a thousand sick here and I am anxious to get away. Our mess got off to ourselves under a large tree and were doing pretty well but two more squads moved here today, and I fear that we will be crowded. We have plenty of good water but wood is scarce. I can walk anywhere and help cook now.

I wrote Alex about getting my shirts. I am so proud of them I can hardly see strait. Everybody admires them and wants them. I am well fixed in the clothing line now, two shirts and two pr. drawers is as much as I want at a time. I am having my undershirt washed today for the first time in five weeks, only dabbled out in cold water and no soap once. I have on both the shirts you sent me now. I will put on my undershirt as soon as it gets dry. Fortunately I carried two pr. of socks with me on the tramp, but they need darning. I doubt whether you would know me or not hardly if you were to see me now. My old hat

---

[45] MHF thought the 45th Ga. had gone to Gordonville, Va., to join troops under Thomas J. "Stonewall" Jackson, who had become a Confederate hero with his stand at First Manassas and campaign in the Shenandoah Valley. By this time the 45th Ga. had been combined with the 14th Ga., the 35th Ga., and the 49th Ga. to form a brigade under the command of Brig. Gen. Edward L. Thomas. Thomas' Brigade was in the division command by Maj. Gen. A.P. Hill.

[46] Tenting material.

has about ten holes in it which I have sowed up with white thred. I also let down the top and sowed it in with white thread, and I have not shaved since I left Macon. But all this I bear cheerfully, if I can be of any service to my country. I want no overcoat or blanket till cold weather for I would be almost certain to lose them if I had them.

I earnestly hope you all will make a good crop. You must send out Jennie all the time you can possibly spare her.[47] Alex had written to me about the negroe frolic. It made me broil to think of it. I think I shall have to whip some of them yet if I ever get back.

I looked in vain in the pockets of my shirts for a letter. Doc wrote me that Pap had a letter for me, and he told him to mail it to Richmond to me, but I have never received it.

When the new crop of corn comes in, if the Ray Guards has any friends in old Crawford, I want them to send us some meal. I am not so tired of biscuits as the others but I want a change. If we had meal we could make mush and bake good bread without greece. We buy a little meal sometimes and pay at the rate of $8.00 per bus. Butter $1.25 cts per lb., Sugar from 75 cts to $1.00 per lb. Molasses $6.00 per gal. Milk 40 cts a qt. Gingercakes 25 cts apiece, Chickens $1.25 cts apiece and so with everything else. It is hard (I think) for the poor soldier to have to pay these prices with his hard earned wages, but he often has it to do, or suffer with hunger. This I know from experience. I regret very much having to spend my money and think I am treating my family unjustly, but I cannot suffer with hunger. Write soon.

Your husband,
M. H. Fitzpatrick

ॐ

A. P. Hill's Division Hospital *(Letter Number 12)*
Near Richmond, Va.
August 10th, 1862

Dear Amanda,

I wrote to you not long ago but have concluded to write again. I was improving when I wrote to you but have been very sick since, and am quite weak now though not suffering with any accute pain. I do not

---

[47] Jennie was a slave belonging to his mother. By "send out" MHF probably meant have her work in the fields rather than in the house.

know what is the matter with me, unless it is a kind of protracted spell of Colic. I take no medicine, in fact there is but little medicine given here and what is given does more harm than good. I can walk about a little now and earnestly hope that I will get well soon.

I wrote to Alex to send me a hat, but I have bought one from the Executor of one of our Comp. that died recently. So he need not send it. It is a very good hat. I bought it at auction and paid $3.50. I also bought a pair of socks so you need send me only one pr. I wrote you when I first came here that this was a Brigade hospital and that there was about a thousand sick here, but I soon found out it was a Division Hospital with 2,700 sick in it, but half or more have been sent away, some to their Regiments and the others to Richmond, and they are still getting them away as fast as possible and say they are going to break it up as soon as they can. I fear I will have to go to the hospital but I hope all will be for the best. It is the hottest weather I ever felt in my life. I fare tolerably well as we are under a tree and have a negroe to cook for us.

I want to see you and my boy bad enough, and all of you. Oh how I wish I could see him walking and hear him jabber, and I hope from some indications I see that we will soon have peace and then I can come home. Our Regiment is or was a few days ago five miles this side of Gordonville. You must continue to write and direct to Richmond and the letters will go the Reg. no matter where it is. If I go to the Hospital I will write to you immediately, and you can direct your letters there. Our Comp. has lost about 25 with sickness and one with the bullet.[48] Pray for me. Write soon.

Your husband,
M.H. Fitzpatrick

꒰꒱

---

[48] Those from Co. K who died of disease from March 4 to August 10, 1862 included: 3rd Corp. Mathew H. Myrick, 4th Corp. E. W. Hicks, Pvts. Green W. Carter, Andrew J. Cates, W.B. C. Cates, James L. Causey, Cicero C. Cloud, John W. Cloud, Cunningham (first name unknown), Charles Jefferson Goodin, Joseph T. Goodin, S.F. Hartley, William Johnson, J. S. Leadingdam, J. H. Powell, A.M. Rigby, Jonathan E. Ross, J.L.T. Sawyer, E.F.N. Shirley, John A. Slocumb, Jefferson Smallwood, William C. Sullivan, John T. Taylor, Styles Taylor, B.F. Thomasson, James E. Webb, R.J. Williamson. Pvts. J.A. Lightfoot and John W. Sandifer were killed on June 30, 1862 at the Battle of Frayser's Farm. The five-month mortality rate for Co. K was almost twenty-six percent. Not until their last battle would the company be so hard hit.

Near Fairfax Courthouse, Va. *(Letter Number 13)*[49]
September 2nd, 1862

Dear Amanda,

I eagerly embrace this opportunity to drop you a letter which I will send by Jack Adams.[50] I am well at this time and through the mercy of God am alive. It would take ine two days steady writing to tell you what I have been through. I have been in three fights recently and have come out safe so far. I wrote to Mother the day before I left the Hospital and I suppose she has received it before this time, and no doubt all of you have been anxious to hear from me again. I found a letter from Alex when I got to the regiment but have forgotten the date of it and I had to burn it up. It took me eight days to get up with the regiment after I left Richmond. We rested the next day and then marched two days of the hardest marching that was ever known almost. My feet blistered and sometimes when I would start, I would have to lean over on my gun and the tears would involuntarily gush from my eyes. We got to Manassas the day after it was captured.[51] We captured an immense quantity of army supplies there. We feasted for once, but the greater part were burnt. I witnessed the burning. The town and a train of cars nearly a mile long were burnt. We then marched on beyond Centerville, and found the Yanks in strong force. The fight opened late one evening & we were not called in, but went into it early the next morning. We got a strong position behind a railroad embankment, fought them for about an hour and drove them back. Before a great while they charged our position and flanked us at the same time. Gen. Hill had sent a Curior previous to that for us to get out from there but we failed to get it. Our brigade fought like heroes, our Reg. was in the centre. The first we knew both wings had given away and the 45th was nearly surrounded. The last fire I made I stood on the embankment and fired right down amongst them just as they were charging up the bank about fifteen ranks deep. I turned and saw the

---

[49] This letter will describe MHF and the 45th Ga.'s part in the Second Manassas campaign. John J. Hennessy's *Return to Bull Run, The Campaign and Battle of Second Manassas* (New York: Simon and Schuster, 1993) provides a good detailed account of this campaign.

[50] A.J. Adams, a private in Co. K, was wounded at Frayser's Farm and discharged due to disability on September 1, 1862.

[51] The vast Federal supply depot of John Pope's Army of Virginia was captured on August 26, 1862. The feasting of the hungry Confederates was something they never seemed to forget. It is mentioned often in letters and memoirs.

whole Reg. getting away, and I followed the example in tribble quick time.[52] They charged over the road and fired on us but were met by Branch's Brigade and were driven right back over it and about a mile the other side. I went to where I fired last and three of the devils were lying there. I got me a good yankee zinc canteen which fortunately was nearly filled with water. I rallied again with the Brigade but we were not in the fight anymore that day. It told heavily on our little comp. We went in with 10 men and lost 1, wounded Jim Moore, and Lieu. McCrary, Henry and Frank Knight, and Tom Lewis were taken prisoners, at least they have not been seen or heard of since. They were placed behind some rocks in [a] gap of the Rail Road. The next day I skirmished all day which is pretty ticklish work. I took a prisoner about dark, a great big strapping fellow weighing about 200 lbs. I marched him in with some little pride. There was hard fighting done that day but our Brigade was not engaged till nearly dark when they charged a battery and took it by firing only a few shots. The next day we marched on this road and got into a fight here, we were not engaged but a little while, but had to stand picket and it rained from the time the battle commenced till late in the night. It was an awful night, to me. It is a beautiful day today and we are resting. I got a good pr. shoes, haversack &c on the battlefield.[53]

I left my haversack with Henry Pope's negro, who has charge of a wagon.[54] I had to do that or throw it away and I am pretty certain it will

---

[52] MHF meant "triple quick time."

[53] On August 29 Jackson's Corps took a defensive position along an unfinished railroad cut crossing and then running roughly parallel to the Groveton-Sudley Road on the battlefield of First Manassas. Throughout the day, piecemeal Federal attacks failed to break Jackson's lines. At about 3 p.m. the Federal brigade of Brig. Gen. Cuvier Grover struck the left of the Confederate line at a gap between Thomas' Brigade and Maxcy Gregg's South Carolina Brigade. As MHF described, the Federal assault stormed through, flanking the Georgians and causing the collapse of Thomas' line. Thomas rallied the 49th Ga. and elements of the 14th Ga., 35th Ga., and 45th Ga. to a second line of defense but this too was breached. This serious threat to the left of the Confederate line was met by Gregg swinging his brigade to attack Grover's Federals. Dorsey Pender's North Carolina Brigade joined the Confederate counterattack. This forced Grover's Federals to retreat with heavy casualties. Although MHF gave Branch's North Carolina Brigade the credit, it appears Gregg's and Pender's brigades played a larger part. The next day Pope attacked Jackson's lines again, not realizing that Longstreet's Corps had arrived and was on the Federal left. Longstreet's assault that afternoon routed Pope's army. As MHF describes, Jackson's Corps joined in the attack, helping to inflict a complete defeat on Pope. See Hennessy's *Return to Bull Run, The Campaign and Battle of Second Manassas,* 243-270.

[54] Pvt. Henry B. Pope served in Co. K, and apparently brought a slave with him.

be all safe. I will have to close as Adams; but just then he said he would not start before morning. Tip Hammock was left behind sick. I do not know what became of him but I suppose he is at some private house. Jack Wilder is with us now. He came to us yesterday morning. I learn the 27th Ga. is near here, but I almost know Doc is not with them. We have whipped the yankees every fight yet and I hope will soon close the war. We have fared pretty badly in the eating line at times, and would have suffered if it had not been for roasting ears. My feet has got well and my general health is pretty good considering what I have to go through, but I try to bear up cheerfully and do my whole duty to my country. Many have fell around me but it has pleased God to spare my life so far. I fear and know that I am not as thankful as I ought to be. I want you to trust in God and continue to pray for me. I have wandered far from the path of duty as a Christian, and am often troubled much about it. I still hope that I will one day return home to you, sweet wife and see my darling boy again and my dear old Mother, and go to meeting at old Elim[55] again and tell you all about my ups and downs. I know you have written to me but there is no chance to get a letter, but you must write again and maybe I will get them at some time.

I have changed much in my feelings. The bombs and balls excite me but little and a battlefield strewed with dead and wounded is an every day consequence. I have seen old Stonewall often and was near Gen. Lee yesterday evening. We had liked to have been caught in a trap like we did on the night of the 3rd of June, yesterday evening, but we were more watchful this time and instead of our men going to see who they were, a Major General from their side came riding swiftly up to our ranks thinking we were Yanks. As soon as he saw the mistake he turned to go back but was instantly brought dead to the ground. We fired on the Yanks and they run quick. The General's name was Cony.[56] I will close. Train up our boy to be a man in the true sense of the word.

Your husband,
M.H. Fitzpatrick

---

[55] Elim Baptist Church, Crawford County, Ga.

[56] MHF is describing the death of Maj. Gen. Philip Kearny at the Battle of Ox Hill or Chantilly, September 1, 1862. Kearny was shot much as MHF wrote. Kearny had lost one arm in the Mexican War and was admired by friend and foe. His body was returned to the Federals.

ॠ

Near Martinsburg, Va.[57] *(Letter Number 14)*
Sept. 27th, 1862

Dear Amanda,

I have just received from the hand of John Wilder yours and Alex letters dated Aug. 30th and am truly glad to hear from home again, but sorry to hear of the death of your brother Thomas, of which I had been informed a few days before by Col. Simmons. I have a strong hope that he is in a better world.[58]

I am sorry to learn that my darling boy had been sick but I hope he soon entirely recovered. You say he gets more and more like me. You cannot conceive how bad I want to see him and all of you, but I have never regretted coming to the war and I feel proud that I have been of some service to my Country. I am well and doing finely at this time. I hardly know how to begin to write unless I knew whether or no you have received my letters. I have written several. The last I wrote while at Harper's Ferry and gave to a negroe wagoner to carry to Winchester and mail it there.

Our Brigade was left at Harper's Ferry to guard the place for four days.[59] We then came up the River about 7 miles and rejoined our Division. The next day, Saturday, we marched out five miles to meet the enemy. We were on the extreme right. A call was made for two skirmishers from each company. Being just hotheaded enough to love the excitement, I volunteered immediately. We sallied forth and had gone but little ways before we routed the Yankee skirmishers. Bank! Bank! went the guns. Whiz! Whiz! went and came the bullets and the Yanks trotted handsomely, while our boys poured it into them thick. To

---

[57] Martinsburg, Va. (now West Virginia) is about ten miles west of Sharpsburg, Md. This was probably the farthest north MHF went.

[58] Amanda's next oldest brother, Thomas J. White, moved to Louisiana sometime before the War. He enlisted in Co. B of the 4th Battalion Louisiana Infantry on June 4, 1861. In June 1862, he was wounded during the James Island and Seccessionville campaign near Charleston, S.C. Taken back to Crawford County, he died of his wounds on August 12, 1862. David Lee's family history, *The White Family of Crawford County, Georgia*, 25, provided these details on Thomas' military service.

[59] The Battle of Sharpsburg or Antietam was fought on September 17, 1862. Near the end of the day, Lee's Army was saved by A.P. Hill's Division, which had marched with great speed from Harper's Ferry. Thomas' Brigade had been left behind in Harper's Ferry, so MHF missed this battle.

my greatest mortification my gun failed to fire, but I soon recollected that it was charged with a Yankee cartridge which had to be ramed hard. I drew my stick gave it a hard ram tried it again and went clear as a whistle. On we went still routing them till we drove them across the river. We halted at the edge [of] a woods and about 400 yds. to my right near the bank of the river lying under a tree were about 12 or 14 Yanks. Myself and two more scouts had our own fun shooting at them. We raised our sights, took deliberate aim and soon made them O skeedaddle handsomely, and it was _____ left one there. We were all the time exposed to the heaviest shelling I have ever seen or heard. Our Brigade followed in the rear. We lay there the balance of the day with nothing to do, but the left wing of our Division had a hard fight, but came off victorious.[60]

The next day we moved farther up the river and there I again saw Jim Wilson and Cicero Futrel. They said they left Doc at a good private home three miles from Frederick City in Maryland. What his fate is God only knows, but we must hope for the best. Cicero and Jim was in the hard fighting on the other side of the river and Jim received a slight wound on his chin. Their Company lost heavily among the killed were Henry Hancock.[61] Cleveland's Comp. lost heavily. Dick Bazemore had his leg cut off near his body. Tom Walker and Henry Harris were killed and many others. Oh, how it grieves me to think of them.[62] Last Sunday evening we moved two miles to this place. Sunday night I was sent as Sergeant of the Guard with three men to guard this house and premises, and have been here ever since, which is three days and nights. They feed us high and I am getting fat. That is the rule when we guard a house, make them feed the guards.

The division is half a mile from here. I have no idea when we will leave here or where we will go. I have heard nothing from Tip Hammock since we left him before we went into the Manassas fight. John Wilder left the things you sent me at Gordonville and I am glad he done it. Tell Alex the hat I have got now will last me probably till

---

[60] This paragraph describes MHF's part in the final action of the Sharpsburg campaign, when A.P. Hill's Division defeated two Federal divisions which had been sent across the Potomac in pursuit of Lee's Army. This engagement took place on September 20, 1862.

[61] Jim Wilson and Cicero Futrell were with Doc in Co. C, 27th Ga. Doc's Compiled Service Record does not state he was left behind when Lee's Army retreated. Henry Hancock, Sr., was killed at Sharpsburg.

[62] Co. E, 6th Ga. was raised by Wilde C. Cleveland (the son of a wealthy Crawford County family). Co. E was mauled at Sharpsburg. Nine men were killed outright, four more died of wounds, eleven others were wounded and four were captured and later paroled, making twenty-eight casualties.

the war ends, as it is a good homemade wool hat. When we go into winter quarters I will be glad to get the suit of jeans you are preparing for me, as this suit is getting thin and thredbare. But I will not grumble if I cannot get them.

I am writing this with the hope of getting a chance to send it to Winchester to mail as they are sending the sick from here there. Write and direct to Richmond. May God bless you all.

Your husband,
M.H. Fitzpatrick

༄

Camp Near Berryville, Va. *(Letter Number 15)*
Nov. 7th, 1862

Dear Amanda,

I received yours of Oct. 19th a day or two ago and was truly glad to hear from you again and to hear that all were well and that Henry was so fat. He must be a little backward in talking, though. I do not know about that. As you say, he will be great company to you when he learns to talk well. I want to hear him jabber and see him walk bad enough but it cannot be so yet awhile and the best way is to submit without a murmur. If it should be the will of Providence that I should never return, I want you to start him to school by the time he can walk there almost and keep him going till he gets an education if it's possibly in your power, and instill the true principles of manhood in him from the beginning. A grown up man with boyish principles is anything but pleasing.

You spoke of being lonesome. I know you must spend many lonesome hours and I truly sympathize with you; but you must visit more and form the habit of reading a great deal and you will find it a great help to drive away the blues. I hope that Mr. White succeeded in the salt enterprise. If they fail on the coast I do not know what you all will do about meat. But it will be better to do without meat altogether than submit to yankee rule. We were tight run for salt here for about a week but we get plenty now. We also got pretty scarce of flour for awhile. We only got one ten cent tin cup light full a day to the man, and a good many times I quit eating hungry and it made me feel pretty bad, but I thought anything for liberty. We draw a plenty now, and occasionally get a good ration of pork, and then we have greece to put in biscuits. We have quit putting tallow in biscuits, we had to buy it from the butcher and they got to selling it so high that we quit the business. I went to a mill near here the other day and bought some shorts at 4 cts per lb. that went fine.

I am looking everyday now for my clothes. I wrote Lou to tell you not to send a vest but I do not know whether you got the letter in time or not. The reason I did not write for bedclothes is that I feared you would have none to spare and also feared if I got them before we quit moving so much, I would loose them, and another thing, our wages are raised to $15.00 a month and we are to be clothed by the government and not draw any more computation money.[63] At least that is the opinion of many. If that is the case, I will get no credit for anything you send me and it will be best to draw altogether from the government except socks. I wrote Lou in my last letter to her for you to send me an overcoat, but I now countermand the order, for I suppose I can draw, if not I can make out very well without it. We can draw clothing here much cheaper than they can be bought in Ga. Some of the boys have already drawn good clothing at reasonable prices and excellent blankets at $4.00.

I wrote to Lou a few days ago. We were then about 10 miles above here. We staid there two nights and came here. We are in Clark County, I believe, about 2 miles from Berryville and about the same distance from the Shenandoah River. We have been here four nights and have been, and is yet under considerable excitement about a fight. Our whole Brigade stood picqet day before yesterday and the night following. The Yankees are on the mountains on the other side of the river. They bombed us pretty sharply that evening at a long distance and wounded one man. I hear that our batteries opened on them yesterday and drove them from their position but cannot vouch for the truth of it. We were ordered yesterday evening to put on our accoutrements and be ready to march at a minutes warning. We continued so for some time and were ordered to lay off our equipments, cook up our rations and be ready to march early this morning, but it is about 1 o'clock now and we are here yet, but occasionally I hear the booming of canon and would not be surprised to receive marching orders at any moment.

---

[63] In 1862 Confederate infantry and artillery privates were paid $11 per month.

We have drawn no money yet and cannot till Lieu. McCrary[64] gets here, all the other companies in the Regiment have drawn. I will send you some the first chance I get. It will be six months tomorrow since I left home. It seems but yesterday that I told you goodbye. I can but wonder if it will be six months longer before I return to your sweet embrace. But let what will come, let us bear it cheerfully and do the very best we can under all circumstances. You wrote me once to know something about gloves and I never could think to say anything about it. I have a most excellent pair that I found during the Richmond fights. You must write me a long letter. I am in fine health. May God bless you.

Your husband,
M.H. Fitzpatrick

☙

Near Berryville, Va.
Nov. 10th, 1862 *(Letter Number 16)*

Dear Brother & Sister,[65]

I received your kind and interesting letter of October 18th a short time ago, and was truly glad to hear from you again, but sorry to hear of your ill health and also of Henry's and the baby's sickness. I fear Henry will never stand a camp life but I hope he will be able to procure a discharge if necessary. I am in as good or better health than I ever was in my life and am gaining weight every day, for which I should be very thankful.

I had heard before I received your letter that Jim has got home. It done me more good than anything I have heard since I joined the Army. I was glad to hear that he was on a visit to you. I want him to

---

[64] 1st Lt. William R. McCrary of Co. K.

[65] This unusual letter is the only one in the collection addressed to someone other than Amanda. It may have been written to Burwell and Mary Greene, MHF's brother-in-law and sister. If so, then "Henry" is likely their son, a member of Co. A, 10th Battn. Ga. Inf. The baby would be their much younger son Burwell. "Jim" may be MHF's brother James, whom MHF almost always called "Doc."

stay there till he fully recovers. I am writing on the last piece of paper I have and I do not know where I will get an envelope.

(The remainder of this letter is illegible. The following note was written on the back of the same paper.)

August the 30th m m

if I get kiled I wante you to write a letter to my wife stateing to here that I want here to get Mr. _____ Evans to get my moneye what is duie or boute 44 dollars _____ to Forte Vallye Ga. To _____ A. Evans ine ceare of Mr. Evans.
A. S. Evans[66]

꿍

Near Guiness Station, Va. *(Letter Number 17)*
Dec. 4th, 1862

Dear Amanda,

I received yours of Nov. 5th some time ago and was truly glad to hear from you and to hear that all were well. I am well, but about worn out marching and about to get barefooted and naked too. We have been marching hard for twelve days. We started from five miles above Winchester, and got here about 12 o'clock yesterday and will probably rest here for awhile. We are about half way between Guiness Station and Fredericksburg, and about 60 miles north of Richmond.[67]

I wrote to Alex the third day after we started on the march, and sent the letter by Lieu. Jenkins[68] of the Taylor County Company to be

---

[66] A.S. Evans was a private in Co. K. Perhaps he had written this note before a battle and, surviving, gave or sold the paper to MHF.

[67] The Federal Army of the Potomac, now under Maj. Gen. Ambrose Burnside, began moving from Warrenton, Va., toward Fredericksburg on November 15, 1862. Gen. Lee followed, first with Longstreet's Corps and then with Jackson's. Jackson's men began moving south from the Winchester, Va. area on November 21. The buildup of both armies across the Rappahannock River from each other at Fredericksburg set the stage for battle.

[68] Wesley H. Jenkins enlisted as a private in Co. E, 45th Ga. He was elected 2nd lieutenant of the company on September 25, 1862 and then resigned on November 15, 1862. He probably carried this letter with him on his way home. Jenkins will enlist in the Georgia militia in 1864.

dropped in an Office somewhere near home. I also sent $65.00 by him to you. He lives near Dr. Greene's in Macon Co. and said he would forward it to Bro. Burwell's, and you could get it from there.[69] The Wilder boys, Jim Drew, and Tom Smisson all sent money by him to be forwarded in the same way, and they want Alex to get it and give it to those it was sent to. I told them I knew Alex would attend to it promptly. Jim Drew sent $25.00 to his Sister, the widow Crutchfield.[70] The Wilder boys sent $85.00 and Tom Smisson $175.00. I want you to pay Alex the $10.00 he sent me by Northrop Smith,[71] and use the other as you think best. I do not know how to advise you unless I was there, but you must cheer up and manage the best you can. You will have to pay our tax, &c. Alex will fix some way to get shoes for you. By rights we will draw money again in a day or two. If we do I will send you some more by the first chance.

We had some pretty rough weather on the march, but considering the time of year we were greatly blessed. I suffered more with sore feet than anything else. I threw away my old socks and took it without any and done much better than with the old holey things. I bought a pair and wore the two last days and got on very well. I paid a dollar for them. They had been worn some and I nearly finished them just in two days.

My feet are nearly well now. My shoes are nearly worn out. I would wear out any thing the way we had to march and the kind of roads we had to go over. A great many are entirely barefooted. My coat caught on fire one night while I was asleep and nearly burnt out one of the pockets and burnt a considerable hole besides. I learn that Capt. Browne[72] is in Richmond with our clothes. I would be happy to get mine just at this time, but it is all for the best that he did not get to us before we started on this march. They say we will draw shoes soon and I will get a pair then. The things you sent by John Wilder are in Gordonville yet. I may get them after awhile.

Rumor says that a fight is anticipated near here soon, but I can tell nothing about it. I would like to give you a full history of our march, but I took down no notes and cannot do it from memory, but I recollect well we had to march in the daytime and cook at night regular on for

---

[69] "Bro. Burwell" was MHF's brother-in-law, Burwell Greene, Jr., and "Dr. Greene" may have been one of his relatives.

[70] Probably Elizabeth Crutchfield, who in the 1860 Census was thirty-two-years old and the head of a household with three children.

[71] Probably Pvt. J.N. Smith of Co. K. The Wilder boys, Jim Drew and Tom Smisson were all friends of MHF in Co. K.

[72] Capt. John T. Brown was quartermaster of the 45th Ga.

twelve days and nights. We came from Winchester down the Staunton road to New Market Town, then turned across the mountains. We first crossed the North Mountains then the Blue Ridge. The scenery on the Blue Ridge was the grandest I ever beheld in my life. The road went winding like a snake and we ascended up and up till we reached the snowy cliffs. It was a fair day and tolerably pleasant, but the snow and ice would not give way to the rays of the sun there. As we marched on I gazed upon the scene with the wildest imagination, and longed to stay there to rove and dream awhile, but onward we had to march. It rained hard one night while we were on the march and I was trying to cook in a spider[73] without any lid. It out-done me, but I made out a large cake and cooked it in the ashes and it done finely. We fared tolerably well in the eating line on the march but it is coming quite scarce just at this time, but I think they will get straight and draw full rations soon. Our whole force are around near here.

It will be seven months tomorrow since I left you and my darling boy. Oh! how I want to see you again, but it cannot be so now. Write me all about my boy, all about how he talks and what he does. I will close. May God bless you.

Your husband,
M.H. Fitzpatrick

Near Guiness Station, Va. *(Letter Number 18)*
Dec. 5th, 1862

Dear Amanda,

I wrote you a long letter yesterday and gave it to one of my mess to mail, and he found a man living near Griffin, Ga. and gave it to him. He will mail it in Griffin so you will get it about the time you get this. I write again today because one of our company Mr. James Martin[74] has got a discharge and will start home today or tomorrow and I concluded to send $10.00 more in money to you. I want to send you all I can

---

[73] A frying pan with legs, allowing the pan to be placed above the hot coals of a fire.

[74] James H. Martin was a private in Co. K.

possibly spare, and I will risk that much more at any rate. Martin will leave it with Jim Ray[75] and he will send it out to you.

I wrote all the news yesterday and hardly know what to write this morning. I am well and feel considerably refreshed after a day's rest. My feet are about well again. I marched so much that it wore the ends of my toe nails down to the quick, blistered my feet, and made them sore generally, but upon the whole I stood up to it finely and often enjoyed a real hearty laugh. It is useless for a man to say what he can stand and what he cannot stand until he tries and I find as much depends upon the energy and spirits of a man, as his strength. We are drawing full rations now and doing some big eating. From the general appearance I think we will stay here several days. I am looking every day now for Capt. Brown to come with my things. None of you have written to me exactly what you sent, you must write in your next so that I will know whether I get all or not, and if I do not get some shoes pretty soon I will have to write home for some. I cannot afford to go barefooted as long as there is any other choice.

The Yanks are about 6 or 7 miles from here on the other side of Rappahanock, and I think not much danger of an immediate fight. Thoug of course I cannot tell about that. D. H. Hill's Division is not very far from here I learned, but I have seen none of Doc's Company in a long time. Tell Doc to be sure not to leave home till he gets entirely well, but when he does come, to come to see me before he goes to his Reg.[76]

As I have nothing better to write about I will give you a riddle that was given to us last night.

In a garden there strayed
A fair young maid
As beautiful as the morn
The first hour of her life
She was made a wife.
And died before she was born.

The answer to this is composed of three letters and the fifth letter of the alphabet is the first and last letter of the answer. You must all write oftener to me, _____ got letters yesterday, but in vain did I look for one. Direct your letters to Richmond all the time and they will be forwarded to the Reg. no matter where it is. Kiss my boy and tell

---

[75] James J. Ray, clerk of the Court of Crawford County.
[76] This letter would seem to confirm that the "Jim" of the unusual "Brother and Sister" letter (Letter 16) was Doc, who after Antietam recovered at a private home in Maryland and then at his mother's home in Crawford County.

him his pa is well and is coming home to see him after awhile. Be sure to write often. May God bless you.

Your husband,
M. H. Fitzpatrick

๛

Near Fredericksburg, Va. *(Letter Number 19)*
Dec. 15th, 1862

Dear Amanda,

I received your kind and interesting letter of Nov. 30th late yesterday evening and through the providence of God I am permitted to answer it, for we have had another severe battle and it came very near closing the war with me. I received a wound in the left side from a Sharpshooter while lying down. The ball tore through my havresack and glanced against my ribs braking the skin and bruised me severely and gave me the worst shock I ever imagined of. I received the wound late on the evening of the 13th. I am now at the old camp and am improving fast. But in order for you to understand it, I will give you a sketch of the whole affair.[77]

Early on the morning of the 11th heavy canonadeing was heard in the direction of Fredericksburg about six miles from here. We were ordered to be in readiness to march at a moments warning and remained so all that day. Early on the morning of the 12th we took up the line of march toward Fredericksburg. We moved slowly and cautiously and constantly could hear the booming of canon and the

---

[77] In this letter MHF gives an excellent description of Thomas' Brigade's role in the Battle of Fredericksburg on December 13, 1862. As part of A.P. Hill's Division of Jackson's Corps, Thomas' Brigade was in reserve when the Federal Divisions of George Meade and John Gibbon found a gap in Hill's lines. The Federals pierced Hill's lines and threatened the Confederate position on the right of the battlefield. Thomas' Brigade, then Gregg's, Lawton's, Trimble's, and Early's, pushed the Federals out and secured the Confederate lines. Thus ended the best Federal attack of the day. After succeeding waves of Union soldiers crashed against the entrenched Confederate lines, the Army of the Potomac suffered 12,653 casualties to only 5,309 for the Army of Northern Virginia. (E.B. Long and Barbara Long, *The Civil War Day by Day, An Almanac, 1861-1865* [New York: Doubleday & Co. Inc., 1971] 296.) The two armies then settled into winter camps on opposite banks of the Rappahannock River at Fredericksburg.

sharp crack of the skirmishers rifles. We moved on about three miles and took a position in a thick wood as supporters. All day we could hear canonadeing and skirmishing but no general engagement. We remained in that position till about 2 o'clock the next day which was the 13th. Canonadeing and skirmishing was still kept up, getting nearer and more vigorous, and occasionally they would salute us with a bomb and sometimes with dangerous consequences. About half past 1 o'clock the deafing roar of thousands of small arms and whistling of bullets all around us told us that the ball had opened in earnest. We staied there some 20 or thirty minutes and were ordered to another place about 3/4 of a mile to the left. We doublequicked the most of the way and when we reached the place formed a line of battle or tried to in a thick low cedar growth, and marched into it. We had gone but little distance before the bullets came whistling thick and fast and the heartrending cries of the wounded were constantly heard. On we went but still could see no Yankees, but soon the right wing of our regiment fired a deafening volley which told that they were in sight of the blue coats. In a moment more we could all see a plenty of them. I raised my rifle took deliberate aim and fired, loaded and fired again. The Yanks retreated and we followed with a rush and a yell and poured death in their ranks at every step. They retreated about five or six hundred yards and made a stand or tried to, but we charged on and soon made them run again. The Yanks were then in an open field, we followed them a short distance in the open field and halted and fired on them as they retreated till they got beyond our reach. We then ceased firing and took our position there in line of battle. We could see thousands of blue coats to our right but all was still near us except a few skirmishers to our left. The regiment to our left sent out skirmishers to rebut against them but the fire of the Yankee scouts was right towards us. We were ordered to lie down. About a dozen balls one after another whistled close by me. I had my blankets folded in a narrow belt tied together at the ends and had them across my shoulders as is usual for soldiers to carry them. I was lying rather on my side with the fold of the blankets against my head. A ball struck the blankets right against my head but did not go clear through the blankets and did not hurt me. I moved a little lower down and was lying on my left side, in a few moments another ball came and struck me on the left side on the lower part of my ribs which knocked me nearly senseless. I have never had any thing to hurt quite so bad before. I jumped up and halloed that I was wounded. Two of our boys bore me quickly away, one under each arm. I had gone but little ways before a dizziness came over me with the strangest feelings I ever had came over me. The boys poured some water on my head and face and it soon passed off and we went on, till we came to the ambulances. They put me in one, and carried me to the hospital which was on the ground in the woods. They took me out of the ambulance made a pallet with my blankets and I lay down. Fortunately I got near one of my own company that was wounded. I suffered considerably, but after awhile went to sleep and slept soundly for several hours. When I awoke I felt greatly refreshed but just half of my head and one arm and leg felt sore and stiff. I was tired lying and by rubbing and twisting and trying pretty hard to my great joy I got up by myself and walked about some which helped me the most in the world. The shock I received had passed off and I was comparitively a well man to what I was a short time before. It is strange to me how a ball can shock a man in that way, but I do not wish to gain any more knowledge about it from experience.

The next morning I could walk about right well but was awful sore. The Doctor took down my name and where I was wounded and told me to go to the old camp. I put out and got here after hard work and a long time but I was about worn out when I got here, I assure you, although I had only 1 1/2 miles to come. That was yesterday, last night I slept soundly and feel tolerably well today. When I cough it pains me very much and all that side feels sore and lifeless but I hope I will soon recover. I had on my overcoat and old jeans coat but the ball did not enter them atall. The ball went right between me and the ground I reckon is what made it hurt worse. Five of our company besides myself were wounded, none killed. Lieu. McCrary[78] was dangerously wounded in the lower part of the bowels. Joe Powell[79] severely in the leg, John Wilder[80] shot through the upper joint of the left forefinger. E.R. Webb[81] and Tom Smisson[82] slightly shocked. There was no fighting yesterday except canonadeing and skirmishing and I hear of no fighting this morning up to this time, but they are still in battle array near each other and a great battle anticipated. I do not know the results of the battle of the 13th but I think we got the best of it. At least we drove them back all along where I was wounded the ground was literally covered with dead and wounded Yankees. Tip Hammock went through safely but the hottest time may be to come yet.

I saw Old Stonewall twice on the morning of the 13th and Gen. Lee once. We have more confidence in Old Stonewall than any of the

---

[78] Lt. William R. McCrary of Co. K died on December 16, 1862.
[79] Pvt. Joseph M. Powell of Co. K died in a Richmond hospital on February 6, 1863.
[80] John A. Wilder was a corporal in Co. K.
[81] Enoch R. Webb was 3rd corporal of Co. K.
[82] The Thomas Smisson diary does not have any entries for Fredericksburg.

Generals. He has command of a Corps, and our Division constitutes a part of it. In fact we have been under him in all the tramps since we left Richmond. We are blessed with good weather at this time. If it was cold like it has been many a wounded soldier would freeze.

I received Lou's and Ma's letter of Dec. 3rd yesterday at the same time I did yours. It had been a long time since I had received a letter and it done me much good to get them and to hear once more that you were all well and getting on as well as could be expected under the circumstances, and to hear that my boy was growing fast and learning to talk. When I read that he would go to the door and call me as loud as he could, I could not help from crying like a child. It is useless to talk about how bad I want to see him but I will bear it with cheerfulness and still hope on that I will get to see him ere long. The prisoners that we took at the late fight say that they are making the last desperate effort to take Richmond and if they fail they are going to give it up. I have but little doubt but what they will fail and I have a strong hope that we will then have peace.

The 6th and 27th Ga. are somewhere near here, but they were not in the fight. One of our Company saw Jim Wilson[83] and talked with him, just before night on the evening of the 13th. He was well and was detailed as provost guard.

I was glad to hear through your letter that Babe and Rufus and Matt had joined the church.[84] I hope the Lord will bless them in it. As to my part I have gone entirely wild and if I ever get back I shall have my name taken off the church book for it is a shame and disgrace to the cause of Christ for it to be there. But the Lord has spared my life so far for some purpose I know not what. I want you all to continue to pray for me but look upon me no longer as a worthy member of the church.

I have written several letters home recently all of which I hope will be received in due time. I wrote to Mother on the 10th inst.[85] and told her all about my clothes, &c. If I had not got my shoes overcoat and blanket I would have fared but midling by this time. As to old

---

[83] James Martin Wilson was a corporal in Co. C, 27th Ga.

[84] "Babe" was Samantha White, one of Amanda's younger sisters. "Rufus" was one of Amanda's younger brothers. "Matt" was a neighbor and friend, Martha Knowlton. The minutes of Elim Baptist Church show all three joining the church "by experience" in 1862. (See Tina C. Hortman, "Elim Baptist Church Proceedings," *Central Georgia Genealogical Society Quarterly* [1989] 114.) "By experience" meant that they were uniting with Elim based upon their previous church membership and earlier baptism.

[85] By "10th inst." MHF meant 10th of the same month.

Brown's[86] coming with our clothes I have about given that out. I get along pretty well now. I wear both pairs of my britches and have been wearing them for nearly two months. The outside pair got nearly impossible but I worked on them late the other day and they do finely now. The great misfortune here the most of the time is we have nothing to patch with. I have been without a handkerchief for some time till yesterday evening. One of our company burnt a hole in one of his shirts and throwed it away or rather gave it to any of us here (there being a few of the sick and wounded here) to patch with. It was a pretty good checked shirt. I took the back off and hemed it with loud stitches washed it and made a first rate hankerchief. I have saved enough to patch my coat pocket and the hole that was burnt in my coat that I wrote you about, which task I expect to perform now pretty soon. Tell Lou and Ma I will write to them soon. Be sure to write soon, and write me another long letter. May God bless you.

Your husband,
M.H. Fitzpatrick

ॐ

Royster, or General Hospital No. 20 Richmond, Va. *(Letter Number 20)*
Dec. 24th, 1862[87]

Dear Amanda,

Knowing that you like to hear from me often at any time and especially while I am here wounded I concluded to write you a few lines this morning. My general health is very good and my wound I think is improving fast, but I cannot lay on that side yet. The Doctor seems to think that I am much worse off than I think I am but I do not tell him so. It is useless to say much to the Doctors here, they go their own way about things generally. He told me this morning that I must keep in bed a while longer. I made no reply but between his visits I lay in bed but little. He told me yesterday morning that he would give me a furlough after awhile. Those that know says he will be certain to do

---

[86] MHF was still awaiting Capt. John T. Brown, the quartermaster of the 45th Ga., who is mentioned in Letter 17 as being "in Richmond with our clothes."

[87] MHF's Compiled Service Record shows he was admitted to General Hospital No. 20 in Richmond on Dec. 17, 1862.

whatever he promises, but I think it very uncertain about getting one. So you must not look too anxiously for me and if I do not come, you will not then be so sadly disappointed. I am getting anxious to hear from you again and to hear whether or not you received your money safely. I have written to Mother & Lou both since I have been here, I wrote Lou about hearing from my clothes. I hope they will be safe for me when I return to my Reg. I do not think it hardly worth while for you to write and direct a letter here as I will be almost certain to be away before I could get it, but write and direct to Richmond as usual and I will get it at the Reg. But, if it should be necessary for you to write to me here direct your letter to General Hospital No. 20, care of Dr. Harris.

Well, Cout, this is Christmas Eve but little does it seem so to me. I see no indications of Christmas at all, no more than for Sunday which is simply none. I have heard from none of our boys that are here wounded since I wrote Lou. I expect Lieu. McCrary is dead.[88] They give no pass here consequently there is no chance for anybody to get out to hear or see anything. Cicero Cloud and John Spillers are in this Hospital, or was till this morning. Cloud was sent to Camp Winder and Spillers was detailed here as nurse or wardsman or something of that sort.[89] Money is pretty scarce with me now. I only have $6.90 cts. but I can draw here at any time whether I get my furlough or not but I thought I would wait awhile and see.

Tobacco is nearly all I spend money for, it cost $2.00 per pound. I had a three Dollar bill that I could not pass here and I sent it back to camp by Lieu. Rutherford's negroe, to the one I got it from. I will get that when I go to the Reg. If I could get a pass I would buy many little nicknacks so I expect it is best as it is. I send out by the Negroe attendants to get tobacco. We get plenty to eat, enough to make out very well with the exercize we take. If I get off home I will try to bring you and my boy a Christmas present of some sort. It is useless to talk about how bad I want to go home but I will try and not think about it too much. I will close. Remember me in your prayers. May God bless you.

Your husband,
M. H. Fitzpatrick

ɹ❧

---

[88] William McCrary of Co. K died on December 16, 1862.
[89] Pvts. Cloud and Spillers were in Co. K.

General Hospital No. 20 Richmond, Va. *(Letter Number 21)*
Dec. 29th, 1862

Dear Amanda,

If you have received the letters that I have written recently, no doubt you are looking for me at home, but I fear you will be disappointed. There has been a change of Doctors in this ward. The one that was attending here when I first came as I wrote you promised me a furlough when he thought it safe for me to start. But he left day before yesterday and another has taken his place. I asked the one we have now this morning what chance there was for me to get a furlough. He said the last recommendations for furloughs that they sent up were about to be refused, or at least had not returned them and they would have to wait and see the result before they sent up any more.

So you see the _____ thing is working and it is extremely doubtful now about my getting off. Perhaps it is all for the best, but at least we will have to take it so which ever way it works out.

I am getting on very well. My whole left side pains me some yet but not much. I cannot sleep on that side yet. The Dr. permits me to go about now inside the enclosure but no patient is permitted to go outside. The boys say it is the only hospital in the place but what a pass can be obtained but that I do not know or care about. Every thing is kept very neat here, and they feed very well. My appetite is excellent and I eat about all I can get. They serve lightbread, beef, soup, pees and occasionally _____ . We get coffee for breakfast and supper, _____ for supper and soup for dinner. It is often the case the plate is not filled, and we eat our own and then fall in for a patient's plate. I very seldom eat without getting other men's rations.

They have hospital underclothes, that is, shirt and drawers for us to wear all the time we stay here, so I had to pull off my shirts and drawers the first night I got here and it will be a very rare occurence if I ever see them again, but when I leave I will get either them or others in their stead. The first shirt and drawers I got hold of was worse than get out but I did not keep them long before I made a negroe get me a good sett. They are the most singular made shirts I ever read of. The tail is as long almost as I can remember and are split up very little ways on the sides. They have no colar but a button that buttons in the bosom, and no wristbands or buttons at the ends of the sleeves.

I have heard nothing from any of our wounded since I wrote you last. You do not know how anxious I am to hear from you again.

Immediately after receiving this I want you to write me a long letter and write me all the news from away back whether you got your money or not &c and direct it to General Hospital No. 20, Richmond, Va. Care of Dr. Harrison, not Harris as I wrote you before. Be sure to do this as it will do no harm if I do not get it and I think I will stand a chance of getting it for if I am sent to the Reg. before it gets here, it will be forwarded to me.

Kiss my boy for me and tell him all about me. Tell him we have got the yanks nearly whipped and that I will be at home after a while. May God bless you.

Your husband,
M.H. Fitzpatrick

Letters
1863

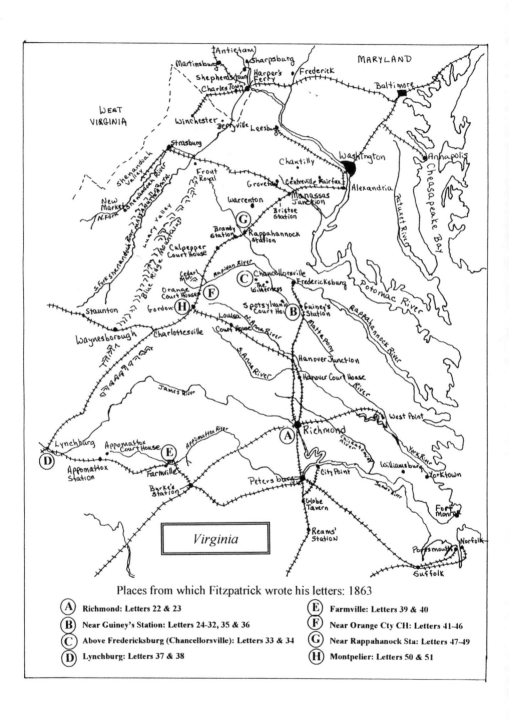

Places from which Fitzpatrick wrote his letters: 1863

(A) Richmond: Letters 22 & 23

(B) Near Guiney's Station: Letters 24-32, 35 & 36

(C) Above Fredericksburg (Chancellorsville): Letters 33 & 34

(D) Lynchburg: Letters 37 & 38

(E) Farmville: Letters 39 & 40

(F) Near Orange Cty CH: Letters 41–46

(G) Near Rappahanock Sta: Letters 47–49

(H) Montpelier: Letters 50 & 51

Camp near Guiney Station Va. May 16th 1863

Dear Amanda,

I received yours of Apr 29 a few days ago and as I wrote to Lou immediately I have waited till now to write to you. I wrote two letters to you while on the tramp and (one soon — a mistake) after we stopp[ed] all of which I hope you received in due time. I know you all have suffered much uneasiness but I suppose your fears in regard to Dec O. & myself have been quelled ere this time. I am well and getting on finely at this time. I was truly glad to hear that you were all well, and that your chickens garden pigs &c were doing so well. But truly sorry to learn of the death of Sarah Rickerson, her death has grieved her brother Tom a great deal. I am sorry to learn that your cards are nearly worn out. I do not know what you will do about it, but if you can do no better you must try to muster up money enough to buy another pair, let the cost be much or little. We will draw money again this evening and I will try to send you a little more home the first chance I get. I hope you succeeded in getting thread from the factory. The women at home have a hard time now and I truly sympathize with them, but I hope God will bless our efforts and we will all yet see better and brighter days. You no doubt before this time have heard of the death of our brave and beloved General Stonewall Jackson. We gained a glorious and brilliant victory, but his death has cast a gloom over that brilliancy that cannot be easily erased. I was near him when he was killed but did not know it at the time. He was shot on Saturday night, by his own men, the North Carolinians. He and his staff were galloping near

Letter of May 16, 1863, in which MHF describes
the wounding and death of Gen. Stonewall Jackson
at Chancellorsville
Photo: Rene Victor Bidez, Fayetteville, Georgia

Ferguson Hospital Lynchburg Va July 6th 1863

Dear Amanda.   Another week has passed and no letter from home and I am still here at the hospital. I am disappointed in both. I was sure almost that I would have been gone from here before this time and also sure that I would have received a letter from you or some of the home folks by this time. I am about well now and expect to leave here soon. I am waiting to draw my money before I report for duty. I learn that we will get it today but do not know how true it is. The pay rolls have been made out and we have been sworn in and I do not know what it is to hinder them from paying us. There is some excitement here about the safety of Richmond and many convalescents have been sent from the hospitals here to defend it. I was sure the Doctor would send me but he examined me and said I said I was too weak yet. That was the first of last week. They are sent to Richmond and formed into Companies and Regiments and will probably stay there till the Yankees leave from about there or till Lee's army falls back from the north. I do not know whether they will send any more to Richmond or not. I do not want to go there, but much prefer being sent to my Reg. But I had rather go to Richmond and join the mass forces there than to stay here when I am able for duty.

Letter written while MHF was hospitalized during
the Gettysburg campaign.
Photo: Rene Victor Bidez, Fayetteville, Georgia

General Hospital No. 20 Richmond, Va. *(Letter Number 22)*
Jan. 2nd, 1863

Dear Amanda,

I write to you again to let you know how I am getting along. My wound is improving fast, and I think it will soon be entirely well so that I can rejoin my Reg., but I have been a little sick for a day or two extra of my wound, but I hope it will soon wear off. It is a dull heavy feeling, with a loss of appetite, and restlessness at night. I bought a quarter's worth of sausage from a negroe this morning for breakfast which tasted delicious to me and not a great while after I lay down and slept about two hours of good sound sleep and I feel better this evening.

My getting a furlough has entirely played out. I asked the Doctor this morning about it and he said there was no chance in the world now. At first they would not give me one because the trip would hurt me and now I am too near well. I know you will be disappointed but you must bear it like a true heroine as you are, and we must hope it is all for the best, as our actions are governed by an all wise Being. And I have a strong hope of returning home soon to stay which will be joy indeed. My hopes are founded on the recent victories in the South West (at least so far as we have heard) and our late victories here, which I think will turn the scale in our favor and be the means of our gaining our independence soon.[1]

I have not heard from any of our wounded since I wrote you last, but I suppose that John Wilder got a furlough as he was wounded in the hand. If he is at home you had better, I reckon, send me some shirts on his return, if you did not sent me any by Capt. Brown, for it is doubtful about my getting more than one when I leave here and it may be of not much value. Do not go to the trouble of making new ones, just any sort will do.

In the last letter I got from you, you wrote that you had nearly broken yourself down at work and had made some money. This you deserve great credit for and I am proud of you, but you must not brake yourself down. You also wrote that your cards were nearly worn out.

---

[1] By "recent victories in the South West" MHF may have meant William T. Sherman's defeat on December 29 at the Battle of Chickasaw Bayou, near Vicksburg, Miss., and, perhaps, the Confederate victory at the first day of the Battle of Stone's River, near Murfreesboro, Tenn., on December 31.

This I am sorry for, as it cannot be easily remedied. Cards[2] are worth $25.00 a pair here, but I hope they are cheaper there. But you must get them when yours wear out no matter what the price is, if they can be found.

Yesterday a new year was ushered in upon us and it was as pretty a day as I ever beheld. With the new year comes new hopes and new prospects, and let us resolve to live better and do better than we did in the past year. The 8th of this month will be eight months since I pressed you in my arms and bade you good-by. It has been eight months of great excitement, toil and fatigue to me and I have undergone more than I once thought I would ever be able to stand, and with the entrance of the new year I can but wonder how long this will endure, but we cannot dive into the future so we must be content with the present and hope for the best.

I sent you a new year's present yesterday, The Magnolia, a weekly literary paper published in this place.[3] I subscribed for it for six months. I hope it will be a great pleasure, profit and pasttime to you. Be sure to write me whether or not you receive it. I have bought two copies of it since I have been here and am highly pleased with it. I sent you half of one copy of it in the last letter I wrote you, and if it does not make my letter too large I will send the other half in this letter and the next copy you will get by mail and by that means you will get all of the tale of the Vow of The Duelist. Write me in your next whether or not you take the Recorder[4] yet. I want you to take it till I get back for from it you can learn much about the war and of the whereabouts &c. of our army. You can get somebody to send on for you and let it continue to come in my name.

I wrote you in my last to write to me immediately and direct it to this place, which request I hope you have complied with. I do not know how long I will stay here but I hope not long, as I had much rather be with my Reg. but you must write again and direct here, and if I leave before it gets here I can have it forwarded to the Reg. I get pretty lonesome here at times but generally I am cheerful and I spend a good portion of my time in waiting on the sick, and there is almost

---

[2] "Cards" were used to separate and align the fibers of cotton and wool that were about to be spun into cloth. Each card contained hundreds of metal teeth about a half inch long mounted on a wooden rectangular paddle complete with a handle. The teeth wore out, requiring the cards to be replaced. MHF knew cards were essential to Amanda's production of homespun fabric.

[3] *The Magnolia* was a Richmond literary magazine begun in 1862. (See Bell Irvin Wiley and Hirst D. Milhollen, *Embattled Confederates: An Illustrated History of Southerners at War* [New York: Harper & Row, 1964], 213.)

[4] The Milledgeville, Ga., newspaper previously mentioned.

always a book or paper that I can get to read. Well, as I cannot get home to make my boy a present you must make him one of some sort in my name. Write me if you have made him any britches yet. Tell Doc to stay at home till he gets well but when he does come to be sure to come to see me before he goes to his Reg. May God bless you. Write soon.

Your husband,
M.H. Fitzpatrick

꒞

General Hospital No. 20 Richmond, Va. *(Letter Number 23)*
Jan. 5th, 1863

Dear Amanda,

I have just been fixing up to start to my Reg. and I tell you my heart throbs with joy at the idea of again being with my comrades in arms and getting to wear my new suit of clothes. I will start this evening but am told will have to go to a place they call the soldiers home and be sent from there to my Reg. and will probably have to stay there tonight.

When I wrote you last which I believe was only three days ago, I was a little sick and expect you have been uneasy about me, but I have got straight again, but I tell you I am keen to get away from here. There is so much sickness here and all the time a loathsome stench from the wounded. I did not get my own clothes back, but I come out pretty well at least better than I expected. I got two pretty good white cotton shirts. One of them is a shade too small and the other a shade too large but they do finely. I got a very good pair of white cotton drawers, but they are a little too short in the legs and I had to sew up one of the legs the first thing I done, it being ripped nearly all the way. Upon the whole they will all do finely as I am not quite so particular as I once was, and I hardly think it necessary for you to comply with the request I made in my last letter about sending me shirts, in fact, I had rather you would not send them till I see how things are going to work and I write for them.

I will write to you again as soon as I get to camp. The boys sometimes laugh at me about writing home so often but I think I know best about that, and I want you all to write to me now right away and direct to the Reg. as usual. Now, Cout, don't sit down and wait till you hear from me again before you write, but write me a long letter as soon as you get this. No doubt you have written to me and directed to this place, but it is uncertain about ever getting it so you must write me the news from away back again.

My wound, I think, is almost if not entirely well. The Hospital is a good place for the sick and wounded at least much better than the camp, but it is the last place in the world for a well man of my disposition. This hospital is a large three story brick building and was originally a tobacco Factory. The first floor is used for a dining room, the second and third for the sick.

Well, Cout, it is nearly night and I am at the Soldier's Home. I did not get to finish my letter at the hospital before I had to start. Only two of us from that hospital left for the camps.[5] They carried us first to a place they called the Barracks I believe, and then brought us here, under guard all the time. It looks pretty hard but I reckon it is all for the best. There are about a hundred of us here now. We are in a large room and will have to sleep on the floor which I assure you is not noted for cleanliness, but anyway will do a soldier. We will take the cars in the morning at 5 o'clock. I learn the army is near Guiness Station. You no doubt have heard all about our victories in the West.[6] There is strong talk of peace here on the strength of it. God grant it may come. It is getting dark and I will have to quit. Remember me in your prayers. May God bless you and my darling boy. Be sure all of you to write soon.

Your husband,
M.H. Fitzpatrick

ॐ

---

[5] MHF's Compiled Service Record shows he returned to duty January 5, 1863.

[6] Again, MHF is probably referring to Sherman's repulse at Vicksburg and to what was reported as a Confederate victory at the two-day battle of Stone's River at Murfreesboro, Tenn. The later battle was actually a draw that ended with the Confederates under Braxton Bragg retreating to Tullahoma, Tenn.

Camp Near Guiness Station, Va. *(Letter Number 24)*
Jan. 8th/63

Dear Amanda,

I got here day before yesterday, and received your letter of Dec. 29th a short time after I arrived. I was truly glad to get it as I assure you and to hear that all were well. I am well and getting on finely now. I found my clothes all straight, I put them on right away and felt like a new man. They fit me exactly; and it is given up by all that it is the prettiest suit there is in the Company. My shirts are just the idea and my comfort cannot be beaten, my gloves are also fine, but I had a good pair already. I was offered a dollar for my old pair, but thinking they were worth more I laid them away in my knapsack for harder times. I was truly sorry you sent the coverlead,[7] as I had two good blankets. I sold it for $10.50. I hated the worst in the world to do it but I could not carry it and rather than run the risk of losing it, I sold it. We may stay here a good while, but it is very uncertain. Tip Hammock and I sleep together now. Tip had a good coverlead and a blanket, and we sleep very comfortably. We have one tent and some flys[8] now and we are doing pretty well. Four of us are hard down at work today building a chimney to our fly. We are about 8 miles east of Guiness Station. I got a letter from Doc when I got back here dated Dec. 14th which I will answer soon. I wrote to you while in Richmond just before I started here, and wrote several letters before that, while in the Hospital.

I know you were uneasy when you heard I was wounded, but you are posted all about it before now. I am glad to hear you had your money all safe, and also glad to hear that you had got salt, and that Betty[9] had pigs and Doc wrote that your cow had a calf which will be a great help to you. I do hope you will get along well.

You wrote me to know what I charged for Lydda. I do not know how much Jennie worked out but I thought both together would make one hand and draw a fifth of the crop.[10] I will write to Alex about it and

---

[7] Probably a coverlet or quilt.
[8] Tenting material.
[9] Apparently the Fitzpatrick sow.
[10] The 1860 Census shows Nancy Hill Fitzpatrick owning four slaves. The Census does not name them. "Thornt" was certainly one, and Lydda and Jennie probably were two others. It seems from the letters that MHF and Amanda rented Jennie, and possibly Lydda. But it's also possible that MHF was in charge of his mother's slaves. It's even possible he owned or co-owned them by this point, although there's no supportive evidence in the letters.

straighten it. You must just do the best you can about the debts, &c., like you I wish I was there to attend to it but it cannot be so now. I did not draw any money in Richmond but will draw here today. I will send you some more money the first chance I get. I subscribed for a newspaper for you while in Richmond, The Magnolia, which I hope you have received before now. Cout, I am afraid you will be mad with me about the coverlead and I am almost sorry I sold it but I did not know what to do. I sold it to the highest bidder. One of our Company bought it that was needing it very bad.

Lieu. McCrary is dead but I suppose you have heard it . Lieu. Slatter has been promoted to lst Lieu. and Rutherford to 2nd and they elected old man Evans 3rd Lieu. while I was gone. He is a poor choice sure.[11]

Since I wrote the above I have drawn my money. I drawed $77.00, I now have $58.00. I want to send $25.00 to you by the first safe chance.

We draw a plenty to eat now and some sugar. We make sassafras tea and wheat coffee, &c. We are busy at work, I must close for this time. George Wright's[12] wife is out here and is going to start home tomorrow. Andrew Wright,[13] one of our company, is going to see her tonight and I will get him to take this letter and send it by her. Do not send me any more clothing till I write for it.

I find one good pair pants a plenty at one time. I am so glad Henry has learned to talk, I know he is much company to you. Write me a long letter and write all the news. I think your sample of cotton jeans excellent. Write me the answer to the riddle I sent you some time back. May God bless you.

Your husband,
M.H. Fitzpatrick

Editors' Note: From January 18 to February 18, 1863, MHF was granted the first of two furloughs he had during the War. After visiting his family, he returned to Virginia and wrote the following to Amanda.

---

[11] "Lieu. Slatter" was Thomas J. Slater, who had been 2nd lieutenant. "Rutherford" was Williams Rutherford. "Old man Evans" was Allen S. Evans who was elected 2nd lieutenant of Co. K on Feb. 17, 1863. Evans, who was 36 at the time of the 1860 Census, was considerably older than most of Co. K.

[12] George W. Wright was a private in Co. E, 6th Ga. On February 19, 1863 he was discharged after supplying H.C. Harris as his substitute.

[13] A private in Co. K and George Wright's brother. See *1850 Census of Georgia, Crawford County*, compiled by Rea Cumming Otto, 1986, copyright: Rhea Cumming Otto.

૨ⅅ

Camp Gregg near Guiness, Va. *(Letter Number 25)*
Feb. 19th, 1863

Dear Amanda,

I arrived here safely day before yesterday, and am happy to inform you that I am well and hearty and in fine spirits. I made the connection all the way through, and had but little trouble. I brought my box safe through. It cost me $5.00 to get it here, but the boys have paid it back to me, except three of them that have not got the change. The boys were overjoyed to get their butter &c. It was after dark when I got here, each one met me with a hearty grasp of the hand and a welcome voice that made my bosom swell with gratitude. As soon as I got warm and dried off a little, nothing would do but I must open the box and it was an interesting spectacle to see them get around, eager to receive something from home. I found the boys in the same place I left them. It was a mistake about their moving.

I carried my box in the car with me a portion of the way, but at some places they would not let me pass with it and then I had to put it on the baggage car. I had to get a passport in Petersburg before I could get on the cars, which I obtained with little trouble. When I got off the cars at Richmond the guards halted me. I told them my furlough was not out and that I had a box of clothing to take to my company. They then told me to pass and go where I pleased. I went to the American Hotel deposited my box and went to draw my ration money. The Office was closed and I could do nothing. I then went to the passport office, and applied for a passport. The Clerk told me he could not give it that I must report at the Soldiers Home. I told him I had a box of clothing at the Hotel to carry through. He looked at me a moment, then wrote out the passport and handed it to me. I then went back to the Hotel with one of our Reg. and failing to get a bed, we got permission to sleep on the floor where we rested finely till the next morning. It was after dark when we got to Richmond. The guards got Bridges[14] right away, but he went through straight the next morning to Guinea's. I took the cars for Guinea's at daybreak the next morning. When I got to Guinea's I failed to find any of our wagons, but found other wagons and got one to haul my box to the Church 1 1/2 miles from here. There were two or three of

---

[14] Probably Thomas Bridges, a private in Doc's company.

my Reg. with me, that had trunks and boxes. Some of them came on to the Reg and sent a wagon to meet us, which brought us right on. It was snowing rapidly and the roads are too bad to talk about. Yesterday it quit snowing and went to raining. Today it is cloudy but is not snowing or raining.

I went to see Doc yesterday. I found him well and getting on finely, but I had the worst walk I ever had in my life. I sent his comb and toothbrush to him by Bridges, which he had received safely. He had my handkerchief which he gave to me. I went up this morning to draw my ration money. They sent me to the Brigade Commissary. He told me I would have to wait a few days till he got an answer from the Secretary of War, as he had written to him on the subject, but he said there was no doubt but what I would get it, and it would be 33 1/3 cts. a day, which is more than I could have got in Richmond. I could have gotten it in Richmond by staying there another day, but there was danger of losing my box, and getting into other scrapes. Tell Lou I had no chance to enquire anything about Henry.[15] None but those that have been to Richmond can know how mean a place it is or how glad a man is to get away from there.

All the boys have chimneys now, but several have come in from the Hospital and we are pretty badly crowded. Salt has nearly played out here, and rations are short, but it is owing, I suppose to the bad roads between here and the station. They are building a pole road from here to there, but it is not finished yet. When it is completed wagons can pass with comparative ease. It is not very cold now but it is awful muddy. The boys are in high spirits with the prospects of peace. The boys say I will get my transportation money back when we draw money again, or at least it was so read out on dress parade. I have 12 1/2 dollars in money now.

Well, Coot, I will close. I have thought a great deal of you and Henry since I left. Poor little fellow I left him in tears that morning. I shall never forget his look. Cheer up and do the best you can and may God bless you both. Be sure to write soon. No letters came for me while I was gone. Doc has received no letters yet.

Your husband,
M. H. Fitzpatrick

---

[15] Lou's younger half-brother, Henry C. Greene, a private in Co. A, 10th Ga. Inf. Battn. He was sick for much of his military career. Although MHF did not know it when he wrote this letter, Henry had died on January 4, 1863 from pneumonia at General Hospital No. 16, Richmond.

꙰

Camp Gregg Near Guinea's Station, Va. *(Letter Number 26)*
March 5th, 1863

Dear Amanda,

I wrote to Alex today and sent the letter by mail. One of our Company Henry Sanders[16] is going to start home on sick furlough tomorrow morning, and although I have just written by mail, it will never do to miss this good a chance to send a letter home.

I received a letter from Alex of Feb. 18th a short time ago, which I answered today, and received yours of Feb. 19th yesterday, which did me much good to read and learn that all were well and that you were getting on so well weaving. I am also truly glad to hear that Henry's cough was getting well, and that he was so pert. Poor little fellow, no doubt but what he missed his Pa, and looked for him every morning, but alas! in vain as you say, for we are many miles apart now. It looks hard and it almost breaks my heart to think of you and him there alone, but these troubles are upon us and we must try to submit cheerfully.

I am in fine health, and am nearly the only man in the Company but what is complaining, more or less. I hardly know what to write unless I recapitulate what I have written to Alex, which I will do partly, as you will be apt to get this first. Cicero Cloud died today, at the Division Hospital about a mile from here.[17] He died of smallpox. I wrote some of you about his taking the smallpox and that he was sent to Richmond, but I was mistaken. This I fear will have a tendency to render you all uneasy about me, but it need not, as I was not in the tent with him and all that were with him have been sent off about half a mile from us. There were 12 sent off which makes duty very heavy on what few well ones there are of us here. We have pretty fair weather of late, and they have got to drilling and doing guard duty again, but this I do not mind atall when I am well. I have got another good Enfield rifle and excellent equipments, which I am very proud of. I have washed once since I got back, I got my clothes clean with but little trouble because I had soap. I do not mind washing atall now. One of my overshirts have commenced wearing out already. I patched it good

---

[16] Pvt. Henry W. Saunders, Co. K.
[17] Pvt. Cicero C. Cloud, Co. K.

the other day. I can patch fine now. I drawed a pair of pants yesterday. They were sent here by a Relief Society and did not cost me anything. They had no buttons and but one pocket, and no buckle on the strops and the strops would not meet behind. I have been working on them late. I put on buttons and fixed the strops behind and put on a buckle, and started to put in another pocket, but I am about to stall on that. I got a pocket from an old pair I found lying out of doors. It is nearly dark, and I will have to quit. Be sure to write soon. Pray for me. May God bless you and my darling boy.

Your husband,
M. H. Fitzpatrick

᠀

Camp Gregg (*Letter Number 27*)
Near Guinea's Station, Va.
March 8th, 1863

Dear Amanda,

I wrote to you only a day or two ago and sent the letter by Henry Sanders one of our Co., but Col. Simmons[18] is going to start home in the morning and I will write again. I sent you $20.00 by him which you will use as you think best. As I told you when at home, I owe Cleveland $10.00 and Fickling for the lumber for our house, which is all I believe. No! I owe Joab Willis for working on our house.[19] Just use your own discretion about paying out, but be sure to keep some by you. If you pay Joab, make him knock off the interest if you can. I drawed $26.70 cts. today, and had $11.00 before.

I am in fine health and getting on finely. I received a letter from Jim White today, in regard to the death of Henry Greene. I will enclose it to you, give it to Lou and tell her to send it to her Pa, by mail or some way as soon as she can.[20] I thought it would be the best way. I saw Jack

---

[18] Thomas J. Simmons, a lawyer, commanded the 45th Georgia from October 13, 1862 until the surrender at Appomattox.

[19] Probably Washington C. Cleveland, a prominent Crawford County planter and Primitive Baptist preacher. "Fickling" was likely C.F. Fickling of Crawford County. Joab Willis is listed in the 1860 Census as a fourty-four year old mechanic.

[20] Henry Greene was Lou's half-brother who had died in Richmond of pneumonia. "Jim White" was one of Amanda's older brothers, who served as 2nd lieutenant of Co. C, 59th Ga.

Hancock this morning, one of Doc's company, who is on Provost Guard.[21] He said he was at his Reg. yesterday, and Cicero Futrel had just got back from home. He said Cicero brought some letters for this Comp. I am in hopes he has one for me. I am going up there tomorrow.

Yesterday was our pickette day, but in the morning I was detailed to guard at the Brigade Headquarters and so I missed it this pass. I fared finely over at the Headquarters. We had a tent to sleep in, and we sent to the butcher pen and bought a beef liver and heart and borrowed a spider and had some old time eating. We drawed a pound of beef to the man yesterday. It is quite a treat for us, it having been three weeks since we drawed any. We draw 1/4 lb. of bacon a day and do not eat all of that. It is so strong and old it is not good.

I wrote you in my last about my pants, I have fixed them up finely. I had liked to have stalled on the pocket but I kept working on it till I got it all right. They are coarse but they are just the idea to wallow in in camps, and I got them in a good time, for my others were wearing off thin rapidly. I am all right in the clothes line now.

We had a pretty heavy rain about two hours before day this morning and it is cold and cloudy now. We had preaching today, the Chaplain of the 49th Ga. preached for us. He is an excellent preacher and preached a good sermon. Today is Sunday, as you may judge from there being preaching. Our preacher has gone home on furlough.[22]

I wrote Alex about the election. It has not come off yet. Bill Loman came in today from home and is a candidate.[23] Well Coot it is corn planting time in Ga. and no doubt buds are putting forth, and the merry warbling of birds is heard, all indicating that stern winter is loosening her tight grasp. But there are no such indications here nothing but cold cold winter yet.

I will close. Cheer up and brave the storm of adversity with all the energy you can put forth and with the hope that brighter days are not far ahead. Write soon and write all about my boy. May God bless you both.

Your husband,
M. H. Fitzpatrick

---

[21] Probably T.J. Hancock, 3rd sergeant of Co. C, 27th Ga.

[22] The chaplain of the 49th Ga. was John James Hyman. Edward Benjamin Barrett began serving as chaplain of the 45th Ga. on January 4, 1863 and continued through Appomattox.

[23] "Bill Loman" was William G. Lowman, 2nd corporal of Co. K. The election was probably for lieutenant.

ɜͩ

Camp Gregg (*Letter Number 28*)
Near Guinea's Station, Va.
March 15th/63

Dear Amanda,

I shall try to write you a few lines this morning. I am sorry to say to you that I am quite sick and have been ever since last Monday night. I have got the mumps, and I think some kind of fever with them. I have had high fever and sick stomach nearly all the time. I tried to throw up one night and fainted and they had to carry me in the tent. I think I am getting some better now. I can eat a little and sit up a good part of the time but I am so weak. The Dr. done nothing for me, said he had no medicine.

Today is Sunday and is my birthday. I went to the 27th last Monday. I saw Cicero Futrel and got my letters.[24] Doc was well. Col. Simmons[25] started home last Monday. I sent a letter with $20.00 in it to you which I hope you have received.

I will have to quit, I am too weak to write now. I hope I will get well soon.

May God bless you and my boy. Write soon.

Your husband,
M.H. Fitzpatrick

ɜͩ

---

[24] Futrell was elected 2nd lieutenant of Co. C, 27th Ga. on February 12, 1863.

[25] Thomas J. Simmons must have been going home on furlough. He had succeeded the first colonel of the 45th, Thomas Hardeman, Jr., who resigned because of wounds received at the Battle of Frayser's Farm.

Camp Gregg Near (*Letter Number 29*)
Guinea's Station, Va.
Mar. 18th/63

Dear Amanda,

I wrote to you a day or two ago. I was quite feeble at that time, I am much better now. I have but little fevor now, and sit up some days all day. My jaws have gone down to nearly their natural shape. My jaws were pretty sore but I suffered but little from them, compared with the headache and sick stomach with which I suffered so much. I did not know before that the mumps made anyone so sick. I do not know how or where I caught them. One other of our Company took them at the same time with myself. They have fallen below on him and are giving him fits. I have escaped that awful part of it so far and hope I will go through without it. My appetite is very poor yet. The boys have been very kind to me in waiting on me and trying to get me something I could eat. I got several potatoes which was a great help to me. I also got some rice which we had all drawn, but which they gave me, and I made me some rice batterbread which was good. Yesterday evening I borrowed a cup of meal, and this morning I bought 75 cts worth of sausage and had a first rate breakfast.

I was truly glad to get your letter from Cicero[26] of March 1st and to hear that all were well and doing well. I am so glad to hear that your seed came up well. I hope you will have a fine garden. I was somewhat surprised to hear that you had weaned Henry, but I expect it is best for him. I expect you had a pretty rough time with him at first. I was glad to learn that Sister Mary and her family came to see you all. Henry, I know, was in _____ with the children. I received a letter from She and Bro. Burwell yesterday, they were all well. I can get a letter from them quicker than from home at anytime.[27]

Well, I suppose Alex has left you, but I have since heard that he returned. I hope under the circumstances he will not have to stay away long. Doc has not been to see me since I have been sick. I think a little hard of him. Several have passed since I have been sick and told him about it. I went to see him a week ago last Monday and came back by the 12th and 4th Ga.s. At the 12th I saw Capt. Carson, Bob Jolly and

---

[26] Cicero Futrell of Co. C, 27th Ga.
[27] "Sister Mary" refers to MHF's sister Mary, who was married to Burwell Greene, Jr. Their family consisted of Lou and six children, including some quite young.

John Price,[28] at the 4th I saw Warren Dickson and Bart Hicks.[29] The two latter received me very kindly indeed and I conversed with them some time.

I wish you would all write to me oftener. Write me all about my boy. Do not be uneasy about me. I will write again soon.

Your husband,
M. Hill Fitzpatrick

꿩

Camp Gregg   (*Letter Number 30*)
Near Guinea's Station, Va.
March 22nd, 1863

Dear Amanda,

According to promise I write you again. My health is still improving. In fact, I am nearly well now except weakness, and I am rapidly gaining my strength. It will be two weeks tomorrow since I was taken sick, and by being careful now I think I will soon be straight again. It has been more than a month since I wrote my first letter to you after coming back and I have received no answer to it yet. It is true I have received four letters from home, two from you and two from Alex, but none in answer to letters that I have written, and I have almost despaired getting any. Henry Scarborough[30] got back yesterday evening. His father sent me word he wanted the money on a note he holds against me for some shingles. The note is for $15.00 I think. The next time we draw I will try to save enough and send it to you to pay it. I had forgotten that I owed it, but it is a just debt. We have more snow and cold weather. It snowed along slowly for three days. Today it is warmer and cloudy but is not snowing. Today is Sunday but it does not look much like Sunday here. Col. Simmons I suppose will start back in about two weeks from now. If you could get some of them to see him for

---

[28] Capt. John T. Carson, Pvt. John R. Jolly and Corp. John W. Price of Co. C, 12th Ga.

[29] Warren Dixon was 3rd sergeant of Co. I, 4th Ga., and Bart Hicks was probably William R. Hicks, 1st sergeant of the same Taylor County company.

[30] Pvt. Henry James Scarborough, of Co. K.

you, I expect he would bring me a snack of something to eat. Just anything that you could send would be very thankfully received.

The election for Third Lieut. has all played out. Evans held his position as Third Lieut. and a Second Lieut. has been appointed. They appointed Orderly Hatcher,[31] but he has not received his commission yet, and the appointment is not yet fully confirmed, but I suppose there is no doubt but what Hatcher will get it. That will leave a vacancy in the Sergeants which I learn they are going to give me but I do not know how true it is. The Present Second Sergeant is to be Orderly and I am to have his place, is the way I believe they are fixing it up.

We have had no more cases of Small Pox and I think the danger is about past now. I am a little uneasy in regard to Alex having to leave you all, but You must do the best you can and I hope God will provide some way for you to make a living. I am anxious to get a letter from you and to hear from my darling boy. I expect he can say almost anything now, and can go to see his Grand Ma by himself. Write me how your pigs are doing and everything you can think of. Pray for me.

Your husband,
M. H. Fitzpatrick

꒰ꔫ꒱

Camp Gregg (*Letter Number 31*)
Near Guinea's Station, Va.
Apr. 17th, 1863

Dear Amanda,

I received yours of Apr. 2nd from the hands of Col. Simmons day before yesterday, and was truly glad to hear from you again and to hear that all were well. I received one from Alex at the same time and also one for Doc which I carried to him yesterday. I found Doc well and hearty and getting on finely. I received my pants also from Col. Simmons, which I am sorry you sent, as I have a plenty without them, but I am thankful to you as I know you did it with the best intentions. I tried to sell them but could not get more than half their worth offered

---

[31] Probably G.A.L. Hatcher, original first sergeant of Co. K It appears from this paragraph that the first sergeant acted as company orderly.

for them, but I shall try again and may get a good price for them yet, if not I shall take care of them the best I can. Titus,[32] Pope's boy, says he will take care of my knapsack again when we start to march. You can scarcely imagine the waste there will be in clothes when we leave here, and we are expecting to leave constant.

The last letter I wrote home was to Lou about 10 days ago. I have been very sick since then with the bloody flux.[33] I suffered a great deal but it did not last but three days, but I have had the diareah ever since, which I suppose is nothing amiss as it would not do to stop it too suddenly. I am nearly well now, and have reported for duty. It seems that I am unfortunate since my return from home but I hope I will get straight now and keep so. There are a good many cases of bloody flux in the Reg. and some of them very serious, among which is Orderly Hatcher here in our tent. I do not think he will live long without a change for the better.[34]

I am glad to hear that Henry improves so fast in talking. I know he is much company to you. You say he eats so much like me. I would like the best in the world to see him eat and to help him when it comes to chickens and eggs. It makes my mouth water to read about your chickens and eggs. My advice to you is not to sell one, but eat them and make your meat go farther by it; and I would not try to raise a great many, as corn is scarce. I am truly glad to hear that you have a good garden. I hope it will be of great advantage to you and I am glad to learn that your pigs are growing fast. You must be a real hand at the loom from the number of yards you have woven but you must not break yourself down at it. If it were not for the patriotism and industry of the women the Southern Confederacy would soon come to nothing. Many a soldier can now realize the value of woman's work that thought but little or nothing about it before the war commenced. I am glad to hear that you have been visiting since I was at home. One of our Company, Loucious George[35] said he saw you and my boy down at your Aunt Sarah's[36] not very long ago. He said Henry was the finest looking boy out. He came to the Reg. last week. I expected you would give me a full description of your visit there in your next letter but you said nothing about it. I am glad that you are so well pleased with the Magnolia. I hope it will be a source of pleasure and profit to you. I read

---

[32] Apparently the slave of Pvt. Henry B. Pope of Co. K.

[33] Dysentery.

[34] Henderson's *Roster* states that Hatcher "died of fever at Camp Gregg, Va., April 20, 1863."

[35] Pvt. Lucius H. George, Co. K.

[36] Unidentified by the editors.

the two you sent me by Bud Robinson[37] with much interest and was highly pleased with the conclusion of the Tale in them.

Well, I suppose Matt & Japp has a fine son.[38] You must give me a description of him when you see him. I was surprised and sorry to hear of the death of the two Mrs. Morgans.[39] I read the other day in the Index (a copy of which happened to stray in our Camp) the death of Mrs. John Ellis, which I regretted much to learn. The Index excited many pleasing recollections in my mind and I read it with much interest.[40]

Lieut. Rutherford, Andrew Wright, John Spillers, and Jerry Lewis all came in last week. [41] John Spillers gave Tip Hammock a good new Bible, which is the first one I have ever seen in the Company, though we have had a good many Testaments. Our preacher has come back and we have preaching every Sunday when the weather is not too bad, and prayer meeting round among the Companies at night.[42] We had prayer meeting here in our Company last night, which was the first that has been held since we have been out. We had a heavy snow soon after I wrote to Lou but it did not last long. We have the prettiest weather I almost ever saw now and it is very pleasant. I saw some peach blooms today, but there are no buds putting forth yet. We draw plenty to eat now, and the flour is much better than we have been getting formerly. We draw pickled beef now which eats fine, and occasionally get some rice, sugar and syrup. Lieut. Evans has resigned, and gone home. He left the first of last week, so we will have to have another Lieut.[43] I do not know who it will be. Some think there is a chance for me but I think there is but very little if any chance atall. I

---

[37] Unidentified by the editors.

[38] "Matt & Japp" were Martha Wallis and William Jasper Knowlton of Crawford County who had been married by the Rev. J.V. Gordon on May 8, 1862 (see William Henry's *Marriage Records of Crawford County, Georgia, 1823-1899* [Warner Robbins, Ga.: Central Georgia Genealogical Society, 1989] 98).

[39] Unidentified by the editors.

[40] MHF refers to the April 6, 1863 issue of *The Christian Index*. (Vol. XLII, No. 14). *The Christian Index* was a weekly newspaper published in Macon by the Rev. Samuel Boykin. It championed the interests of Missionary Baptists in Georgia. Mrs. Ellis' obituary states that she was Elizabeth Ellis, wife of John W. Ellis of Crawford County, and that she died at age forty-one.

[41] Apparently Lt. Williams Rutherford and Pvts. Wright, Spillers and Lewis, all of Co. K, had returned from furloughs home.

[42] The Rev. Edward Benjamin Barrett was chaplain of the 45th Ga. from Jan. 4, 1863 until the surrender at Appomattox. Barrett attended Mercer University and served as pastor at Baptist churches in Irwinton and Providence, Ga. before the War. A fine biographical sketch of Barrett is included in *History of the Baptist Denomination in Georgia* (Atlanta: Jas. P. Harrison & Co, 1881) 22.

[43] 2nd Lt. A.S. Evans resigned on March 24, 1863.

have no influential friends to urge my claims if any claims I have. It does not bother my mind. If I can get through this war with the name of a good private it will be honor enough for me. I will close up. I am going to quit begging you all to write to me and see how that plan will work. May God bless you.

Your husband,
M. H. Fitzpatrick

P.S. I collected my ration money the other day, $9.90 cts.[44]

∼

Camp Gregg (*Letter Number 32*)
Near Guinea's Station, Va.
Apr. 27th, 1863

Dear Amanda,

I received yours of Apr. 11th a few days ago, and yours of the 19th from the hands of John Wilder[45] day before yesterday both of which I was truly glad to receive. I was very sorry to learn from yours of the 11th that Henry was sick but glad to learn from your last that he was well again. I am well and getting on finely. John had several letters for the 6th and 27th Ga. and I went up with him yesterday which was Sunday to carry them. I found Doc well and in fine spirits generally, except a little scarcity of something to eat. Cicero & Jim were also fat and hearty.[46] They moved about 3/4 of a mile a short time ago. They moved chimney and all and are well fixed again. We are going to move tomorrow or next day. We will move, I understand, about two miles from here. It is thought it will be more healthy and wood will be more convenient. I am glad to hear that you are getting on so well weaving, but sorry to learn that you will be scarce of salt and meat. You must stretch it as far as you can and do the best you can under the

---

[44] In MHF's Compiled Service Record there is a note showing he received this money for "commutation of rations while on furlough of indulgence, from Jan. 18, 1863 to Feb. 18, 1863."
[45] Corp. John A. Wilder, of Co. K.
[46] "Cicero" is probably MHF's friend Cicero Futrell, 2nd lieutenant of Co. C, 27th Ga., and the editors assume "Jim" is Amanda's brother, James R.S. White, 2nd lieutenant of Co. C, 59th Ga.

circumstances. We may expect hard times but we must bear up under them with fortitude and be willing to suffer almost anything, to gain our liberty. I am sorry that I cannot be with you in these times of trial to aid and comfort you, but this too we must submit to with the best fortitude we can put forth.

I was glad to learn that Ma and Lou had paid a visit to our relations in Macon County. I hope it was a great source of pleasure to all of them.[47]

We are doing pretty well in the eating line now. The flour we draw is excellent and we have drawn shad twice recently. The shad went fine sure. We had a first rate breakfast this morning. Tom Smisson[48] gave us a good sized piece of butter, and we had a dozzen eggs for which we paid two dollars, and some wheat coffee without sugar. We boiled the eggs and put a good quantity of salt, butter, and red pepper on them, which made them too good to talk about. I still keep my same old mess-myself, Drew and Webb.[49] $2.00 a doz. for eggs is high living, but Drew was sorter sick and wanted some and we all pitched in. I paid a dollar for a drink of brandy one morning not long ago, which was my first pull at that price and, will be the last, but I was a little sick and naturally wanted some anyhow.

You said you hoped I would get home in time enough to eat some of your nice chickens. I can but hope so myself. The boys in the 27th Ga. think we will have peace soon. We whipped the yanks last Summer. They gained nothing the past winter, a great many of their soldiers time is up the first of May and Lincoln is not going to conscript. All these reasons I think bring at least a glimmering ray of hope for peace.

This Brigade held a political meeting day before yesterday, I attended it. The Brigade was but partially represented and the whole concern proved to be a mere farce, at least in my opinion. The proceedings will be published in the Ga. papers and you probably will see them. They passed a set of preamble and resolutions which were very good, and which raked Joe Brown pretty deep. Capt. Wallace offered a resolution opposing reconstruction forever, a heated discussion arose from it. The majority thought it was treating the idea of reconstruction with too much dignity, and it was voted out. Col. Grice proposed Gen. Colquitt as a candidate for Gov. of Ga. and it was voted down, and they broke up with a row, and a big laugh. I think the

---

[47] Lou's father and step-mother, Burwell and Mary Greene, lived in Macon County, as did other relatives.

[48] Pvt. Thomas Smisson of Co. K.

[49] MHF's friends and mess-mates, Jim Drew and E.R. Webb.

election should be left with the people at home as the soldiers mind is not in the proper condition to attend to such things.[50]

I wrote Alex about buying me a knife from Hatcher or his brother rather. Since then I had my old knife fixed by getting another blade put in it and sold it for $2 1/2 dollars. It cost me 50 cts to get it fixed. None of the vacant offices in our Comp. have been filled yet. They seem to be slow in filling them. I will not grumble any more at you for writing as long as you do as well as you have recently. So write again soon and may God bless you and my boy.

Your husband,
M.H. Fitzpatrick

ᕤ

The battlefield of Fredericksburg, Va. *(Letter Number 33)*
Apr. 30th, 1863

Dear Amanda,

I seat myself to drop you a few lines under rather gloomy circumstances. We are now in line of battle near the same place we fought the last Fredericksburg fight, and know not what moment the same dreadful scenes may be reenacted. I am in fine health and in as good spirits as a man well could be with the surrounding prospects.

We moved our Camps on Tuesday, and Wednesday morning which was yesterday morning. We were surprised by receiving orders to be ready to march at a minutes warning. A few minutes afterwards we received orders to fall in. We marched here and formed a line of battle and have been here since. It is now about four o'clock in the evening. We are on the second line, there being another line between us and the enemy. The Yankees have crossed the river at, or near the same place they crossed before. I went down there this morning and could see and hear them plain. I went over the ground we fought on before and saw the place where I was wounded. Our pickette line extends half mile

---

[50] Joseph E. Brown was governor of Georgia and an extreme advocate of states' rights. Brown's failure to cooperate with the Confederate government was not always appreciated by the Georgians fighting in Virginia. "Capt. Wallace" was William Sharp Wallace, of Co. E, 45th Ga. "Col. Grice" was Lt. Col. Washington L. Grice of the 45th Ga. and "Gen. Colquitt" was Alfred H. Colquitt, who commanded the brigade of which Doc's 27th Ga. was part.

beyond the railroad. Our first line of battle is behind the railroad.[51] I went a few hundred yds beyond the Rail R. in the old field. The field is literally covered with graves now. I saw the arm of a dead Yankee sticking out of a grave that had not decayed. We will take the front line in the morning so I learn, and will probably be in the opening of the battle. The booming of canon can be constantly heard but I have heard no small arms yet. We had no time to cook any rations, but detailed men yesterday evening to cook for us and they brought us a supply this morning. I left my knapsack at the camp with the sick. The orders were to bring everything with us but I could not toat mine. I brought my blankets, a shirt, pair of drawers and a pair of socks besides what I have on. The boys we left said they would take care of it if they could and if they could do no better would leave it at a private house. We left several there among whom were Mose Colvin, Tom Rickerson and John Wilder. I had no time to carry my knapsack to Titus, it being about four miles to where he was. I will send you enclosed in this my old furlough and passports, which you can keep as a relic, and will probably do you some good in future should I be killed.[52]

The 27th Ga. is here below us I learn and I suppose Doc is with them. I had hoped for peace but there seems to be no peace for us soon. Do not grieve for me, even if I should fall, but remember me as one dieing to save his country.

I have thought much of my darling boy today. I acknowledge my weakness. It almost breaks my heart, to think of him. I love him perhaps too dearly. God grant that he may live to be a good and useful man and that his path through life may be smoother than his unworthy parents.

Dear Mother, do not grieve for me and Doc. I hope we will come out safe. I know you see much trouble about us and will be sorely troubled till you hear from us again, but cheer up the best you can. I will write again soon if permitted. May God bless you all.

Yours truly,

M.H. Fitzpatrick

---

[51] Unknown to MHF, the Federal Army of the Potomac, now under Maj. Gen. Joseph Hooker, had gained a strategic advantage over Lee's Army of Northern Virginia by crossing the Rappahannock River upstream from Fredericksburg. Hooker left 40,000 Federals behind in Fredericksburg, diverting Lee's attention. By this letter, Hooker with 70,000 men was well into the Virginia Wilderness, on Lee's left flank. Lee would begin moving to confront Hooker on May 1.

[52] Pvts. Colvin, Rickerson and Wilder were all good friends of MHF's in Co. K. "Titus" was the slave of Henry B. Pope of Co. K. Amanda preserved this furlough and the "passports" (actually passes allowing him to travel to and from Virginia). They are pictured on page xxvii.

ॐ

Battlefield above Fredericksburg, Va. *(Letter Number 34)*
May 4th, 1863

Dear Amanda,

I wrote to you the day after we left camp and I snatch this moment to drop you a few lines again. Through the kind providence of God, I am safe so far. I was in a pretty hard fight yesterday morning, but I did not get hurt.[53] Two Of our Co. wounded[,] Henry Knight, very slightly, Jerry Lewis severely, none killed.[54] I saw Doc after the fight, he was not in the fight. He broke down before he got there.[55] One man killed in his Co., Bill McNease.[56] I saw Cicero Futrel. He was not hurt. We are away up here above Fredericksburg somewhere, I do not know where. We have whiped the yankees badly so far. We are expecting to fight again every minute. They moved our Brigade this morning about three miles. We came here throwed up breastworks and are waiting the approach of the enemy. We drove the Yanks from their breastworks yesterday, and run them a mile.

I am in fine health, but am awful tired. I will write again if permitted. May God bless.

---

[53] The Battle of Chancellorsville, May 2-4, 1863, was Robert E. Lee's most impressive victory. Thomas' Brigade was near the rear of the column on Jackson's famous march around the Federal right flank on May 2. They were not a part of the flank attack led by Robert Rhodes' Division in the late afternoon of May 2, but were brought up as reserves that evening. Following the wounding of Stonewall Jackson and A.P. Hill during the night of the 2nd, Maj. Gen. J.E.B. Stuart was placed in temporary command of Jackson's corps. Stuart led repeated attacks against the Federal breastworks that eventually caused the Federal retreat. MHF, in Thomas' brigade, was a part of these victorious attacks. See Ernest B. Furgurson, *Chancellorsville 1863: The Souls of the Brave* (New York: Alfred A. Knopf, Inc., 1992) and Stephen W. Sears, *Chancellorsville* (New York: Houghton Mifflin Company, 1996) for excellent accounts of the role of Thomas' Brigade in this battle.

[54] 1st Sgt. Robert H. Knight and Pvt. Jerry Lewis were in Co. K. Lewis died of his wounds at home in Crawford County on June 22, 1863.

[55] Colquitt's Brigade, of which Doc's 27th Ga. was a part, was vital to the famous charge by Rhodes' Division on May 2, 1863. The charge led to the collapse of Federal Maj. Gen. O.O. Howard's XI Corps.

[56] Henderson's *Roster* shows McNiece was killed at Petersburg, Va., on June 9, 1864, but there is nothing about his even being wounded at Chancellorsville.

2nd P.S. May 5th [57] We are still at the place we came to yesterday. We are awaiting the attack with cool determination. I did not get to send this off yesterday evening. I now have a chance to send it off. I am well and pretty well rested now. May God bless you.

M.H.F.

ʒ❧

Camp near Guiness Station Va. *(Letter Number 35)*
May 16th, 1863

Dear Amanda,

I received yours of April 29 a few days ago and as I wrote to Lou immediately I have waited till now to write to you. I wrote two letters to you while on the tramp and one after we stopped (a mistake I believe upon reflection) all of which I hope you received in due time. I know you have suffered much uneasiness but I suppose your fears in regards to Doc and myself have been quelled ere this time. I am well and getting on finely at this time. I was truly glad to hear that you were all well, and that your chickens, garden, pigs, &c. were doing so well, but truly sorry to learn of the death of Sarah Rickerson. Her death has grieved her brother Tom a great deal.

I am sorry to learn that your cards are nearly worn out.[58] I do not know what you will do about it but if you can do no better you must try to muster up money enough to buy another pair, let the cost be much or little. We will draw money again this evening and I will try to send you a little more home the first chance I get. I hope you succeeded in getting thread from the Factory. The women at home have a hard time now and I truly sympathize with them but I hope God will bless our efforts and we will all yet see better and brighter days.

You no doubt before this time have heard of the death of our brave and beloved General Stonewall Jackson. We gained a glorious and brilliant victory but his death has cast a gloom over that brilliancy that cannot be easily erased. I was near him when he was killed but did not know it at the time. He was shot on Saturday night, by his own men,

---

[57] Judging from this reference to a "2nd P.S." it appears that this letter was mailed by MHF with the preceding letter.
[58] MHF continues to be concerned about Amanda's cards, which were essential to making homespun fabric.

the North Carolinians. He and his staff were galloping near them and they thought it was the Yankee cavalry and fired. They were not in the front line and did wrong to fire.[59]

We are now camped at the same place we left to go to fight. We staid five days at a camp about seven miles above here and then came back here. I have seen Doc since I wrote to Lou. He was well and hearty. We returned from pickette yesterday evening. We had to go about 8 miles. It rained a great deal the evening we got down there, and at night faired off cold. I was on post that night. Tip Hammock and I stood together. We stood about three hours and did not have to stand any more that night. It was pretty cold and lonesome. We stood from 10 to 1 o'clock. We both had overcoats and a blanket, and stood it pretty well. We got lots of fine fish while we were down there but had to buy them. It was quite a treat to me. I love to go on pickette and have a change of scenery and excitement. In fact, I like a little adventure anyway after staying still awhile.

Several of the sick we left here have come back to us from Richmond among them Tom Rickerson. Tom is quite feeble yet but is improving. When he left here he took two pair of my pants out of my knapsack and saved them for me. I gave him one pair and took the new pair you sent me. I was proud to get them again sure as I was certain they were lost. My knapsack soap, &c. is lost for good. I have a plenty of clothes again in fact more than I can carry on a march. I wrote Lou about getting an overcoat and bed quilt. We are well fixed up in the sleeping line now. Drew, Webb and myself, have a Yankee tent just large enough for us three to sleep under.[60] We put up a few logs and covered them with the tent and have quite a snug little place. Each of us have an oilcloth and then my old quilt is just the idea to sleep on. I have one good blanket that I expect to keep, the one I carried home with me. Doc gave me an oilcloth, it is light and is the very thing to keep my blanket dry on a march.

I have had my hair cut since the fight, and have washed up all my clothes neat and clean. I am a splendid hand to wash. I expect I can beat you out of all hollow. The first thing I done this morning after breakfast was to get shaved. Then I took a general wash, feet, neck, head and all

---

[59] The night of May 2, after the great victory of the flank attack, was very confusing. In trying to press the advantage, Jackson, A.P. Hill, and their staffs were attempting to scout the Federal lines when they were fired upon by the 18th and 37th North Carolina regiments. Jackson's shattered left arm was removed that night. He appeared to be recovering, but pneumonia took his life on Sunday, May 10, 1863.

[60] MHF refers to Jim Drew and E.R. Webb.

and then put on a clean shirt and drawers and then washed the ones I pulled off and then sit down to scribble you a letter.

Well I reckon you think I have about run out of something to write, at least it is so whether you think it or not. I got me another canteen in the fight which I do not believe I told you about. It is just like my old one only it is not mashed up and it was full or nearly full of cool water when I picked it up, which was a great help at the time. I have not heard from Jerry Lewis since he was sent to Richmond but it was thought he would not recover. I felt a shudder pass over me when he was shot, which was the first time I ever felt scared while I was fighting, but it passed off in an instant. I was ambitious to be the first or among the first to mount the breastworks, but I fired my rifle just before we got to them and while I was loading half the company were across.[61] They are trying the men today that skulked out of the fight. So help me God Cout, my bones will bleech the hills of Virginia before they shall have me up for that.

Lou wrote me that you were going to make my boy some breeches. I want you to write me all about it in your next and whether he goes in his shirttail any or not, in fact all about him. You wrote he had his something that would bark but I could not make out what it was. Write in your next what it was. Be sure to write soon and write me a long letter. I am due Alex a letter I believe but the tramp made me forget how it was. I will write to him or Mother soon at any rate if we do not get into another fight.

Your husband,
M. H. Fitzpatrick

ॠ

Near Guinea's Station, Va. *(Letter Number 36)*
June 3rd, 1863

Dear Amanda,

I received your kind and interesting letter of May 10th some time ago, but as I wrote to Alex immediately I postponed answering it till now. I wrote to Alex and sent the letter by Capt. Gibson. I sent you

---

[61] MHF was describing the fighting on May 3, when Jackson's Corps, under Maj. Gen. J.E.B. Stuart, broke the Federal lines after incurring severe casualties in very heavy fighting.

$15.00 in money and sent $25.00 for Doc, which I hope has gone through safely. I am anxiously looking for a letter from home now, as I have received no answer to any of the letters I have written since the late battle.[62]

My health is not very good at this time, nor has it been since the fight. I was off duty for three or four days, but am on again now. I have severe cold and diareah caused I suppose by exposure during the tramp. I have taken no medicine for it yet and I hope to get well soon without taking any.

A badge of honor and distinction is to be given to one man from each Company in our Reg. for gallantry and bravery displayed in the late fight. Your unworthy husband was selected from our Company to receive it. The badges have not come yet. I shall be right proud of it as a relic of the past and will try to preserve it for my little soldier boy.[63] But I suppose he is to be Pa's man when he gets his breeches on. How I would like to see him struting about with them on and hear him talk. You must write me all about it.

The Brigade that Doc is in has been sent to Kingston N.C. but I suppose you have heard it before this time. He wrote me a long letter after he got there and I have written to him. I regret much being separated so far from him but I hope it will be for the best, as I do not think they will have so much marching and fighting to do there. I saw him two days before he started but did not know he was going at that time.[64]

We have real summer weather here now, and the leaves on the trees are about grown. I was sorry to learn from your letter that our wheat had the blast. I hope that it did not injure it very much. I reckon you have some ground by this time. We have a kind of protracted meeting going on here now. We have preaching every night and Sunday. Several have joined the church. The news we get from Vicksburg seem to be very vague and uncertain. If we succeed well there, I think we will have peace soon. I learn that nearly all the troops from Ga. have been sent out there even the State Troops, but I hardly believe this.[65]

---

[62] Capt. Aurelius W.Gibson, of Co. K, must have gone home to Crawford County on a furlough.

[63] At the request of Robert E. Lee, the Confederate Congress authorized "medals of honor" for one man from every company of the regiments that fought in the Battle of Chancellorsville. It appears that the medals were never actually struck, although the names of the men selected were published.

[64] Doc's 27th Ga. went to North Carolina to share in the defense of the coast.

[65] MHF was correct in his assessment of Gov. Joseph Brown of Georgia. Brown refused to allow state troops to fight outside of Georgia.

Write me if you ever hear from Billy Miller[66] and how he is getting on. Be sure to write soon and write me a long letter. Use the money I sent you as you think best. I would like for you to pay Scarborough if you can.[67] Remember me in your prayers. May God bless you.

Your husband,
M.H. Fitzpatrick

᠊ᡐᢀ

Ferguson Hospital, Lynchburg, Va. *(Letter Number 37)*
June 15th, 1863

Dear Amanda,

No doubt you will be surprise and grieved at the caption of this letter, but I will explain. I wrote to you, I think, about the 4th of this month. I was not well then and soon got pretty sick. On the 6th inst. our Reg. received marching orders, and I much against my will had to be left behind. I had high fever nearly all the time and was quite weak. I was sent on an ambulance to Guinea's Station, then on the cars to Hanover Junction, staid there one night, then on the cars to Gordonsville. Staid there one night, then to this place traveling all night and arriving here at daylight. From this place we were sent on a Canal boat to Buchanan a place 70 miles above here. When we got there the Hospitals there had been broken up and they sent us back here on the same boat. We were then put in this hospital. It is badly crowded and nothing extra anyway. We got here yesterday morning. I have fever more or less every day but I am stronger and much better I think than when I left camp, and I hope to be well soon. I regret very much not getting to stay at Buchanan as it would no doubt have been a better place than this. Four of our Comp are with me, among them is Jack Wilder.[68] He is pretty sick with fever, but is mending some, I think. I received a letter from you just before I left Camp dated 29th May I think, which I have lost, and at the same time one from Lou

---

[66] Unidentified by the editors.
[67] In his March 22, 1863 letter, MHF mentioned a debt of $15 that he owed to the father of Pvt. Henry J. Scarborough of Co. K.
[68] Pvt. Andrew Jackson Wilder of Co. K has been mentioned several times already in these letters.

dated 28th May. I was truly glad to get them but was almost too sick to read them at that time. I have got Lou's yet and will answer it soon. We had an election in our Comp for 3rd Lieut. just before I left it. Tom Smisson was elected. I run my name but was too sick to do anything about it and got badly beaten, but I suppose I would have been beaten anyhow as Smisson belongs to the ruling squad. It was said he would not be accepted but I cannot tell yet. I do not think he deserves it. Jon Walker is 2nd Lieut., he was appointed.[69] Office does not bother my mind now, what I want is to get well. Direct your letter to Ferguson Hospital 3rd Ward Lynchburg, Va. Be sure to write soon as I want to hear from home before I leave here. May God bless you.

Your husband,
M.H.F.

ॐ

Ferguson Hospital, Lynchburg, Va *(Letter Number 38)*
July 6th, 1863

Dear Amanda,

Another week has passed and no letter from home and I am still here at the hospital. I am disappointed in both. I was sure almost that I would have been gone from here before this time and also sure that I would have received a letter from you or some of the home folks by this time. I am about well now and expect to leave here soon. I am waiting to draw my money before I report for duty. I learn that we will get it today but do not know how true it is. The pay rolls have been made out and we have been sworn in and I do not know what it is to hinder them from paying us.

There is some excitement here about the safety of Richmond and many convalacents have been sent from the hospitals here to defend it. I was sure the Doctor would send me but he examined me and said I said was too weak yet. That was the first of last week. They are sent to Richmond and formed into companies and Regiments and will

---

[69] Smisson, according to Henderson's *Roster*, was elected "Jr. 2nd. Lieutenant" on June 4, 1863. The same day Joel A. Walker was elected 2nd lieutenant of Co. K. Smisson's diary mentions nothing about the election.

probably stay there till the Yankees leave from about there or till Lee's army falls back from the north. I do not know whether they will send any more to Richmond or not. I do not want to go there, but much prefer being sent to my Reg., but I had rather go to Richmond and join the mass forces there than to stay here when I am able for duty.

I have not heard a word directly from the Reg. since I left it, but I suppose they are in Maryland or Pennsylvania at this time, and from what I can gather from the papers are living high on Pennsylvania goodies.[70]

I have written four letters home since my arrival here. The first was written on the 15th June. Twenty one days ago, and I cannot see why I have received no answer. I received a letter from Doc last week which did me much good. He had a letter from home written the 14th of June, and I was glad to hear from that, that you were all well at that time.[71]

Jack Wilder is here yet. He is nearly well and is going with me to the Reg. or wherever we are sent to. If we go [to] the Reg. we will go on the cars to Staunton, and will then have to march 150 miles to get to them.

Six months of the year 1863 have passed and with it the Fourth of July. Preparations were made to have a celebration late in the evening at a College near here, but a heavy rain storm broke it up. An address was to have been delivered and the new Confederate Flag to be thrown to the breeze from the College dome, and it saluted with firing of canon. I was sorry it was a failure. Just before night they raised the flag and fired four or five rounds but it was raining so hard they quit.[72]

Yesterday was Sunday. Day before yesterday a man died in this hospital, and was buried yesterday. It is the custom at this hospital when a man is sent off to be buried to detail 6 men to march behind the bier. I was among the number yesterday. It was the first regular soldiers graveyard I ever attended. It is an old field nearly a mile from here. The graveyard is laid off in wards or squares, and fifty one buried in each square. A Book is kept in which the name of the man, his Comp., Reg., &c is sit down and the number of his grave, so that he can be readily found by his friends. The graves are dug just wide

---

[70] Because of this illness, MHF missed Gettysburg. Thomas' Brigade and the 45th Ga. were not heavily involved in that battle.

[71] The only surviving letters from Lynchburg are this and the previous one.

[72] This was the "old" Lynchburg College, an institution of the Methodist Protestant Church. It existed from 1855 to 1869. None of the buildings have survived, although "College Hill" in Lynchburg is the site. The new Confederate flag that MHF refers to was the Second National Flag. It had the Confederate Battle Flag (red field, blue St. Andrew's Cross outlined in white and thirteen white stars) in the upper left-hand corner with the remainder of the flag white.

enough to let the coffin in from the top to the bottom and are about 12 inches apart, except between the squares where there is a space of about 6 feet. The work is done by negroes and no tear of sympathy falls as the poor soldier is lowered to his narrow home in his mother dust.[73]

We have almost a continual flood of rain here. It scarcely misses a day without a drenching shower, and has been so for two weeks.

We are doing better in the eating line now. We get fresh beef and mutton, and pees.[74] Not green garden pees but regular old fashoned red dried corn field pees. They go fine I tell you, and the beef or sheep is what I long have sought.

I have two shirts two pr. Drawers, 1 pr. Pants, one blanket, one small oilcloth, and my overcoat with me. I have the last pants you sent me. They gave the boys in our Reg. just before the last march [a] choice to have their tents hauled or a portions of their knapsacks. Of course they all preferred the knapsacks. They carried one knapsack for every five men. I put a pair of pants and some other little tricks in one and sent them on. I think one of my company that is here will get a furlough before long. If he does he will carry my overcoat home for me, or will carry it to Knoxville and you can get it from there. I shall leave it here with him and if he does not get off home he can sell it for something and save the money for me. There was a general waste of things when our Reg. left the camp. I picked up a nice light blanket, and brought it here with me, besides the heavy blanket of my own, but knowing that I could not carry it on the march, I sold it the other day for $2.00

I have three pr. Socks with me, I have not wore any hospital clothes here. They have our clothes washed for us gratis once a week.[75]

I am keen to hear from my boy again. It does seem like it has been a long long time since I heard from any of you and especially from my soldier boy. I expect he can just talk almost anything now, and go any where by himself if permitted. You must just write me everything about him, and all about how you are getting along with your little affairs and how you are doing in the eating line. Write soon and write me a long letter, now don't put it off because you think I will never get

---

[73] This cemetery, now called "Old City Cemetery," is a Lynchburg landmark.

[74] Peas.

[75] By this time, the Confederate Medical Service was greatly improved at preparing food, providing hospital clothes, washing those clothes and maintaining clean wards. Lynchburg had three "general" hospitals treating many kinds of illnesses and wounds. H.H. Cunningham's *Doctors in Gray, The Confederate Medical Service* (Baton Rouge: Louisania State University Press, 1958, 1986, 1993) is an excellent source on Confederate hospitals and field medical service.

it but write and Direct to Richmond as usual and it will be mighty apt to come to hand. May God bless you.

Your husband,
M.H. Fitzpatrick

༄

General Hospital-2nd Ward 3rd Division *(Letter Number 39)*
Farmville, Va..
July 16th, 1863

Dear Amanda,

I received yours of June 24th a few days ago, and was truly glad to hear from you again and to hear that all were well. I received Lou's letter written May 29th before I did yours and answered it yesterday. You see from the caption of this letter that I have not started to my Reg. yet, and that I have changed positions. I will explain. Today is Thursday. Last Monday I drawed my money. I drawed $22.00. I reported for duty the next day. The Doctor much to my surprise and disappointment, examined me and said that I had not fully regained my strength yet and that my digestive organs were weak yet, and it would be better for me to wait a few days longer.[76]

Yesterday they received orders to transfer forty men from that Hospital to this place immediately and Jack Wilder and myself were among the number sent. We arrived here late last night. I told the Doctor this morning that I wanted to go to my Reg. He said he would send me in a day or two.

I am very well pleased with this place. It is a small neat village and is about fifty miles from Lynchburg on the railroad running from Petersburg to Lynchburg.

I directed Lou's letter to Reynolds as I suppose she is at her Pa's at this time.[77] I knew nothing about coming here when I wrote to her.

---

[76] MHF's Compiled Service Record shows he was admitted to Division No. 3, C.S.A. General Hospital, Farmville, Va. on July 15, 1863 and returned to duty on July 20, with the diagnosis of "debilitas," or weakness.

[77] "Reynolds" is a town in Taylor County, Ga. Because Lou's father, Burwell Greene, Jr., is listed in the Census of 1860 as living in Macon County and he died before the Census of 1870, this reference to his living in Reynolds is puzzling.

There are several wounded soldiers here that were in the Gettysburg battle. One of them who belongs to our Division says that Thomas' Brigade was in the fight Thursday and Friday which is all that I have heard from our boys yet. He could tell me nothing about the casualties. I long to be with them again and hope I will not be disappointed in getting off this time. I will write again before I leave. I sold my overcoat yesterday for Four Dollars. I saw no chance of sending it home and Four Dollars is better than nothing. I am glad that you are getting on so well making dresses and with your garden, chickens, pigs, &c. Like you I hope you will soon be able to raise your own meat.

The Yankees have got Vicksburg and I see no immediate prospect of peace now but it will never do to shrink for a moment or even get low spirited about it.[78] I am so proud to hear that my boy is doing so well and is so smart to talk. I long to see him with his breeches on, and talk with him, but I must wait patiently. Pray for me.

Your husband,
M.H. Fitzpatrick

❦

General Hospital (*Letter Number 40*)
2nd Ward--3rd Division
Farmville, Va.
July 20th, 1863

Dear Amanda,

I wrote to you only a day or two ago but as I shall leave tonight for my Regt. I will write again this evening, not knowing when I will get the chance again. This is Monday - I told the Doctor again this morning that I wanted to go to my Regt. and he said all right. Jack Wilder is going with me.

My health is very good, but I do not believe that I would ever fully regain my strength in a hospital. I think marching and the excitement of change will be an advantage to me. I do not know where we will find the Regt. The last account I had of Lee's army they had recrossed the Potomac and were anticipating a fight near Winchester.

---

[78] Vicksburg, Miss., fell on July 4, 1863.

I have been fixing up for the trip today. I have my blanket, oilcloth and clothes out sunning. I have just washed my meat bag and the inside of my havresack, and have them out drying. I had a shirt, a pr. of drawers washed last Saturday, so I will have clean clothes to start with. I have three very good pair of socks. I have learned to darn first rate and I find it a great advantage.

There are three large fine churches in this place--Baptist, Presbyterian, & Methodist. I attended the Baptist Church yesterday and last night.[79] I was well pleased with the services and especially with the singing. They had a splendid Choir but no instrumental music. There were some good looking girls there and if I had had my shoes blacked and had on a cravat, I should have gone home with some of them as long as they did not know I was married, provided you know they would have permitted me. Well, enough of this foolishness.

We have some pretty weather now which is a rarity to us. I hope it will continue till I get hardened to Camp life again. Our prospects are not so bright as they were a few weeks past and I expect the people in Ga. are pretty low spirited. This should be avoided as much as possible. It just fires me up to fight the harder, and I am told by those just from the army that the soldiers are in fine spirits and ready for another fight. I have never learned yet the casualities of our Company or Reg.

I see one bright ray in these dark times. There was a general insurrection in New York a short time ago, caused by trying to enforce the draft. Also in Connecticut and New Jersey. Now if the Yankees will fight among themselves and let us alone it will please me the best in the world.[80]

Well I quit writing and went down to the river and went in a washing and have just got back, fixed up my blanket and havresack, eat supper and drawed two days rations. I have my discharge from the hospital. Our transportation is all fixed and we will leave at 11 o'clock tonight. We will go from here to Lynchburg, from there to Charlottsville and from there to Staunton and will foot it the balance of the way which is the mournful part of the tune. I will write to you again on the way or soon after I get there, but you must not be uneasy if you

---

[79] Farmville Baptist Church was founded in 1836.

[80] The Draft Riots of New York City took place on July 13-16, 1863. Upwards of 1,000 people were killed or wounded and property damage was estimated at $1.5 million. The governor of New York called in state troops to quell the riots. Lesser riots also took place in other northern cities. See E.B. Long with Barbara Long, *The Civil War Day By Day, An Almanac, 1861-1865* (Garden City, N.Y.: Doubleday & Company, 1971) 384.

do not hear from me regularly and often now, for there will be much difficulty in sending off letters till the Army is settled again.

I hope to find several letters at the Regt. for me. Now do not neglect it but be sure to write me a long letter as soon as you get this, and direct to Richmond as usual. I shall be anxious to hear from home again when I get to the Reg.

Watermelons, peaches and many good things are plentiful in Ga. now at least, I hope so, for I want you all to enjoy these things if I am temporarily deprived of them. You must write me all about it and what my boy says about it and whether he is fond of them or not. You must get him a knife if he has not got one, and write me if he has a hat, and how fast he grows and all about him. I often long to be with you and him, especially when Sunday comes, but we must wait patiently and probably by suffering more, we will the more prize our liberties when gained.

I thought I would only write you a few lines this evening but I want to see you and talk with you so bad that I have kept on writing one stuff or other. Write me if Babe has returned home but I suppose she has before this time, the last I heard from her she was in Ala. Also write me when you heard from Greene and how he is getting on and also from Jim.[81]

Remember me in your prayers. May God bless you and my noble boy. Be sure to write soon.

Your husband,
M. Hill Fitzpatrick

৯৩

---

[81] "Babe" was Amanda's sister Samantha, younger by four years. "Greene" was one of Amanda's older brothers, Joshua Green White. Before the War, he had moved to Troy, Ala. Green enlisted as a private in Co. H of the 18th Alabama Volunteer Infantry Regiment, part of the Army of Tennessee. "Jim" in this paragraph is another of Amanda's older brothers, James R.S. White, 2nd lieutenant of Company C, 59th Ga. Infantry.

Camp Near Orange Court House,[82] *(Letter Number 41)*
Aug. 23rd, 1863

Dear Amanda,

Jeff Reins is going to start home on furlough in the morning and I
haste to drop you a few lines to send by him.[83] It is Sunday and the sun
has just sunk below the western horizon, the shades of night are
approaching and I will have but little time to write. I received a letter
from you of Aug. 3rd and if I mistake not, another which is misplaced
at this time which I have not answered. I wrote to Alex last week and
should have written to you sooner, but was waiting for Jeff's furlough to
come so I could send it by him. It came a few minutes ago and he will
start early in the morning. I will send Henry a pair of brass martingale
rings, which you must tell him is to put on his martingales, and ride his
pony with when he gets a little bigger.[84] Give them to him to play with
and if he looses them of course, it makes no difference. I send you some
buttons. They are not much account if any, but I know you will be glad
to get anything from me.

I am sorry I have no money to send you this time but I hope to have
some before a great while. They have given two men out of every one
hundred furloughs. I was surprised at it. Jeff has promised me to go to
see you and Ma, and he can tell you all the news. I intended to write
you a long letter and answer yours in full but I will have to put it off. I
am always so glad to hear from you and my soldier boy and to hear
that you are well. Bless his little soul how I want to see him and help
him eat millwaters[85] and peaches. Cout I want you to send me some
sewing thread. I have used all that black you gave me and the white
ball, of which I have a good deal yet, is too coarse for any of the needles
I have now. Also a little red pepper, not much, for I shall loose it. Do
not send any clothes. I have as many as I can take care of. I patch my
clothes and darn my socks regular and they last more than twice as
long by it. I also wash them regular now and can wash as clean and
nice as anybody. We draw some soap and I bought 50 cts worth so I
have a good supply, now.

---

[82] This and the following five letters were all written from the camp of the
45th Ga. near Orange Court House, Va., just west of the Wilderness and
Chancellorsville area, on the Orange and Alexandria R.R. These letters were
written during the lull in active campaigning following Gettysburg.

[83] Pvt. Silas Jefferson Raines of Co. K.

[84] Martingale: A horse's strap, attached with rings.

[85] Culinary historian Terry Ford of Ripley, Tenn., believes "millwaters"
would have been a porridge made with fruit.

I am Sergeant of the guard today and will have to be up the most of the night. It is about dark, and I must quit. May God bless you. Write soon and write a long letter. Pray for me.

Your husband,
M.H. Fitzpatrick

ข๛

Camp Near Orange Court House, Va. *(Letter Number 42)*
Aug. 28th, 1863

Dear Amanda,

I wrote you a few days ago and sent the letter by Jeff Reins. I hope he has arrived safely at home by this time and delivered your letter. I am in fine health at this time and getting on finely. I wrote to you in a hurry and forgot to mention anything about your type[86] of which you was so kind to write me in yours of 3rd inst. I am anxious to get it, and I want you to send it to me by Jeff Reins. He promised to bring it for me. I told him the morning he started to tell you that I forgot to write for it, but to make it sure I write again.

I received a letter from Alex of Aug. 13th a few days ago, which is the only letter I have received in answer to any that I have written since I returned to camps. I have written a good many. I have looked for a letter from Lou for some time. I cannot see why she does not write. I am also looking for a letter from Mother. Alex promised to write again in a day or two and write more fully is why I have not answered his of 13th inst. I received a letter from you of July 23rd in answer to the first letter I wrote you after I went to Farmville, which I have forgotten for certain whether I answered or not. However, it makes no material difference now, I try to keep my correspondence straight but get it a little entangled at times. You have discovered that I started this letter on the wrong page, but I reckon you can get it straight somehow. I wrote to Pat and Camilla the first of this week. They wrote to me some time ago

---

[86] Probably an ambrotype or tintype, early forms of photographs.

so I learned from Sister Mary, but I missed getting the letter, so to keep them from being disappointed I wrote them anyhow.[87]

We are kept pretty busy now. We have two Battallion drills a day and have to sweep the yards everyday except Sunday.

It makes my mouth water to read of your having so many peaches. I never see one, and only a few inferior apples, which sell from one to two dollars per doz. I see a watermelon occasionally. They sell for from five to ten dollars a piece. Groundpees sell readily at a dollar a qt. which is thirty-two dollars a bushel. I hardly ever buy anything of the kind. We are doing better in the eating line than usual. We draw about equal quantities of flour and meal, beef and bacon which is much better than altogether of either. We put soda in the meal as regular as we do in the flour. It helps it the most in the world. You ought to try it once or twice with just a little soda. Soda cost $ 5.00 per lb. We only eat twice a day. My appetite is excellent now and I enjoy eating to the utmost.

Mose Colvin and I mess together. He is an excellent messmate, and I tell you we have some fine dishes occasionally.[88] We never put greece in biscuit. We save the bacon greece to fry beef steak. Well enough of this condognimity.

We have some fine weather of late. We have cool nights and pleasant days; which is quite an agreeable change. We are still remaining here and I hear no talk of moving soon. Of course it is only guess work how long we will stay anywhere. Castle George is getting well, John Wilder is improving slowly.[89] He has applied for a furlough and I think will be successful. The health of the Comp. with the exception of these two is the best I have ever know it.

Gen. Lee has issued an order to put a stop to speculating except by sutlers,[90] and all gambling. This is an excellent thing if it is carried out. There is not half the gambling and swearing among the soldiers now as there was last year. I was glad to hear that you had had a revival at Old Elim, and that Mr. Rigdon had joined the church.[91] I should have liked

---

[87] "Pat and Camilla" were MHF's nephew and niece (and Lou's half-brother and sister), Alexander Fitzpatrick "Pat" Greene and Amanda Camilla Greene. In the 1860 Census Pat was twelve years old and Camilla was ten. "Sister Mary" was their mother, MHF's sister.

[88] Before his recent hospitalization, MHF had "messed" with Jim Drew and Enoch R. Webb. While MHF missed Gettysburg, Drew was wounded there and Webb was captured at South Mountain, Md. on July 5, 1863.

[89] "Castle George" was Pvt. J.C. George of Co. K. Corp. John A. Wilder had been wounded in the left hand at Fredericksburg.

[90] Traveling merchants who sold to soldiers.

[91] The minutes of Elim Baptist Church for 1863 state that Bro. Stephen Rigdon was received into the church by experience (See Tina Hortman, "Proceedings of

to have been there, but alas, it is useless to talk about wanting to be at home now. It is my duty and I yield obediently to remain here now. I hope all the boys will get off home this winter that have not been and then they will start around again and I will have a showing.

I am glad always to hear that my boy is growing fast and improving every way. I hope he will make a great and good man. I want to see him so bad to see how large he is and hear him talk. I see no immediate prospect of peace but I can but hope that God will bless us soon in answer to the many fervent prayers that have been sent up for our Country. I will close. Write soon and write me a long letter. Pray for me. May God bless you.

Your husband,
M. Hill Fitzpatrick

ᔐ

Camp Near Orange Court House, Va. *(Letter Number 43)*
Sept. 10th, 1863

Dear Amanda,

I received your kind devoted and interesting letter of Aug. 20th day before yesterday and can assure you that I was more than glad to get it and to hear that all were well at that time. I have been quite sick for three or four days with diareah but got a good nights sleep last night and am about well this morning. I have been off duty but shall not report on the sick list this morning.

Tom Smisson is going to start home this morning on furlough and I have commenced to write as early as I can see how, in order to have my letter ready. I had become real uneasy before I got your letter, it had been so long since I had heard from you. Your letter was about 18 days on the way when it ought to have come in five or six. I hope they will come more regular in the future. I have written several letters to you recently, all of which I hope you received in due time.

I am sorry to hear that you suffered so much with toothache. I hope you will be rid of it since you had your tooth pulled out. I am glad to

Elim Baptist Church," Central Georgia Genealogical Society Quarterly [1989], 114).

learn that Greene had visited you. I should like the best in the world to see him. I am sorry to hear that Frank was sick.[92] I hope he has recovered by this time and am also truly sorry to learn of the death of Frank Fitzpatrick.[93] I know it almost broke the hearts of his folks, they doated on him so much. I am glad to hear of such great revivals of religion in our settlement. I hope it will do much good. It is truly time that all were turning to the Lord for to him alone we must look for help and deliverance from our great troubles.

Well, Cout, like a true and heroic Southern woman, I suppose you are making my clothes anyhow. I shall appreciate them the more when I get them because you worked and made them for me, but really I did not intend to burden you with that task, but you say and I know it is so that it is a pleasure to you to fix my clothes for me. I am proud of you and often say and know that I have the best wife in the world. Do not send them to me yet as we may have much marching to do before we go into winter quarters and I do not need them now nohow. You need not make me a coat as the one I have will last me another winter. There is not a crack in it yet except a small hole in the tail which I neatly patched. I will need a vest, make it military style buttoned straight up in front. As to overshirts I believe I had rather you would not make any atall, for I will have to throw them away when we start to march and when I pull them off I catch cold sure so I had rather do without them altogether. I tell you the less a soldier is burdened with the better he can get along. We have drawn no money yet. The payrolls are all ready but the Q Master has no money yet.

I am sorry you can get no shoes. I do not know how to tell you to manage but you must have some, no matter what price.

We are going to have a convention this morning of the three companies in this Regt. representing Crawford, Taylor and Houston County to see whether we will run Col. Simmons or Lieut. Col. Grice for Senator. They do not want to oppose each other and have agreed to leave it to these three Companies to see which shall win. I think Grice

---

[92] "Frank" was another of Amanda's older brothers, Benjamin Franklin White. Although he had enlisted in Co. E, 6th Ga. Infantry in May 1861, he was discharged with a medical disability that August. At the writing of this letter, Frank was farming in Crawford County (See David E. Lee, *The White Family of Crawford County, Georgia,* 21).

[93] "Frank Fitzpatrick" was MHF's first cousin, the only son of Bennett and Eliza Fitzpartick. He enlisted as a private in Co. F, 57th Ga. Infantry on May 3, 1862. He was captured when Vicksburg fell and was paroled on July 22, 1863. He died at home in Crawford County on August 22, 1863, but the editors do not know if he died of illness or wounds. He was eighteen years old.

will get it. If the convention comes off before Smisson leaves I will P.S. the result.[94]

Well, Cout, I have written about all I can think of. You must cheer up. I know you get lonesome and low spirited often and I truly sympathize with you. I think of you and my darling boy often and sometimes get real childish. I want to see you so bad I shall know how to appreciate home and the loved ones there if I can ever get there again. Write me a long letter. I want to know how they all get on making syrup and everything of the kind. Be sure to write soon. Pray for me. May God bless you.

Your husband,
M. Hill Fitzpatrick

P.S.
Grice got the nomination. The vote stood Simmons 22; Grice 46.

≥●

Near Orange Courthouse, Va. *(Letter Number 44)*
Sept. 15th, 1863

Dear Amanda,

I received your kind and interesting letter of Sept. 6th day before yesterday and was truly glad to hear from you again and hear that all were well. I am in fine health at this time. I am looking for Jeff Reins back tomorrow and would wait till he comes before I write,[95] but we are under marching orders now and are expecting to leave every moment and learning I may not get the chance of writing to you again soon or probably not atall till God only knowing, will write now.

Night before last we received orders to cook what rations we had and hold ourselves in readiness. Yesterday evening we drew more rations with orders to cook them immediately. We were almost certain we would have to march last night but it is about 10 o'clock AM and we

---

[94] "Simmons" was the colonel of the 45th Ga., Thomas J. Simmons, and "Grice" was Lt. Col. Washington L. Grice. Apparently the "convention" was nominating one of them for the Georgia Legislature.
[95] The letter dated Aug. 23, 1863 was carried home by Pvt. Jeff Reins of Co. K.

are here yet, but as I have said are expecting to leave every moment and go into a regular fight.

There was a Cavalry fight and considerable canonadeing yesterday and the day before not far from here.[96] The result and particulars of which I am not able to tell you and it is generally conceded that a regular battle is imminent. I can but sincerely hope that if the trial comes our arms will be crowned with a glorious victory and that the same hand that has lead me through so many firery ordeals will safely preserve me through this. But if I fall, as I have told you before, grieve not for me but think of me dieing for my Country and my all.

I wrote you all about my clothes in the last letter which I sent by Tom Smisson. I do not need any socks now and I had rather not get them yet but if Jeff brings them I will try to take care of them. I would be glad [if] Jeff could bring me some syrup. It would be quite a treat to me. I have never found out yet how Mother came out making syrup. They have all quit writing to me. I do not nor cannot imagine the cause of it. If I knew the cause I would try to remove it.

I am glad that you have some more pigs. I hope they will do well. You have wove a quantity of cloth sure, and deserve great credit for it. I am glad that Henry is so well pleased with his rings and I hope I will yet see him ride with them. I rec. a long and interesting letter from Doc yesterday written Sept. 8th. He was in fine health and just passed through a severe crisis on Morris Island. The particulars of which no doubt you have learned before now.[97]

We have had several grand reviews recently of which I have given no items I believe. We first had a Division review. The Division was formed in a straight line on an old field and our new Major Gen. Wilcox, attended by Lieut. Gen. A. P. Hill and his aides rode in a handsome gallop down in front of the line and back in the rear of it. The line was about a mile long. The Generals then took their positions on an elevated place and we passed near them in Column of Companies.

---

[96] The Army of the Potomac advanced from the Rappahannock River to the Rapidan, occupying Culpeper Court House, Va. MHF was probably referring to the skirmishing that accompanied this advance on September 13-15, 1863.

[97] Doc's 27th Ga. was involved in the defense of Charleston, S.C. On the night of September 6, Battery Wagner and Battery Gregg on Morris Island were evacuated. These important earthworks had been besieged by the Federals since early July and were the scene of terrible fighting. Although Morris Island was abandoned, Charleston itself, and Fort Sumter, continued to hold out.

I intended to write you before now but neglected it that we are in Wilcox's Division now. He is from Ala.[98] You should bear this in mind. Thomas' Brigade, Wilcox's Division, Hill's Corps. Soon afterwards we had Brigade review which was conducted on the same plan only as a smaller scale.[99] The next day we had Corps (pronounced Core) review which was grand indeed. Our Corps is formed of three Divisions-Wilcox, Heths, & Andersons which was formed in three separate lines about a hundred yds. apart and each a mile or more in length. Gen. Lee, attended by Lieut. Gen. Hill and their aids, also each Major Gen. as they came to their Divisions, rode in front and rear of each line in a spirited gallop. Gen. Lee is the best rider I ever saw. He was mounted on a fine gray horse. I cannot look at him with his gray hair and beard only with feelings of awe and almost devotion. The Generals then took their position on an elevated place and we all passed them in Column of Companies. It took a long time for the whole line to pass. We had excellent music and all passed off finely. Gen. Thomas has gone home. Col. Simmons is acting Brigadier.[100]

Write soon. May God bless you.

Your husband,
M. Hill Fitzpatrick

        ⅀

---

[98] Maj. Gen. Cadmus M. Wilcox was promoted on August 3, 1863 to the command of a division in A.P. Hill's Third Corps of the Army of Northern Virginia. Thomas' Brigade was a part of this division. Wilcox was a native North Carolinian and a West Pointer, but he won early fame by commanding a brigade of Alabama infantry, which is probably why MHF thought he was from Alabama. Ambrose Powell Hill, a Virginian, had commanded Thomas' Brigade first as a division commander in Stonewall Jackson's Corps. Following Jackson's death, he was given command of the newly organized Third Corps, which included Thomas' Brigade.

[99] MHF and the 45th Ga. had been under Brig. Gen. Edward L. Thomas since the Seven Days Battles. Thomas was a native of Clarke County, Ga., a graduate of Emory College of Oxford, Ga., and a veteran of the Mexican War. A prominent planter, Thomas first commanded the 35th Ga., and was promoted in June 1862 to command a brigade consisting of the 14th, 35th, 45th, and 49th regiments of Georgia infantry.

[100] Douglas Southall Freeman described this review of the Third Corps as taking place on September 11, 1863. The Second Corps, under Lt. Gen. Richard S. Ewell, had been reviewed two days earlier, about the time Longstreet's First Corps had been sent to reinforce Braxton Bragg's Army of Tennessee. See D. S. Freeman, *R.E. Lee: A Biography*, *Vol. III* (New York: Charles Scribner's Sons, 1948) 167.

Camp Near Orange Court House, Va. *(Letter Number 45)*
Sept. 27th, 1863

Dear Amanda,

I received your kind and interesting letter of Sept. 8 sent by Jeff Raines several days ago, and as I wrote to Ma right away I waited till now to write to you. I was truly glad to hear that you were well, and getting on as well as circumstances would permit. I am well and doing finely now, but we have had a pretty rough time for the last week. I wrote to Ma last Monday. The next morning early we were on the march. We went to guard a bridge about 7 miles off. We staid there two nights. While we were there our Cavalry had a fight on the other side of the river. We could hear the firing and expected to be into it pretty soon, but our Cavalry whipped them out and we had no fighting to do. Only our Brigade went at first but we were soon reinforced by two other Brigades. There was a large corn field near us unguarded and we made roasting ears get up and dust worse than you can imagine. We had had none in some time and were worse than hogs. Officers and all pitched in. Soldiers will steal or press, as they term it, and there is no use to deny it. After staying there two nights we went back to old camp, and staid there about fifteen minutes and were ordered to fall in again. Tired as we were we started again and came about two miles to this place. So we are in new camps now with a prospect of resting awhile. But I have not told you all our tramp last week. The morning after we got here we were ordered on pickette. We had three fords to guard and divided our Regt. into three Squads. Our Company and three others went to a ford about two miles distant. There had been no picketting there before and we had a rich time. Orders were issued for all to stay in Camps but there was no use talking. A large Chinese sugar cane patch was soon discovered a short distance up the river on the Yankee side. A foot log was also discovered to cross on and the result can better be imagined than told. A fine roasting ear patch was also discovered near at hand and the final result the next morning was about two thirds of the Comp. was gentlemanly sick, your humble servant among the sickest. But it being only belley ache it soon wore off. Among the other good things we found were pumpkins which we cook and eat at all stages. If they are green we cook them after the squash order and if ripe after the usual manner of cooking them at home. They eat splendid either way. We got back here early yesterday morning and had been here but little while before we were ordered to fall in again, and now comes the most solemn scene I ever witnessed. We were ordered to witness the death of two men who had been court martialed and sentenced to be shot for desertion. We went to an old field near our old Camps. The whole Division were ordered out and were formed thus [____]and in the open space were placed the men to be shot, or rather first were placed the stakes to which they were to be tied. The stakes were about two feet high with a piece nailed across near the top in this shape †. The stakes were about ten paces apart. The procession then moved out of a skirt of woods near by, and was composed of a band of music, three chaplains, the two prisoners, two or three officers and 20 men that done the shooting. They marched around the whole line the band playing the dead march which was the most solemn music I ever heard. I shall never forget the impression it made on me. After reaching the end of the line, the prisoners were conducted to the stakes, and the guards were placed ten paces in front of them, in two ranks. There were ten men to shoot at each prisoner. Six guns out of the ten were loaded with balls, the others with powder only, but none of the guard knew whether his gun contained a ball or not. After arranging the guard and prisoners, they sung a hymn and went to prayer. The Prisoners were then tied to the stakes. They were kneeling with their face towards the guard and had their arms tied to the cross piece and were blindfolded. The command was then given to fire and they were launched into eternity. The cross piece to which one was tied was shot to pieces. He raised himself perpendicular fell forward and turned over on his back and died instantly. He was pierced through with six balls. The other was struck with only one ball. He turned to one side and was some time dying.

The whole Division then marched near by them. One of them, the one that was struck with six balls, was a Georgian. He belonged to the 14th Ga. in our Brigade. He was a fine looking young man and I learn had a wife and two children at home. He was a gambler and reckless character. He talked a good deal but I was too far off to understand what he said, but I learn he expressed a willingness to die and said he had a hope in Christ. The other was a North Carolinian. He was a sorry looking man, and from what I can learn would talk to no one after he was condemned.

We then returned to camp and last night I got the best night's sleep I have had in some time. Today is Sunday, and is a clear beautiful day. We had preaching today and there is baptizing this evening. The nights are quite cool now. I hope we will stay here for some time now but that is quite uncertain. The yanks peck at us a little every day or two and we have been expecting a fight but they have not made a general advance, but may in a short time. Our Cavalry took about forty prisoners while we were guarding the bridge.

We hear cheering news from Bragg. I hope he will be victorious this time and will keep the yankees out of Georgia and raise the spirits of the people at home, and I also think we will be able to give them a severe flogging here if they advance on us.[101]

I wrote Ma about receiving the things you sent me by Jeff. I hardly know how to thank you, especially for your type.[102] Again and again have I looked at it and mused over it. I value it more highly than anything I possess here. I carry it in my pocket. I have made a kind of case for it of thick cloth. I have lost the ring you gave me. I lost it while on my way to the hospital. I regretted it very much. I have thread enough to last me a long time now. I let the boys that have none have it whenever they want any, and I also do a good deal of sewing for them. Some of them cannot patch yet. My pepper is quite a treat. Mose's wife sent him some pepper and sage too and we have some extra fixed up beef. I forgot to write you for some sage, but fortunately Mose[103] has enough to do us a long time. We have drawn no money yet, but I suppose will before long.

I am glad to hear that you have chickens so plentifully. There is no danger of perishing for meat as long as they last, but of course, I want you to exercise your own judgment about selling them. You can tell best about it. I am glad that syrup is plentiful. I want you to secure 25 or 30 gallons if you can, but you know best about it and I leave it all to you, knowing that you will do the very best you can. I got a long letter from Doc a day or two ago. He had been sick but had gotten over it. I am glad to hear that the conscript is raking some of the Croakers in our County. I think it will help them. Well, I suppose you have had a wedding, Sam Johnson and Sall Revel. I should like to have been at the wedding. I think it is about a match.[104]

We have heard nothing from Drew, Webb or Woodward yet.[105] Write me if you have heard anything from Drew. He may have written to some of his folks there. Drew left a good vest in his knapsack, with our things. It was all that I found that belonged to him when I came to

---

[101] The Battle of Chickamauga, Ga. occurred on September 19-20, 1863, and saw the Confederate Army of Tennessee under Lt. Gen. Braxton Bragg defeat the Federal Army of the Cumberland under Maj. Gen. William S. Rosecrans.

[102] Probably an ambrotype or tintype.

[103] MHF's mess mate, Pvt. Moses F. Colvin.

[104] The editors have been unable to identify Sam Johnson and Sall Revel.

[105] Co. K's Jim Drew had been wounded at Gettysburg, Enoch R. Webb was captured at South Mountain, Md., on July 5, 1863, and Pvt. Council D. Woodward was captured at Gettysburg.

the Regt. I took care of it for him till the other day. Our Quarter Master told us we must reduce the number of knapsacks, and only 5 were allowed to be hauled from our Company. I could not get Jim's vest in and a vest is not allowed to be hauled nohow, so I put it on and give away my old one. I do not look for Jim back this winter, if atall, so I will keep the vest, and you need not send me one.

I have given you a long heat, and will now close. You must, must write me a long letter and tell me all about my boy and everything. I want to see him so bad. Write me all about how you are getting on. I am anxious to hear often now and am uneasy since Alex and Mr. White have both gone.[106] Pray for me. May God bless you.

Your husband,
M.H. Fitzpatrick

꿈

Camp Near Orange Court House, Va. *(Letter Number 46)*
Oct. 8th, 1863

Dear Amanda,

I wrote to Lou this morning and sent it by mail, but Henry Pope one of our Company who belongs to the Signal Corps, is going to start home in the morning and by a dim firelight sitting on the ground I will write you a few lines.[107] I wrote Lou all the news. We have three days rations cooked and ordered to be ready to march by 5 o'clock in the morning. As I wrote Lou, our Regt. is on pickette today, but I was excused by being on duty yesterday. I have been hard down at work all day with the others who were left here cooking rations and fixing up to start. I am pretty tired tonight but I fear will be much more so tomorrow night. It is thought that we will have a fight in a short time, and this poor letter may be the last one that you will ever receive from me. But I will hope for the better. From what I can learn we are to be the attacking

---

[106] In July 1863 both Alexander Fitzpatrick and William B. White, Sr. (Amanda's father) joined Co. B, 8th Battalion Cavalry, Georgia State Guards. The oldest white male remaining on the Fitzpatrick or White farms would appear to have been seventeen-year-old Rufus White, Amanda's brother.
[107] Pvt. Henry B. Pope was transferred from Co. K to the Signal Corps in June 1862.

party. But you will learn all about it before you get this. My health is good, and I have a splendid enfield rifle and I hope to be of some service to my country.[108] As I wrote Lou I received your letter of Sept. 20th a few days ago and the one of 1st inst. sent by Smisson yesterday. I will not claim this as an answer to them but will write again soon if I get the chance.[109]

You must cheer up and hope for brighter days. I truly sympathize with you. I know you spend many lonely hours, and have to labor hard. I would gladly share your labor trials and troubles if it was in my power. I send you some buttons which you can put on something for our darling boy or use them in any way you like.

I will close. Write soon. May God bless and protect you and my darling boy. Remember me in all your prayers and if we meet no more on earth, may we meet where partings will be no more.

Your husband,
M. Hill Fitzpatrick

ॐ

Camp near Rappahanock River, Va. *(Letter Number 47)*
Oct. 20th, 1863

Dear Amanda,

We have just been on a tramp of 11 days and stopped here yesterday evening and may stay here a day or two. I seize this opportunity to drop you a few lines. I am well but am pretty well tired down.

We left old camp on the morning of the 9th inst. The day before we left I wrote to Lou, and the night before we left, I wrote you a short letter and sent by Pope, one of our Comp. who belongs to the Signal Corps. I had just received two letters from you then, one by mail and

---

[108] Some 400,000 Enfield rifles were imported from England by both sides. The .577 caliber rifled musket was popular with Confederate soldiers. It is the only rifle MHF mentions.

[109] Smisson began his furlough on September 10, 1863. The day after this letter was written the Army of Northern Virginia crossed the Rapidan River, moving west and north to turn the right flank of Meade's Army of the Potomac and head toward Washington. The Bristoe Station, Va. campaign was under-way.

the other by Smisson, but they got wet and have been destroyed so you see I cannot give a regular answer to them.

We have been in no fight but a portion of the tramp has been rough. We march in a round about way. The enemy being in full retreat before us all the time. Our Cavalry and some of other forces were skirmishing and fighting more or less with the rear of the enemy nearly all the time while we were going up, and at Bristoe Station about five miles this side of Manassas Junction a pretty heavy fight opened just ahead of us. We halted, loaded and put out expecting to go right into it. We had been marching hard all day, and were tired, but had to double quick for a good long ways. Now this is easily told but I assure you not easily done. I kept up pretty well but was tired enough to fall down and give it up, but that would not do. We went up and formed a line of battle. By that time the small arms had about ceased, but they sent a few shells over amongst us and killed one man in Comp. G in our Regt. No others were hurt.[110] We lay there that night and the next morning the Yanks were all gone. That evening we started back and marched late that night through mud and water. Early next morning we started again through a hard rain. We went a short distance and stopped to tear up and burn the railroad. We worked at it all day, it raining nearly all the time, and just as we went into camps there fell the hardest rain I believe I ever was in. We waded branches and mud holes as we came to them. We were drenched to the skin but by hard work got a good fire and it stopped raining and we dried off and lay down and slept sweet and sound till morning. We tore up railroad the next day.

It was a fair day and we camped just beyond the Rappahanock from here. We staid there one day and two nights before we could cross the river. We crossed yesterday morning on a pontoon bridge. Before we started yesterday it commenced raining and rained hard again, and was pretty cold. The roads were a perfect loblolly of mud and water and we again waded mud holes and branches. My poor pen fails to give even a faint description of the sufferings of the soldier. I will leave it for future historians to tell, but never will justice be done the subject. We

---

[110] MHF's description is very accurate. Bristoe was a campaign of maneuver. Lee was frustrated by his inability to attack Meade while on march and before the Federals could establish strong defensive lines near Centreville, Va. On October 14, 1863, elements of A.P. Hill's Corps struck the retreating rear units of the Army of the Potomac at Bristoe Station. Hill was unable to damage the Federals and Lee's Army failed to bring them to bay before they prepared defensive lines too strong to attack.

had to wait a good while at the bridge before we could get over and fortunately for us it faired off, and we now have pretty weather.

We dried off good last night and am comfortable once more, so far as eating and sleeping is concerned, but would like to have some clean clothes to put on. I have not changed since we started, so you may judge I am a black boy by this time. Our knapsacks are in the wagons but I hope they will let us have them soon.

We are now about seven miles above Culpepper[111] encamped in a beautiful piece of woods. We captured a good many prisoners on the tramp, but had no regular engagement. Lee's object seemed to have been to run the Yanks back and tear up the railroad, so as to prevent them from resuming operations anymore this campaign.

I got a letter from Doc and one from Alex last night, both written on the 11th inst.[112] They were both well. I am anxiously looking for a letter from home now and was sadly disappointed in not getting one from some of you yesterday.

We fared pretty well in the eating line the most of the time while on the tramp. One day we all got pretty hungry and eat acorns like rip. We could get plenty of them and they are sweet to a hungry stomach. Cout, I hope you may never feel the keen aching, raving pangs of hunger. It affects me sooner than almost anybody else, and affects my brain immediately. But away with these unpleasant subjects. A good soldier grumbles at nothing, so you must not understand me to be grumbling, but having nothing else to write, was giving you some hints of the soldier's life that may be of interest to you at some future days when peace will have spread her balmy wings o'er the Suny South and Liberty shall have perched herself firmly on our banner and we shall be a free, independent and happy people.

My shoes are about worn out but I will draw some soon I hope. I have the same shoes I wore home. We have drawn no money yet. Be sure to write soon and write me a long letter, and tell me all about my boy and everything. Pray for me. May God bless you.

Your husband,
M. Hill Fitzpatrick

৵

---

[111] Culpeper Court House, Va.

[112] Doc was with the 27th Ga. in the Charleston area and Alex was having his first taste of soldiering with the 8th Cav. Batt. of the Georgia State Guards.

Camp Near Rappahanock River, Va. *(Letter Number 48)*
Oct. 29th, 1863

Dear Amanda,

I received yours of Oct. llth several days ago but as I had just written to you, I postponed answering til now. I am well and doing pretty well now. I wrote to you a week ago and gave you a rough sketch of our late tramp. We have been resting quietly here since I wrote and it has been a delightful rest. The weather has been pleasant most of the time. We have had one rain and it has faired off pretty cold. We were on pickett last night and yesterday. This morning _____ was ice and a large frost. We went on pickett on the Rappahanock about 1 1/2 miles from here. There was some excitement with those that were on post. Our Co. was not on post. The Yankee cavalry came in sight on the other side several times and our picketts fired on them pretty rapidly. I do not know if they killed any. The Yanks would retreat when our men would fire in them. There was also canonadeing going on at intervals some distance off, the result of which is unknown to me. It is thought by some that we will have a fight soon, but I hardly think so. I was glad to learn that all were well at home and that you were getting on as well as circumstances would permit. I hope you will have good luck with your hogs. I think it a very good idea to kill the yearling you spoke of. I am at a loss how to advise you about anything now. Just do the best you can. We will draw money soon I hope and I will send you all I can possibly spare by the first chance. I drawed a pair of shoes this morning which I was needing very bad. I do not think we will march a great deal more this Fall. You can fix my clothes and send them by some safe chance. John Wilder may be coming before a great while.[113] There is a talk of sending Capt. Brown, our Q. M. home on detail to bring clothes to us.[114] If he goes that will be the safest chance. I am in no hurry for them. Be sure to send me some soap. You could send that by Henry Pope if you could get it to Knoxville but you have nobody to attend to such things now.[115]

---

[113] Corp. John A. Wilder had been wounded in the left hand at Fredericksburg and had been at home in Crawford County trying to recover.
[114] John T. Brown was quartermaster of the 45th Ga.
[115] Letter 46 was carried to Crawford County by Pope, as he was going home on a furlough. Knoxville is the county seat.

I am writing with ink of my own make which is simply polk berries squeezed out. I want you to put a little coppera[116] in your next letter for me to put in it. They say it will turn it black and make it more indelible. We got our knapsack the day I wrote to you and I washed and put on some clean clothes, first getting shaved after which I felt like a new man. I have turned out my whiskers. They are about an inch long.

I was glad to learn from your letter that Sister Mary had visited you.[117] I hope you will arrange it so to return the visit. I want you to go about and enjoy yourself whenever you can and look ahead to brighter times, and brood over the present gloomy times as little as possible. I do not think our prospects for Independence gloomy by any means, but on the contrary brightening every day, but of course it is a dark time with the women who are left almost unprotected at home. But as true and patriotic Southern ladies, I hope you will bravely stem the storm and successfully land on the shore of Liberty.

I got a letter from Alex a short time ago. They were all getting on finely then. He is in the same mess with Mr. White. I had been looking for him or Mr. White for some time. Your sister[118] raked me for not writing to Pop,[119] but you must recollect I wrote him the last letter and until he answers that of course it is prudent for me to remain silent. It would be a pleasure to me to correspond with him or any of the family but when a correspondence becomes onesided, I am afraid of intruding, and you know well my independent feelings. I am too much so perhaps but I did not make myself.

I am glad that my boy is improving so fast. I reckon You will have to start him to school next year. Of course, you are right about making him obey you but I know you love him too dearly to whip him too much. I am truly glad that you have all got shoes. You must make Thornt mend them when they need it and they will last much longer by it.

I am glad that Jim Drew has got home and Smisson told me was nearly well. He is a noble fellow and I think a great deal of him. Tom Rickerson is my favorite among the boys here now. Any of the girls would do well to set their cap for him and would do better to catch him. He is a large, well proportioned, noble looking soldier, and has the

---

116 Properly "copperas," a sulfate of crystallized copper, also called green vitriol, used in making ink and pigments. This letter is faint, but very readable, after more than 130 years.

117 MHF's older sister, Mary Fitzpatrick Greene.

118 Samantha "Babe" White.

119 William B. White, Sr.

mind and disposition to correspond with it.[120] It is cold writing and I will close up. Write me a long letter. Pray for me. May God bless you.

Your husband,
M. Hill Fitzpatrick

ॐ

Camp Near Rappahanock Station, Va. *(Letter Number 49)*
Nov. 2nd, 1863

Dear Amanda,

I have written two letters to you since we have been here, and thought I would wait this time till I got a letter from Lou or some of you to answer, but I have waited in vain, and our Quarter Master, Capt. Brown is going to start home in the morning, for the purpose of bringing clothing &c to the Regt., so I will write now so you can have my trick ready to send by him. Tom Rickerson, Tip Hammock, Colvin and I have concluded to have a box sent. So you can see Mr. Hammock or Wiley Rickerson and put my things in a box with them. Wiley Rickerson is to make the box. You can pay him your part of the expenses. Capt. Brown says he will bring us some eatables in with the clothes. The other boys have written for some. I feel a delicacy in saying anything about it knowing that it is scarce with you and we draw a plenty to eat. I know you are willing and anxious to send me some, but as I have said I know it is a hard time with you. If you send anything to eat, do not send but very little and nothing that will spoil. Send me a little more pepper and some soap, but I believe I have written to you or Lou about the soap. Get Lou or some good hand to mark all the things plainly.[121]

We are still quietly resting here. The troops are camped very thick here and wood is very scarce. I suppose we will move soon but I hope we will have no more hard marching this year. It is pretty cold of nights now and in the daytime too some days. I want to go into winter

---

[120] Pvt. Drew had been wounded at Gettysburg and was at home in Crawford County recovering when Smisson was home on furlough. Thomas W. Rickerson was 4th corporal of Co. K.
[121] MHF and his friends Moses Colvin, Tip Hammock, and Tom Rickerson were planning a "care package" from home. Tip's father was Mansel Hammock; "Wiley Rickerson" was Tom's father. The 1850 Census lists Wiley Rickerson as a blacksmith. Mansel Hammock was a successful farmer in Crawford County.

quarters so we can build some huts and have some protection from the rain and keen cold cutting wind. My health is fine at this time and Mose and I can eat a doz. good sized biscuits and beef according at one time and not think hard of it in the least. I throwed away my knapsack or the one that Drew[,] Webb and I had when we started on our last tramp, but I drawed another since we came here. I have no use for a knapsack on a march but they are very useful in Camps. I have just got a letter from Doc which I read with much interest. He was well and doing finely on the good things they had just received from Ga. This makes me think again of our box. It will have to be sent to Macon, I suppose, and Ma can send it by Thort if someone would go with him. However, you can all talk that over and fix it up.

We drawed two months wages yesterday. I drawed $46.00, twelve dollars of back rations which I should have drawn while at the Hospital. I have collected what was oweing to me and paid what I owed, and have $34.00 left. Two of our Comp. went home on furloughs recently, Harvey Locklair on sick furlough[,] Lieut. Walker on well furlough.[122] They both left before I drawed money or I should have sent you some. I did not get to even send a letter by either of them. I will send you some money by the first chance. They owe me two months wages now and over a hundred dollars commutation money for clothing which we will get next January, paid forty dollars transportation money, home and back, which I do not know when I will get. Some blankets and overcoats have come to the Regt. but I will not get any I suppose as there are others needing them worse than I am.

Cout, it is a serious truth that there are men in our Regt. that have been entirely barefooted till a day or two ago, and have but one inferior suit of clothes and not a sign of blanket, overcoat, or anything atall to lie on or cover with. They build a fire and lie down on the ground before it and sleep, when it is cold enough to freeze a man well wrapped up. But they will now soon be supplied with blankets and clothing. Mose and I have fixed some logs all around and put it full of leaves like a hog bed which we sleep on and cover with our blankets. They have quit making wheat or anything else scarcely about here and straw has played out. The health of our Comp. was never better, but there are always some sick. Wash. Piles was sent to the hospital this morning. He is in a bad condition. He has the rheumatism.[123]

---

[122] Pvt. Harvey Lochlear, and 2nd Lt. Joel A. Walker.
[123] Pvt. George Washington Piles was admitted to the General Hospital at Charlottesville with acute rheumatism on Nov. 3, 1863.

I have quite an interested time attending the Lodge here. There are many bright Masons here. I would like you could take some Degrees or all that a Mason's wife is allowed, but as the Lodge is so much thined out by the war it will be a hard matter to fix it up now, but the first chance you get attend to it. It may be of great advantage to you.[124] I hear but little war news of late. The Yanks are not a great ways from us on the other side of the river, but we have forces over there also now, and I saw a good many more going over there this morning. Our men are hauling the railroad iron away from there and I learn that the Yanks have commenced to rebuild the road where we commenced to tear it up and our men want to prevent them from doing it this winter.

The prisoners we took were the sorriest looking men I ever saw. It makes me mad to even think of submitting to such demons in human shape. I can but hope that peace will dawn upon our distracted country soon and nestled in our pleasant cottage in the sunny South, we will yet spend many pleasant, useful and happy days together.

We may have many obstacles to surmount yet and the dark clouds may hang over us for a long time but the more obstacles we surmount and the longer the cloud hangs over us the brighter the Sun of Peace will shine when it does burst forth. Lieut. Col. Grice has gone home. He was elected by a handsome majority. He got 84 out of 85 votes that were cast in the three Companies in this Regt. He is a bright star. He did not have to resign but will return to us in a short time. He told us if he did have to resign he would come back and take his gun as private. He told us good-by with the feeling of a father and they all told him to be sure to come back to us. We miss him a great deal.

Be sure to write soon. I will send this to Macon by hand. May God bless you and my darling boy.

Your husband,
M. Hill Fitzpatrick

---

[124] This is the first of several references to MHF's membership in the Masonic Lodge. Georgia Free Masons responded to the War by chartering lodges within nineteen state regiments, including MHF's 45th. Before the War both MHF and his brother Alex had been active in Jackson Lodge No. 48, in the Hickory Grove section of Crawford County. The original officers of the 45th Ga. lodge were Capt. Richard W. Bonner of Co. F as Worshipful Master, Capt. William S. Wallace of Co. E as Senior Warden, and Capt. Aurelius W. Gibson of Co. K as Junior Warden. See William Henry Rosier and Fred Lamar Pearson, Jr., *The Grand Lodge of Georgia, Free and Accepted Masons, 1786-1980* (Macon, Ga.: Grand Lodge of Georgia, Free and Accepted Masons, 1983) 90-92.

Ʒᴥ

Montpelior, Near Orange, Va. *(Letter Number 50)*
Dec. 10th, 1863

Dear Amanda,

I rec. yours of Nov. 14th soon after I got back from our late tramp, but as I generally answer my letters according to which I rec. first and had written to you just before we started I answered Lou's and Alex's first. I answered Alex's only yesterday and carried it to camp yesterday evening, and found that Lieut. Rutherford[125] was going to start home on furlough tomorrow morning, so not knowing that he was going when I wrote Alex I will write to you this morning instead of waiting awhile, as I thought of doing and send them both by him. I will send you $45.00 in money but will not enclose it in the letter. I suppose he will send or carry the money and letters down to you, but he may mail the letters at some near Post Office and not mail the money in which case you can get somebody to go after the money. I believe I will also send you a few more buttons that I have picked up as I have no use for them and they may do you or somebody more good. The money you can use at your discretion, but as I said before I want to pay our buggy debt in Macon this winter if I can possibly do it and you have enough without it. I will draw a right pretty little pile the 1st of Jan. if they pay us our commutation for clothing as they have promised. I want you to get somebody that is passing down to Macon to see the man. C. Ward[126] is his name I think and find out if he has the note yet, and if he will take Confederate money for it, and if Alex, Mr. White or some of the neighbors who could spare the money would take up the note and have it near you. I think we could manage to pay it pretty soon, but I leave it to you to manage as you think best.

My health is excellent but I feel drowsy this morning as I was at the Lodge till midnight last night. We are looking for Brown[127] with our things in a few days. I begin to need shirts and drawers pretty bad but I keep patching the old ones and make them do. I have got the same shirt and drawers yet that I wore home last winter and they were not new then. And our eatables, if we get any, Mose and I can enjoy finely here to ourselves, especially the syrup if we get any, for we can get

---

[125] 1st Lt. Williams Rutherford of Co. K and Crawford County.
[126] Unidentified by editors.
[127] Capt. John T. Brown, quartermaster of the 45th Ga.

good corn bread to eat with it. The old fellow here says he wants us to stay as long as the Army stays here and we may spend the winter here. I said in Lou's letter that this was the birthplace of Madison but I was mistaken. His parents were living here at the time of his birth, but I see from his history that he was born while on a visit to some of their friends in another county. This has once been a grand and noble place and many traits of its grandeur can be seen yet, but since the war it has been taken but little care of and the beauty of the place, such as the fancy garden, yards &c is almost entirely neglected. The dwelling is situated on a beautiful eminence and commands a grand view of the mountains and the country scenery around. It has been erected more than a hundred years and is built of pure granite. It is a very large house and has about 20 rooms in all. The grave yard is quite interesting to look at. Madison, with many of the family, is buried there. It is enclosed and belongs to the State of Va. The monument over the grave of Madison is about 20 feet high and is of plain granite, nothing showy about it. There is a large library here to which I have free access and which is a source of great improvement and pleasure to me. The old Irish bachelor who lives here is quite a strange character. He has been from Ireland only about two years. He has a polished education and knows much of the world, but knows nothing about the managing of negroes and they torment him and fool him badly. He is very industrious but has no regular habits except to be going here and there all the time mostly on horseback. He has no regular time to eat and very seldom eats when we do. He is kindhearted though and confers many favors on the soldiers. They are holding Court Martial in our room every day now but we occupy it at night. We are on guard all day and have but little use for it. The boys in Camp here have all got good houses built now and are well fixed for the winter.[128]

I will close, but I had like to have forgotten to answer your question about my jeans coat. Tell Rufus[129] that I do not want to sell it as it is the only one I have to wear if I should be so fortunate as to get home again and it would cost more than he would want to pay if you asked him the customary price. I am so glad Henry improves so fast and is so much company to you. God bless his little soul. I hope yet to hear his sweet prattle and spend many happy days with you and him.

---

[128] The first of three letters written from Montpelier, the home of President James Madison. From 1857 to 1881 Montpelier was owned by Thomas J. Carson, an Irish immigrant who had settled in Baltimore and prospered as a banker. During the War, he remained in Baltimore and Montpelier became the home of his bachelor brother, Frank Carson.

[129] "Rufus" was one of Amanda's younger brothers.

Be sure to write soon for I will want to hear if you get the money and write me a long letter. Pray for me. May God bless you.

Your husband,
Hill Fitzpatrick

P.S. Some of the boys have just come over here from camp and say it is very uncertain about Lieut. Rutherford's getting off on furlough, and I will not put in the buttons but will send this to camp to be mailed if he does not get off and will send money seperately so he can hand it back to me if he does not get off. You can tell by where this is mailed whether he carries it or not. MHF[130]

❧

Montpelior Near Orange C. H. , Va. *(Letter Number 51)*
Dec. 16th, 1863

Dear Amanda,

I rec. your kind and interesting letter of Nov. 30th a few days ago but as I had just written to you I postponed answering it till now. I was truly glad to hear from you again and to hear that all were well and that my noble boy was so smart and improving so fast. There is no use talking how bad I want to see you and him and all of you, but I see no chance now for me to get a furlough this winter. My health is excellent and I am still here guarding this house and premises, and am getting on finely. Our Brigade left yesterday evening[,] went to Orange and took the cars, I suppose[,] from what I can find out to go to Staunton for four or five days or probably longer. They left all the sick and unable at the Camps also all the wagons ambulances tents &c, and left Mose and I here. I knew nothing about it till late yesterday evening. I went over to Camps and found them gone. John Wilder was left at our Camp. He said Capt. Gibson[131] who is in command of the Regt. now said for us to remain here, as they would be back in a short time. One Brigade from

---

[130] This P.S. was found on a small loose piece of white ruled paper in the collection of the original letters at the Georgia Department of Archives and History in Atlanta. The editors believe that it was originally sent with this letter.
[131] Capt. Aurelius W. Gibson of Co. K must have been put in temporary command of the regiment in the absence of Col. Thomas J. Simmons.

each Division I believe has gone. I do not know what they are up to. I would have like to have taken the trip. I know the boys will miss me as I am generally the leader for life and action on such a scout.

I wrote to you on 10th inst. expecting to send the letter and some money by Lieut. Rutherford. He did not get his furlough then and I sent the letter by mail and put in an explanatory P.S. He said he thought he would get off in a short time, and also one of the Co. Frank Knight[132] drawed a furlough a day or two ago and would have started home I suppose by this time if it had not been for the tramp. They will both go I reckon when they get back and I will send the money by one of them.

I got a letter from Lou of the same date of yours which I will answer soon. I am grateful to you for sympathizing for me when it is cold, but do not indulge in grieving for me, for often when you imagine I am suffering badly, I am comfortably situated. The winter here has been very mild so far for this country, though we have had ice three or four inches thick, we have had no sleet or snow yet. Capt. Brown has not arrived yet though we are looking for him every day. I am delighted with the idea of getting the clothes and many good things you sent me. I hope I will get them safely. I feel and know that I have got the best wife and the best Mother in the world. They feel for me and do all they can for me, and if all other friends vanish with the wind they will stand alone to comfort, strengthen, and bouy me up. I am sorry you forgot to mark the potatoe Henry sent. If I get them however, I will eat one in his name any how.

Well, I reckon it is hog killing time with you all now, and you are having I hope a rich time on spareribs and chitlings. Some of them wrote you only had two hogs to kill. I thought you had four when I was at home[,] saving for this winter. You must get enough from Ma to do you plentifully this next year as she will have a plenty to spare and I do not want you to be scarce again. Pitch in like a man an attend to it, and everything of that sort. You must be the man and woman both now you know, and get corn to keep your other hogs from Ma, so you can maybe have enough of your own hogs next winter to do you. Do not be anyways backward in getting the corn for Lydda's wages will pay for it, and the meat too, and I know Ma will let you have it.[133]

The old fellow here in this place went yesterday evening and got two more guards. Somebody broke into his mill house and barn

---

[132] Pvt. Archibald F. Knight of Co. K.

[133] Lydda was a slave owned by Nancy Hill Fitzpatrick. She had apparently been hired out to MHF and Amanda.

adjoining it night before last and stole a large amount of wheat. He did not blame me atall for it as the mill is nearly a mile from here and we were not guarding there atall. The two men he got yesterday will guard there altogether. I believe it was citizens or negroes that stole the wheat for soldiers have no use for it. There was corn in there but they took none of it. Soldiers will press corn to make lye hominy or get it ground for bread but they draw plenty flour and of course have no use for wheat.

I have a fine time reading. I am now reading Colton's Life of Henry Clay.[134] It is a large work in two volumes. I take it with me while on guard nearly every day. I will close and go to breakfast. We get just as much milk as we want three times a day. While we are stationed here direct your letters[,] all of you[,] to Orange Court House instead of Richmond, and they will come a day or two sooner I think. I noticed some letters directed there that came very quick.

Tell Henry that there is a pretty little pony here that Pa wants him to have mighty bad and that he must save his rings till he gets big enough to get one like him to ride. Write me if he wears breeches all the time now. Write soon. May God bless you. Pray for me.

Your husband,
M. Hill Fitzpatrick

---

[134] Calvin Colton's *The Life and Times of Henry Clay* (New York, 1842).

Letters
1864

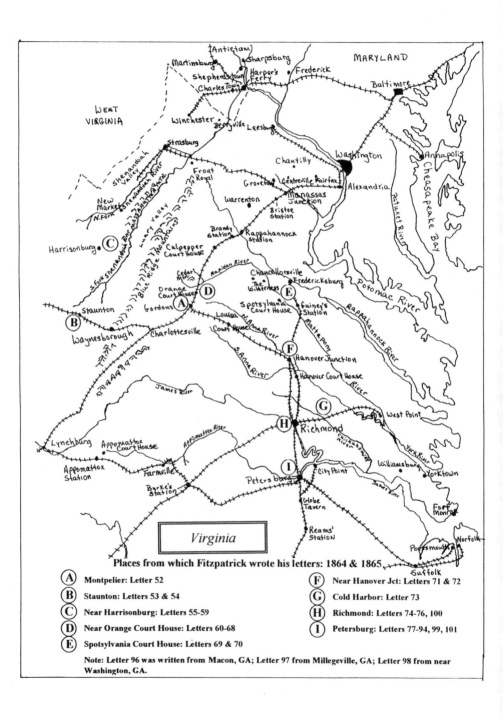

Places from which Fitzpatrick wrote his letters: 1864 & 1865

(A) Montpelier: Letter 52

(B) Staunton: Letters 53 & 54

(C) Near Harrisonburg: Letters 55-59

(D) Near Orange Court House: Letters 60-68

(E) Spotsylvania Court House: Letters 69 & 70

(F) Near Hanover Jct: Letters 71 & 72

(G) Cold Harbor: Letter 73

(H) Richmond: Letters 74-76, 100

(I) Petersburg: Letters 77-94, 99, 101

Note: Letter 96 was written from Macon, GA; Letter 97 from Millegeville, GA; Letter 98 from near Washington, GA.

Montpelior, Va. Near Orange C. H. *(Letter Number 52)*
Jan. 6th 1864

Dear Amanda,

In haste I drop you a few lines. We have just received orders to be ready to start to our Brigade early in the morning. It is about dark now and I am writing by candle light in our room where we have had such a pleasant time. I have rolled up my blanket[,] fixed up everything, and we will start pretty soon and go to Camp tonight. Mr. Carson is having some rations cooked for us to carry with us. I learn the Brigade is near Winchester. I do not know whether we will go by railroad or not. We may go by railroad to Staunton but then we would have to march a long ways. Capt. Brown[1] came in yesterday evening but did not bring the boxes. He left them in Richmond. He will bring them on to us when we get stationed. I was very much surprised to learn that we had to go to the Brigade as we were looking for them back here every day. All hands[,] wagons and all are going now and break up these Camps.

Well, Amanda, I have not had a letter from you or any of you at home in a long time. The last one I got was written Nov. 30th, 1863. I have anxiously looked day after day for a letter from some of you at home but have to start off now still without hearing from home. I have written every week or oftener since the last fight, and have got letters from everybody that I have written to since then but from you all at home. Do for my sake write to me as soon as you get this, whether you have just written or not. Direct to Richmond as usual and it will be forwarded on to me. My general health is good but I suffered almost beyond endurance last night with a tooth ache and Pneuralgia.[2] This morning by time, I put out to Camp went to the Doctor and had it pulled out. It has been easy ever since. It was badly decayed. It was one of my left upper jaw teeth.

Cout, I am a little low spirited tonight. I want to hear from you so bad and it is not a pleasant idea to think of leaving such comfortable quarters as we have here and take it in the open woods again. But this will soon pass off when I get away, I hope. I have a good pair of shoes, a good blanket and good overcoat and I hope will not suffer much. It is cold now. There is a little snow on the ground now. We had a pretty

---

[1] John T. Brown, quartermaster of the 45th Ga.
[2] Neuralgia, an acute pain along the cranial nerves extending down into the face.

heavy snow a few days ago. I saw some men skating on the pond with skates today, the first I ever saw. Well Cout I will write again soon if I get the chance. I must close and start. May God bless you.

Your husband,
M. Hill Fitzpatrick

ॐ

Staunton, Va. (*Letter Number 53*)
Jan. 13th, 1864
Dear Amanda,

I have just received yours of Jan. 2nd and am more than glad to hear from you again and to learn that all were well. I am well but worn out. You are a little surprised I reckon at the caption of this letter. I wrote to you on the night of the 6th inst. soon after we had rec. orders to come to the Brigade. We did not get off till 8th. We started through the snow, wagons and all, and took it by foot across the mountains. John Wilder, Dave Wactor, Colvin and I camped and messed together.[3] We had a good place to camp the first night, built a big fire[,] raked away the snow, and fared pretty well. The second night, Colvin and Wilder stopped behind at a house and Dave and I had to take it by ourselves. We camped right among the mountains on a steep mountain side. Dave was tight, but not so much but what he could walk tolerably well. I had all the cutting to do and after hard work, and Dave's getting about fifty falls on the snow we got a fire[,] cooked our supper and tried to lay down to sleep. We had only one blanket apiece and it was so steep and rocky that we done but little sleeping. But, as uncomfortable as it was, I could not help enjoying a hearty laugh at Wactor occasionally. He says the way he kept from rolling down the mountain when he was asleep he bent over a hickory sapling and held it in his teeth. The next day we crossed the mountains. The road was covered with snow and ice, and it was hard work getting the wagons over. The next night, Henry Gibson and I put up at a house and staid all night, and fared just well enough.[4] We had a splendid supper and breakfast and a good feather bed to lie

---

[3] "Wactor" was Pvt. David S. Wacter of Co. K. "Colvin" was Pvt. Moses F. Colvin.
[4] Pvt. Henry J. Gibson of Co. K.

on, the first I tried since I left home. They charged us $2.50 apiece. The next night I staid at a house by myself, but did not fare so well, paid $2.00. Early the next morning we come up with the Brigade, coming from Winchester on their way to this place. That was yesterday. We camped two miles from here last night. We got to a place where there was no snow hardly, built a large fire[,] lay down around it and slept soundly. This morning our Comp. was sent here on provost guard, so I am now writing in the City or Town of Staunton. This is a right sharp town nearly as large as Macon[,] situated in a mountainous region. It was thought by our coming here that we were going to take the cars and go back to Orange, but now I do not know where we will go or what we will do. Our Comp. will stay here on guard as long as the Brigade is camped where it is. Capt. Gibson has procured a room for us which we will go to soon. I am now writing in one of the lower rooms of the Courthouse where some clerks stay and write. We stopped this morning here in the courtyard. One third of the Camp is on guard all the time and take up all soldiers that have no passes. I am sorter sick and my feet is sore, but a few days rest will bring me all straight again I hope.

I do not know now when we will get our boxes. I am nearly out of shirts and drawers, but will have to make out somehow. My old ones done pretty well while I was stationed but are about to wear all to pieces since I have been on the march.

I was a little surprised at your not keeping Lydda this year. I thought it would just suit Ma to hire her as she had horses and hands a plenty. I do not like the plans atall, but it may be for the best. I do not blame you in the least. I know you done the best you could, but if I had known it sooner, I think I could have made arrangements with Ma to have kept her. What I wanted her to stay there for was so she could help you but if you can do without her I suppose it will do as well.

Well the least said about it the best now, but I hope to God I will get home some day to stay and I will try to straighten up things a little. Until that time you must exercise your best judgment and manage the way you think best after studying over the matter well and not do the way everybody tells you. This I know you have done and I at least will never grumble at you. So among all your trials you will have one friend that will not desert you and who you can tell freely all about it.

Well, Cout, as I said before, I do not blame you in the least and you are my overseer and manager now and it will all be for the best I hope, so chip in and pitch ahead. I am glad you paid the lumber bill. It looks like I will never get to send you any more money. One of our Comp. went home on furlough since they have been up here in the valley but

I was not here and did not get to send you any by him. I have spent seven or eight dollars on this march for eatables and loaned out $25.00 to the boys since I got to them so I have not much left now. We will draw our two last months wages and our commutation money pretty soon, so they say, so I hope to get to send you some yet this winter.

Well, I am glad you was doing so well on spare ribs and chitlings, and am truly glad that you have a good prospect for meat next winter. I am proud of my boy and glad to hear that he is fat and growing fast and is so smart. I want you to start him to school next year or pretty soon at any rate and keep him going all the time until he gets a good education. I want him to have that if nothing else. I want to see him bad enough but I must wait patiently and hope for better times. Well I want to know what is the matter about getting answers to my letters of late. I wrote to you before the last fight, and then wrote on the 10th of Dec. to you and you said nothing about getting either of them. I also wrote to Lou on 4th Dec and have written to her once since then and have no answers to them yet. I also wrote to Ma about the last of Dec. Write me whether you all ever get them or not if you do not answer them. I got a letter from Alex the other day written just before he started back. He said he had shoe leather to make me some shoes whenever I wanted them. I want you to have them made and keep them ready to send to me when I write for them. I will need them I expect this spring or summer. These I have are too small to march well in and will be worn out I expect by summer. Have them made large eights or nines small, not very small nines either.

Well I will close up[,] write me a long letter and write all the little particulars about everything. I will write again soon. Remember me in your prayers. May God bless you.

Your husband,
M. Hill Fitzpatrick

ॐ

Staunton, Va. *(Letter Number 54)*
Jan. 18th, 1864

Dear Amanda,

In haste I drop you a few lines this morning. We have marching orders and expect to start in a few minutes. It is reported that we are going about 25 miles from here near Harrisonburg and go into winter quarters. I hope it is true. If it is we will get our boxes pretty soon.

My health is excellent. We have had a gay time here on Provost Guard.[5] We are all pretty well rested now. Mose Colvin is at the Hospital in this place. He has been complaining for some time. I think he will get a furlough. Tom Rickerson drawed a furlough since we came here and will start home soon.

I rec. your letter of Dec. 27th the other day. I had just rec. yours of Jan. 2 and answered it, so I thought I would wait awhile before I wrote again. I wrote to you last on 13th inst. which I hope you will rec. and it will post you on my late tramp. I do not know what has got into the mails. I got the one you wrote on 2nd Jan. before yours on 24th Dec. and have no letter from Lou yet.

Yesterday was Sunday. I went to church at the Baptist Church at 11 o'clock and at night.[6] I went to a school exhibition one night soon after we came here. It was a nice thing but cost me two dollars.

It is cold and cloudy and I fear will rain or snow today. We have drawn no money yet. The Payrolls are all fixed up and we would have drawn today if we had staid here.

I saw Bob Jolly and Dawson Rogers the other day on their way home on furlough.[7] All our settlement boys are well. I must quit and be ready to start. I will write again soon. Write soon and write me a long letter. May God bless you and my noble boy. Pray for me.

Your husband,
M. Hill Fitzpatrick

P.S.
The order to march this morning has been countermanded and I will write a little more before I mail my letter. We will start early in the morning. I have just read yours of Dec. 24th again which I did not take time to do while writing the first part of my letter. Lieut. Rutherford has not gone yet on furlough but has one on the way now. I suppose he and Tom Rickerson will get off together. Tom does not want you to say anything about his coming home as he wants to take his folks by surprise. I am glad you were doing so well on hog killing and fixing when you wrote, but sorry that Henry was so near barefooted. I hope

---

[5] A detail of soldiers acting as police.

[6] Staunton Baptist Church was founded in 1853. It is now the First Baptist Church of Staunton, Va.

[7] John R. Jolly and Dawson Rogers of Co. C, 12th Ga. Infantry, were also from the Elim settlement area of Crawford County.

you have procured him a pair of shoes before now, if not get them as soon as possible regardless of cost. I am a little surprised to hear of so many weddings. Write me whether Polly and John M.[8] married or not. Like you I think it would be a splendid match.

I am sorry that Ross would not serve you at Elim this year. I expect Uncle Johny will be the only chance.[9]

Gen. Lee has issued an order that all who will furnish a recruit to their companies shall have a 30 days furlough. The recruit has to come here before the furlough is given. I reckon there is no chance for me to make a rise in that time but if you see or hear of anybody nearly 18 years old that wants to come to the war send them to me if you can and I can then get a furlough. Or if he is over or under 18 so he has never been in service. We have a good Company, and I think as good a Regiment as there is in the whole army. Do not let this trouble you any. I merely mentioned it as I had nothing else to write. Write me or tell Lou to write me Bro. Ben's address.[10]

M.H.F.

❧

Camp Near Harrisonburg, Va. *(Letter Number 55)*
Jan. 22nd/64

Dear Amanda,

Tom Rickerson and Lieut. Rutherford will start home tomorrow or next day, but I suppose they will get off early in the morning. I send

---

[8] Unknown to editors.

[9] Like many rural Baptist churches, Elim extended an annual call to one of the community's preachers to serve as pastor. In the minutes for 1863 the call for 1864 was extended to a "Bro. Ross" but he did not accept. "Uncle Johny" was almost certainly the Rev. John V. Gordon, who had served Elim more than once. See Tina Hortman, "Proceedings of Elim Baptist Church," *Central Georgia Genealogical Society Quarterly* (1989) 113-114.

[10] MHF's brother Benjamin (eighteen years older) moved to Mississippi in the 1840s to teach school. He married Elizabeth Jane Moore in Chickasaw County, Miss., in 1846 (according to the DAR application of Miss Katie Elizebeth Fitzpatrick). He enlisted in Co. C, 31st Miss. Inf. on March 5, 1862 and was appointed assistant quartermaster ten months later. This job, which carried the rank of captain, required much travel and made keeping up with him hard for the Fitzpatricks.

you some buttons and a buckle and $145.00 in money. Lieut. Rutherford wants the money to use on his way home and will send you the amount as soon as he arrives. My health is only tolerable good. I am worsted with our tramp, but I hope we will get to rest awhile now.

I wrote you on the morning of 18th. The next morning we started and arrived here on the evening of 20th. We are four miles east of Harrisonburg, and 29 mile north of Staunton. We drawed money the evening after I wrote you in the morning. I drawed $136.00 and had $33.00 oweing to me which I collected right away. I was in hopes I would have more to send you but I have spent a good deal as I generally do on a march, when I have it and I will keep some for fear of getting sick. Tom has promised me faithfully to go and see you and Ma. You must treat him with the greatest respect for my sake if nothing else but he richly deserves the esteem of all. He is truly a noble highminded young man, and as brave as the bravest. I think a great deal of him as a soldier and companion in arms. He can tell you of many hard struggles we have had side by side amid the clash of arms and the roar of canon, and many camp jokes if you can get him started. Furloughs are being granted freely now. Our Company sent up three more this morning. Tip Hammock, Greene Boman and Berry Frazier got them.[11] They will get off soon as they only have to go to Gen. Early[12] the Commander of our squad here in the valley.

I wrote you that we had a Brigade here from each Division, but I was mistaken. There are only two Brigades here, and we are here close together. As I wrote in my last, I thought we were coming up here to put up winter quarters, but the order is to not build huts, as it is uncertain about our remaining here long. They sent for our boxes yesterday and I hope we will get them now in a day or two. We have tents enough for all to sleep under by crowding a little and are doing pretty well. The snow is melted off but it is cold. I forgot to tell you in my last that I had received your copperas. I acknowledged the receipt of it right away in a long letter to you, in which I sent you a song ballad, but as I have never heard from the letter, I suppose you did not get it. I made some good ink with it. I want you to send my shoes by Tom. I wrote you about them in my last letter. I had rather you would send them by him as he is so careful and I will need them by the time he gets here. But if you cannot get them made in time, just let them miss

---

[11] Green B. Bowman was a private in Co. K and Ellsberry S. Frasier was appointed 4th sergeant in 1863.
[12] Lt. Gen. Jubal A. Early.

till another chance. I had no idea of sending home for shoes till Alex wrote me he had made arrangements for a pair for me.

I tried to get my transportation money for my passage home last winter but failed. It is $40.00. I reckon I will get it some day. Use the money I send you as you think best. Be sure to keep enough for emergencies. As I wrote before, I want our buggy debt paid, but if we can't raise money enough we will have to put it off. If you can pay it, Mr. Miller[13] will attend to it for you. He is a Mason now and I know will do the best he can for you. If they keep furloughing this fast as I hope they will, it will be my time again after awhile. Do not be uneasy about my health for I can eat like rip. I recommend Tom to all the girls, any of them would do well to get him. Write to me as soon as you get this and send me a handful by Tom. May God bless you and my darling boy.

Your husband,
M. Hill Fitzpatrick

ॐ

Camp near Harrisonburg, Va. *(Letter Number 56)*
Feb. 10th, 1864

Dear Amanda,

We got back to these camps from a twelve days march three days ago. Yesterday Tip Hammock started home on furlough. I wrote a long letter to Lou, by him and give a sketch of our tramp. John Wilder, Dave Wactor and Harvey Locklair has all got discharges and will start home in the morning.[14] I sent you a little funnell and Henry an iron ring by Tip. I sent my old pockette book to Henry by Tom Rickerson. I want you to keep it for him till he gets old enough to take care of it himself, in remembrance of the war in which it was worn out. I have a good homemade pockette book[,] a present to me. I sent you my overcoat by

---

[13] Isom E. Miller of Crawford County.
[14] Corp. John A. Wilder was discharged because his left hand had been rendered almost entirely useless from wounds received at Fredericksburg. Pvt. David S. Wacter had been wounded in the left foot and left arm at the Battle of Frayser's Farm. Pvt. Harvey Lochlear was also discharged due to disability resulting from wounds received at the Battle of Frayser's Farm.

John Wilder. Clean it up and take care of it for me till next winter when you can send it back to me by the first chance. Put some pocketts in front outside sorter slanting before you send it back. I would not send it now but Joe Walker[15] has given me a good large warm cape to wear as long as I want it, so I can make out without my overcoat very well, and it is such a good one I hate to lose it.

I found two letters here from you when we got back and rec. another of Jan. 30th yesterday. I am truly glad to get them and to learn that you were well, and that Henry was getting on so well, and improving so fast, but sorry to learn that you lost one of your hogs. I hope that no more of them will die. I am anxious to hear if Tom got home safe, and you got your money all right. I know you will be uneasy about me before Tip gets there, for I had no chance to write or send off a letter on the march, and was longer than I have been since I came to the war in writing home. My health is fine now and we are living high. Mose and I bought a quart of syrrup and the butter that was in our box our settlement boys all eat together, with the understanding that when our butter comes we divide with them. I do not know how long we will stay here or when we will get our other boxes.

I am glad you made some money. I think six dollars is a big pile for you to make in one month and do your other business too. I have made a little money lately. I had $6.50 when I got back to New Market on our tramp here, and now I have $15.50 cents and two plugs of tobacco some paper and envelopes extra. I made it buying tobacco and apples and selling them again. It is my first speculation. I do not like the business and should not have done it if I had not been scarce of cash. I also made a dollar today, sewing. I made a haversack for a fellow. It was his own proposition to give me a dollar for it. I have some sewing of my own to do. I want to patch my old pants and wear them while we stay here and save my new ones. I give away my old shirts and drawers. They were about gone under sure. I am highly pleased with all you sent me. I will sell about half my soap for fear of having to march and it is too much to pack. I can get $3.00 for half of it. It is pretty cold now but is clear.

I will close as I have got to write several letters for the boys. Write soon. May God bless you. Pray for me.

Your husband,
M. Hill Fitzpatrick

~

---

15 2nd Lt. Joel A. Walker of Co. K.

Camp Near Harrisonburg, Va. *(Letter Number 57)*
Feb. 18th, 1864

Dear Amanda,

I have been looking for an answer to the letter I sent by Tom Rickerson for several days, so I could learn whether you rec. the money I sent you or not, &c, but failing to get it so far I will write again. I am sorry to inform you that I have been quite sick for four or five days, and am quite feeble yet. I rested well last night, and eat some breakfast this morning, the first that I have ate for three days that would stay on my stomach. My digestive organs seem to be entirely deranged. I ate too much was what made me sick at first, but if my stomach had been right it would not have hurt me so bad. I had sick stomach and threw up a great deal, and also the diareah at the same time. It worsted me pretty badly sure. The Doctor has attended me, but has not given much medicine. I feel so much better today that I hope I will get well soon now. I learn from letters received by the boys that Tom Rickerson is very sick. I am truly sorry to hear it. His furlough is out today but I am not looking for him back. Unless Col. Simmons brings my shoes I will have to draw a pair the first chance for these have about played out.[16] I sent you a letter and my overcoat by John Wilder which I hope you received safely. We got our other box the day after John left. The potatoes and cakes were rotton. The butter is sound, but tastes pretty rank. I cannot eat any atall of it since I have been sick. I am going to work it over and see if I can't get some of the old smell out of it. The meat Ma sent me kept nice enough. Last winter it would have been worth a great deal to me, but now we are drawing more veal [and] nice pork than we can eat, so I sold it. I got $2.00 per lb. for it from a citizen. It weighed 9 lbs. Mose and I have flour and pork enough now to last us 10 days. We are going to sell some of it. My peaches kept just nice enough. They make splendid pies without any sweetning. I put on my new pants to have my two old pair washed, and burnt them right away. Send me a scrap like them by Tip to patch them with. I got a lady living near here to mend them but the piece she put on is not quite large enough to do well. I had no scizzors and wanted it done nice

---

[16] Thomas J. Simmons, colonel of the 45th Ga., was at home on furlough. This reminds the reader that the Confederate soldier was truly a "citizen soldier." Col. Simmons was first a neighbor to MHF and secondly his commanding officer.

is why I got her to do it. I also got her to bind my hat which had got to flopping, for all of which she would not have a cent of pay.[17]

The day after we got the balance of our boxes, we moved camps about half a mile, and are now camped at an excellent place[,] wood and water both convenient and plentiful. The springs we get water from are medicinal and said to be very healthy and were once resorted to largely by the rich and invalid.

The weather is extremely cold and disagreeable now. A good many have put chimneys to their tents and are very comfortable. My crowd put if off till it is too cold now to work at it. I miss my overcoat but my cape does me finely. I told John[18] to explain to you how to fix the pockets and take out the pocket that is in it. I will want a dress coat and vest next winter, but do not want you to put any buttons on the coat, and I will take the buttons off my old coat and put on it. It is too cold to write so I will close up. Write me a long letter and tell me all about my boy. May God bless you. Pray for me.

Your husband,
M. Hill Fitzpatrick

P.S. - Feb. 19th. I did not get my letter off yesterday and before I mailed it this morning, I want to let you know that I am nearly well again or feel so at least, to keep you from being uneasy about me. I slept well last night and feel like I could eat some grub now.
M.H.F

࿐

Camp Near Harrisonburg, Va. *(Letter Number 58)*
Feb. 24th, 1864

Dear Amanda,

Jack Wilder will start home on furlough this morning and I will send you a letter and $20.00 in money by him. I have been looking for a

---

[17] Hats were very important to soldiers on both sides. MHF seems to have favored soft wool felt hats with a brim, as did most Confederate soldiers. The regulation "kepi" is never mentioned in these letters.

[18] John A. Wilder, who had returned to Crawford County on a medical discharge. The supply and quality of Confederate uniforms was a continual problem. MHF preferred clothes Amanda made, although he took government issued clothing.

letter from you or some of you at home for some time but failed to get it. Tom Rickerson I learn is very sick and I fear will not recover. I regret it much and still hope that he will get well and return to us. Col. Simmons time is out but he has not returned yet. I am anxiously looking for him, hoping he will bring me a letter and my shoes.

My health is excellent at this time. We are still here near Harrisonburg, but it is rumored that we will return to Orange soon, but I hope it is not true. I had rather stay here in the Valley now for the remainder of the winter. We are living high now. Our tricks from home have not given out yet and we draw plenty of good pork and flour, and have some fine eating sure. We have baked a great many pies with our fruits and we sell what we do not want to eat. I have made $8.00 selling pies. I would not send you so small an amount of money, but it is a good chance and we will draw soon or at least it will be draw time soon, and I do not know but what you may be needing it badly. Now I want you to write to me as soon as you get this and not wait till Jack starts back. Furloughs are being granted freely now. Castle George and Jerry McGhee[,][19] two others from our Comp. are going to start this morning. McGhee got a recruit for our Comp. and got a 30 days furlough for it. Mose Colvin has a sick furlough sent up which he will be pretty sure to get. There will then be six left in our Comp. that have not been home atall. After those six gets off, they will start around again, but then I reckon all will draw or it will be a long time yet before I get home again, I fear. But it is prophesied by a good many that this cruel war will end before a great while and then we will all get furloughs. The weather is pleasant at this time, but is very changeable. Sometimes it is cold enough to freeze chinches[20] and then in a short time it is pleasant. The health of our whole Brigade is better than I have ever known it before.

I have been making a little money recently by sewing, patching pants, coats, &c. They come to me and offer me high pay to do it. I hate to charge for it but it takes time and thread and to make a little to buy tobacco, &c. , I accept of the pay. It takes thread like rip and I will have to trouble you for another small ball by the first chance. I have no scizzors and there is none in the Company now and I have to use my knife. It is rough work but soldiers think it very nice. I wish I had a pair of scizzors. I could soon make enough to pay for them by cutting hair and I intend to buy a pair the first chance. When we are in Camps I like to have something of the kind to do to employ my mind. We can

---

[19] Pvts. J.C. George and William J. McGee.
[20] Bedbugs.

get but little to read, and something of that kind to do is much better than playing cards or lolling about. I long for the time to come when I can return to you and my darling boy and spend my time in your company, and in reading good books.

I had been very sick when I wrote you last, but soon got well again. Write me where Alex is, and what he is doing. I learn that their twelve months companies are bursted up and that they will have to go into regular service. I have written several letters to him since he has been in service, none of which I have heard from, so it is discouraging to write again, though I want to get a letter to him on business affairs, which I explained in a letter to Lou which I sent by Tip.

There is some law passed about the Confederate money so I hear, but I do not understand it. If you have any on hand that you do not use immediately, get advice how to work it. I owe Joab Willis $8.00 and the McLendon Estate $10.00. The latter note is or was in the hands of old man Cleveland and I owe the buggy note $140.00 which is all I owe that I know of.

Well Cout cheer up and hope for better times. Write soon and write me a long letter. Pray for me. May God bless you.

Your husband,
M.H. Fitzpatrick

ॐ

Camp Near Harrisonburg, Va. *(Letter Number 59)*
Feb. 28th, 1864

Dear Amanda,

I rec. yours of 13th inst. day before yesterday and was truly glad to hear from you again, and to hear that all were well and that you received safely the things I sent by Tom. It had been a long time since I had rec. a letter from you, and if I was by you I would pinch your ears good for not writing to me as soon as you got the letter by Tom, and for not writing more explicit about Alex. I was anxious to find out where he was, as I wanted to write him a letter on business affairs. You said you would send the money down to Macon by him to pay the buggy debt, and by that I infered that he was at home at that time. I have just written to him and directed to Capt. Blunt's Company Macon, Ga. For fear that he does not get the letter I will explain to you so that you can attend to it if necessary.[21]

He wrote me not very long ago that Ma would pay me all she owed me as soon as she sold her meat. Now I do not want her to pay it unless you realy need it and cannot do without it, and I hope that will not be the case, as I can send you some if I am fortunate and keep well. I have never asked for a cent that Ma owed me and have never wanted her to pay it but had much rather it would remain as it is, especially now, when Confederate money is worth so much less than money was when I worked hard for what she owes me. Just explain this to Ma and I know it will be all right. If Ma has any money to spare after paying all her debts, besides what little she owes me, she could let you have enough to pay Joab Willis and the John McLendon note and it of course it would be all right but I do not want her even to do that, unless she has a plenty to spare.

Col. Simmons and Capt. Gibson came in this evening. I was glad to hear from them as well as from your letter that Tom Rickerson was getting well. My health is fine at this time and I am living just well enough, but it will not be so long, for we have orders to start back to Orange day after tomorrow morning. It will get me all over for I am nearly barefooted and there is no chance to draw any shoes if I wanted to draw and I would hate to draw now as Tip if he has good luck will be here with mine in about six days.[22] I am so glad that Henry is proud of his pockete book and ring. I sent a dollar by Tom to get you some apples and carry to you but as you wrote nothing about it, I reckon he forgot it or could not get any. I also sent a Dollar by John Wilder to get me some apples.

You want me to write all about my things. I believe I wrote about everything but the tobacco which I forgot whether I mentioned or not. I found it in one of my shirt pockets and was glad to get it. I like my shirts the best in the world, but I wrote about it in Lou's letter and all about our long march which I supposed you would read. Mose started home on sick furlough a day or two ago. I sent a letter to Cousin Emily by him.[23]

---

[21] Alexander Fitzpatrick enlisted in Co. B of the 8th Cav. Batt., Georgia State Guards. This company was originally raised for six months. It may be that he then enlisted in "Capt. Blunt's Company," but there is nothing in Alex's sketchy Compiled Service Record about this.

[22] Apparently Col. Thomas J. Simmons did not bring MHF the shoes.

[23] "Cousin Emily" was the second of Bennett and Eliza Fitzpatrick's six children. She was about twenty-three years old.

You say I must get a furlough. There is no chance for me now and no trying to do unless I could furnish a recruit, and I see no chance for that. There are six or seven to go yet before it starts around the second time and then all will draw together I learn so any chance is a long ways off yet.

I had to quit last night[,] it got too dark for me to finish my letter. Last night I got a letter from Doc, written Feb. 18th. They were near Lake City, Florida. I learn that they have been in a fight since that time and am anxious to hear who was killed and wounded.[24] Write me all you know about it. As you say it has been twelve long months since I left home and I long to return again but must take it easy. It is warm and cloudy this morning. It is reported that we will not start tomorrow if it is raining. Write soon. May God bless you. Pray for me.

Your husband,
M. Hill Fitzpatrick

ॄ❧

Camp Near Orange Courthouse, Va. *(Letter Number 60)*
March 6th,1864

Dear Amanda,

Today is Sunday. Last Sunday I wrote to you from near Harrisonburg, and wrote that we would start back to this place on Tuesday. Accordingly Tuesday morning we started and yesterday arrived here where we are encamped within a half a mile of our old Camp.

I am about up the spout.[25] I have not a sign of a shoe to my name, and am worn out, but I did not make the march barefooted. Capt. Gibson had two pair of boots. Henry Gibson[26] wore one pair of them

---

[24] Doc's 27th Ga., as a part of Colquitt's Brigade, had been transferred from Charleston to meet Federal threats in Florida. On February 20, 1864, Colquitt's and Harrison's brigades (approximately 5,000 men), under Brig. Gen. Joseph Finegan, defeated a division of Federal troops (5,500 men) under Brig. Gen. Truman Seymour at the Battle of Ocean Pond, or Olustee.

[25] "Up the spout" was then a popular expression, indicating exhaustion or a hopeless situation.

[26] While it seems likely that Capt. A.W. Gibson and Pvt. Henry Gibson were related, the editors have been unable to document any relationship.

two days, and I wore Henry's shoes. The boots nearly ruined his feet and he had to take his shoes and let me have the boots. I wore the boots till we got here then which was three days, and they broke me down and nearly ruined my feet. This morning I have not put them on atall, nor do I expect to any more if I can help it. I put on an old pair of socks over one of my new pair and am taking it shoeless. I am so stiff that I can hardly walk atall but I hope a few days rest will bring me all right again.

Tip's time will be out tonight. I shall look eagerly for him to come and bring my shoes. The morning we started from the valley it was raining. In the evening it sleeted awhile and then commenced snowing and continued snowing till after dark. We marched about 22 miles that day and camped on the Blue Ridge Mountains near the top. I[t] was an awful time. I with several others got in an old vacant house and fared tolerably well compared with those who staid outside among the rocks in the steep mountainside. The next day was a pretty day and we stopped before night at a good place. The next day we marched 25 miles and stopped after night on a steep hillside. That day we came through Charlottsville. A short time ago the Yanks made a raid above Charlottsville and burnt a bridge across the Rivana River, and we had it to wade. I say we nearly all waded it but I was fortunate enough to get to ride. I was standing on the banks thinking about it when I noticed a field officer belonging to our Brigade sending his horse back from the other side for several men to ride over. I caught him looking at me[,] threw him a Masonic Sign and he sent his horse back for me. The river was wide and pretty deep and I was glad to get over dryfooted. There was an old boat above the bridge that a good many crossed in.

While speaking of the first days march I forgot to mention that we crossed the Shenandoah River, in two flat boats, that were carried over with poles. There was considerable excitement in the Brigade there and along before we got there, in consequence of two young girls that were with some soldiers in the 49th Ga. They were dressed in men's clothes or rather in a soldier's garb and were following the Brigade on foot. It was soon rumored all through the Brigade that they were of the fair sex and their face and hair also betrayed them, and everybody wanted to get a look at them. After they crossed the river Gen. Thomas found it out and had them put back on the other side with orders to remain there. Of course, they were of disreputable character.

Well I believe I had gotten to the third days march. The two next days we did not march so far, and yesterday which was the fifth and last days march, I with one other of our Comp. came by Montpelior and called on my old Irish friend Mr. Carson, got a warm dinner with him and rested about two hours and then came on here to the Camp. We drawed corn meal lard pork and coffee yesterday evening and had patty bread[27] and coffee for breakfast this morning. They have drawn no flour here for four weeks and do not know when we will draw any more. I do not like it much but will not grumble. They have been trying to fight about here for several days but did not make it out. All is quiet here now and the troops have returned to Camp. The yanks made a raid on the railroad above Richmond a short time ago and burnt some bridges and tore up the road apiece, but it has been repaired and the cars I learn passed through again yesterday. The yanks seem to be determined to trouble us all they can.

We could have come a much shorter route from the Valley here if it had not been for them, as it was we had to wind all about and march much farther and harder. When on their raid above Charlottesville they done much mischief. They carried off a great many negroes. In one instance they made the negroes hitch up the horses to their master's carriage right before their master's and mistresses' faces and drive off and they took the rings off the ladies' fingers[,] slapped their jaws[,] struck them with their sabres and took all their meat[,] corn and horses and acted mean generally.

I am anxious to hear from you and my boy again. You must answer this as soon as you rec. it, and give me all the news. I am wearing my new britches now. I shiped my old ones when we started on the march. My gloves are about worn out. Please send me a pair by Jack Wilder or the first chance. I will close up. May God bless you. Pray for me.

Your husband,
M. Hill Fitzpatrick

ɤ

Camp Near Orange Courthouse, Va. *(Letter Number 61)*
March 11th, 1864

Dear Amanda,

Tip came day before yesterday and brought your letter of 3rd inst., my shoes, socks and thread and beeswax all safe. All of which I was glad to get, but I had a piece of wax which was answering my purpose finely, though in sending me that you showed a thoughtfulness for me

---

[27] Bread baked in a small pan.

which I shall never forget. My shoes came in a good time sure for I was without a footcovering at the time. They are a little too large, but it is a good failing. My socks I did not realy need at this time but they are not in the way at the least. My thread I am proud of. I have put up a regular tailor shop, and am making my expenses at least by it. I bought a pair of scizzors the other day with a nice brass chain attached to them for which I paid $10.00. I intend selling the chain for four or five dollars if I can to help pay for the scizzors.

My health is excellent at this time, but I tell you eating is scarce, especially in the meat line. If I had the meat now that I sold in the valley I would not take four prices for it. Tip brought some butter cakes and meat with him which he divides with me. He said Mrs. Miller[28] gave him some of the butter and told him to divide it with me. It is a great treat just at this time sure, and I want you to return my thanks and best respects to her for it. Tip went to see Doc in Macon, and Alex was there and sent a letter to me by him. I had read through a letter rec. from home by Tom Smisson that Doc was wounded and in Macon, and was very uneasy about him. I am still uneasy about him. Tip says he don't think he will be able for duty anymore. I hope he is at home by this time. I am anxious to hear from him again and to get a long letter from him telling all about the fight. I want to hear from Jim Wilson also. I have talked to Tip a heap since he came back and it is a great satisfaction to me. He has told me a great deal about my boy and praises him to the highest pitch.[29]

I rec. a letter from you of Feb. 22nd the day before Tip came was glad to hear that you had my coat all safe. You had done a big days weaving that day sure. You must not hurt yourself at work, because the war's on hand. I am sorry to learn that the cold had killed your garden plants, but by this time I hope you have a fresh start.

Alex wrote me that he could not pay the buggy note. The note had been confiscated as Yankee property and the man could not or would not take the money for it. I wish I had not sent you the $20.00 by Jack Wilder, but as it is you must do the best you can with it. If you still have it on hand let Alex have it with the other if you can send it to him, and he can fund it alltogether. There are two months wages due us now

---

[28] Probably the wife of Isom Miller of Crawford County.

[29] Doc was wounded at the Battle of Ocean Pond, February 20, 1864. According to his Compiled Service Record and to his pension application made in the 1890s, he received a gunshot wound near the left wrist, causing him to lose the use of his left hand. Jim Wilson was a corporal in Co. C, 27th Ga. and was wounded at the Battle of Ocean Pond. Unlike Doc, he would return to active duty.

but we will not draw I learn till two more months are due and then we will draw the new issue.

They are still granting furloughs. Bob Wilder started home two days ago, and two others will start in a short time. I wrote to you as soon as we got back here from the valley and gave you a sketch of our trip, which I suppose you have received by this time. I wrote you in one of my letters to send me a patch to put on my pants, and for fear that you did not get the letter I will mention it again. I want a long patch to put on the leg in front from nearly up to the knee down to the bottom. Be sure to send it by the first chance. If you have none of the same color something else will do, and [if] you have no scraps that are long enough I can sew them altogether and make them do.

You mentioned again about my writing to Mr. White. I want to do anything I can that would give you pleasure, but it is an awkward and up hill business for me to commence a correspondence with him again. I cannot see why he should think hard of you for my not writing. I am almost certain that he is mistaken about writing me the last letter. The last one I wrote him I enclosed a letter to Henry in it. If he answered it I have never rec. the answer, and when I was at home he said nothing to me about answering it or my writing to him. If I was certain he wrote to me last I would write to him.[30] Write soon and write me a long letter. May God bless you. Pray for me.

Your husband,
M. Hill Fitzpatrick

Camp Near Orange Court House, Va. *(Letter Number 62)*
March 21st, 1864

Dear Amanda,

I rec. yours of 13th inst. from the hands of Jack Wilder yesterday evening and was truly glad to hear from you again and to learn that all were well. I have had the belly ache for about a week and have fared pretty badly but am much better now and hope to be well soon. It was not eating too much this time dead sure for our rations are rather slim,

---

[30] "Mr. White" was Amanda's father, William B. White, Sr. "Henry" is Amanda's younger brother.

but still we get enough to make out with finely. We draw sugar and coffee enough to have some nearly every time we eat. We draw corn meal most of the time now.

I am glad you had succeeded in getting out your long piece of cloth, and I hope you will have a rest from weaving for awhile. I am glad to learn that Doc was mending. Jack went to see him in Macon. Jack says the Dr. will not let him go home yet. I was in hopes to hear that he was at home when Jack came, though no doubt it is best for him not to move too soon. I am anxious to hear from him again and to hear that he is at home and doing well. Jack says that Alex was down with the measels and he did not get to see him. I am sorry to hear of it. I suppose he will get a furlough soon and go home. I have written two letters to him recently but rec. no answer to either. He wrote to me by Tip but had not rec. my first letter at that time. It seems to be a hard matter for me to get a letter to him. I have been longer in writing to you or some of you at home this time than I ever have to be still in Camp, but being on the sick order and also looking for Jack to come so that I could hear from Doc again was the cause of it.

I am sorry that you cannot get paper. I hope you have secured some by this time. It is worth $10.00 per quire[31] here.

I got a long letter from Lou the other day. She seemed to be a little low-spirited and I think had rather be in Crawford again.[32] I am glad your garden was doing well. I hope you will raise a plenty to eat, if not you are up the spout for there seems to be no chance to buy. Jim Drew came with Jack. I am glad to see him back again to mess with him. He looks well and is in fine spirits.

We have established a regular sharp shooting or skirmishing Battalion in our Brigade. I joined them immediately. They took from two to four men from each Company. They called for volunteers and if more volunteered than was needed they picked out the best ones from the number. They wanted one non-commissioned officer from our Company. I volunteered and as none of the others did they accepted me readily. They wanted two privates from our Comp. Several offered and they chose John Spillers and Noah Cloud from the number. They are both good scouts. I wish Tom Rickerson had been here and gone into it. We drill to ourselves and do the skirmishing when there is a fight on hand and fall back when the regular engagement opens and do not go into it atall unless it becomes a very tight fight. Skirmishing is ticklish

---

[31] A group of twenty-four or twenty-five sheets of paper.

[32] In Letter 39, MHF wrote that he had "directed Lou's letter to Reynolds as I suppose she is at her Pa's at this time."

business at times, but I like to do it when it has to be done. We are excused from all camp duties and also from pickette duty which is a great help.[33]

It is cold and windy now. We have a good large tent fixed up on logs and tightly dobbed and sleep warm and comfortable. Eight of us sleep in it. We have built no chimney. The boys say they have done without this long and will not build now.

I am glad that my boy is doing so well. Jack says he is a great boy sure. John Collum came with Jack, and Jack will get another furlough before long and go home again. They both look pretty badly worsted. They were eight days on the road. Colvin's time will be out pretty soon now and I suppose he will start before you get this. If not be sure to send my patch to mend my britches by him.[34]

They stopped furloughing a short time ago but it is thought that it will be resumed again pretty soon, and then Jack will get off right away.

I was sorry to hear of the death of Russ Davis.[35] Like you, I often think of the happy times we had there in our young days, and the scene enacted while riding along the road not far from there, when I asked a blushing girl of fifteen summers to be mine, and she would not consent. Well Cout, we have had many trials since then and a hard road to travel, but that was the last quarrel we had. I often wonder how you ever managed to love me. I was so much older and uglier than you but I suppose a woman can do anything she sets her head to.

I was 29 the 18th of this month but the day passed off without my thinking about it. My hair is turning gray fast. I do not think the war is the cause of it, for I commenced turning gray at 22 and I do not take trouble to heart like some folks. I think it was first caused by hard study while teaching school.[36]

---

[33]Although there were specific Confederate battalions called "Sharp-shooters," MHF seems to have been volunteering for a less formal group. Skirmishers were an important part of infantry tactics during the War. Fanning out before the main battle lines, skirmishers fought "Indian style," taking advantage of trees and fences rather than staying in the fixed lines of their infantry companies. The organization of Thomas' sharpshooters seems to have been ordered by the new division commander, Maj. Gen. Cadmus Wilcox, as one way of preparing for the spring campaign. Pvts. John S. Spillers and Noah Cloud were friends of MHF who volunteered along with him.

[34] Pvt. Andrew Jackson Wilder had brought John Collum of Crawford County to Co. K as a new recruit. Hence he qualified for another furlough. Moses Colvin was still on furlough in Crawford County.

[35] Unidentified by editors.

[36] MHF taught school in Linden, Texas, in 1857 and 1858.

Jack says they are well pleased with Cousin Emily as a teacher there. I am glad to hear this and hope she will do well.[37] I have been looking for a letter from her for some time. I miss Lou the most in the world about writing to me about how Ma is getting along farming and things generally. You must write me in your next all about how they are getting on, and how you are getting on also. I fear sometimes that you lack things and really suffer for them and do not let me know for fear it will trouble me. Write me if you have ever got a hat for Henry, and how you are off in the shoe line.

Lieut. Col. Grice has resigned. He had to do it before he could get off to attend the Legislature in Ga. We all regret it much. We will never get another as good as he was. I am sorry now that we elected him.[38] I go over to Montpelior occasionally and get a good dinner which is a great help to me. I also get my clothes washed there. They wash them nice and iron them, which is a great help. I make money enough sewing to pay for the washing and more too, and sewing is easier than washing. I wear gallows[39] now. I find it a great advantage especially on the march. I made me a pair of leggings off my old pants legs which is a considerable preservation to my new pants.

Bill Gardner was here yesterday and last night. He looks well, but is as poke easy as ever. He is trying to get to our Comp, but it is doubtful about his succeeding.[40]

Well Cout, I will close up. I think and highly hope that this war will end this year, and Oh then what a happy time we will have. No need of writing then but we can talk and talk again, and my boy can talk to me and I will never tire listening to him and he will want to go with me everywhere I go, and I will be certain to let him go if there is any possible chance. So, hoping for these good times, let us cheer up and go forth with renewed vigor and energy. Pray for me. May God bless you.

Your husband,
M. Hill Fitzpatrick

֎

---

[37] Where Emily Fitzpatrick taught school is unknown to the editors.
[38] Lt. Col. Washington L. Grice resigned his commission on March 17, 1864.
[39] A pair of suspenders or braces.
[40] There is no soldier with the surname of "Gardner" on the roster of Co. K.

Camp Near Orange Courthouse, Va. *(Letter Number 63)*
Apr. 3rd, 1864

Dear Amanda,

Colvin came in three days ago, and brought me your letter of March 24th and that night I rec. by mail at the same time yours of March 18th and 20th all of which I was glad to get and to learn that all were well. Colvin also brought me a letter from Alex of March 22nd which I was glad to get but sorry to learn that he had the measels.

You are a witch to guess at my wants sure, for the ham of meat and $10.00 was the very thing I was needing and I am glad to get them. Also the gloves suspenders patches and thread and tobbacco, all of which I rec. safely and now return my thanks to you for them. You sent more by double of the patching than was necessary, but I will take care of it, and will no doubt find a use for it. My gloves just fit and are just the idea. The suspenders I could have done without as I had a pair that was given to me. The things you sent me are much the best and I treasure them because they came from you. The tobacco I am glad to get and it chews finely. It is a scarce article here and a high price. The ham of meat is quite a treat sure for we only get 1/4 lb. per day now. We took breakfast off of it this morning as it is Sunday and it went fine sure. The money I was glad to get too as I had none, but I could have borrowed at any time but never do that if I can manage without. When I sent you the last $20.00 I expected to draw again the 1st March but we will not draw till 1st May. I could make money in the valley enough to pay expenses and more too but it is different here. I make some here by patching but have to wait for it till we draw again. I have $13.50 owing to me in little debts and I owe $11.00.[41] I spent four dollars of that you sent me for a toothbrush right away. I broke one some time ago and had to be without till I got your money. I never do without a fine comb and toothbrush if there is any chance to get one. Colvin got the bill you sent changed to fives in Richmond which kept me from losing 33 1/3 percent on it.

My health is excellent at this time and I am getting on finely. Jack Wilder started home again the day Colvin came in. He started early in the morning and Colvin came in that night. I sent a letter to Ma by him is why I was in no more of a hurry in answering yours. I sent Ma some coffee and you a shawl pin just for a project and three or four buttons. I

---

[41] Smisson's diary contains lists of men who owed him money. MHF is on one of these lists.

shall save all of my coffee to send home as I cannot drink it, and I had rather Ma had it anyhow. We are fixing up a nice pudden for dinner. I do not know how we will come out as we will have to put meal instead of flour in it but we have plenty of sugar to put in it. Colvin is not messing with me and Drew, since he came back, but I shall divide the ham with him as long as it lasts for his kindness in bringing it to me. It is nearly fair and tolerably pleasant today, but we have had rain cold and snow in a full supply recently. The boys have decided to put a chimney to our tent tomorrow and I am glad of it. I have not fixed my pants yet, it has been too bad weather. I fixed me a pair of leggings which I wear to preserve my pants from the_____ . I am glad to learn that you were successful in the eggs and chicken line. I should like to help you eat some but see no chance for a long time yet. I do not blame Ruffus atall for going to one of his brothers although if it could have been agreeable all around I would have been glad for him to have come here.[42]

I am a little surprised at the apple scrape. John was mistaken about my having some to send you and getting them stolen. I care nothing about the amount of it, and no doubt they will straiten it, but I wanted you and Ma to get them for the rarity of the thing. I gave Tom a dollar to get you some and John a dollar to get Ma some.[43] I am sorry you were caught with $2.00 in Confederate Money on your hands at that time. I reckon you have disposed of it in some way before now, but I had sure rather it could have been funded before this time, or which would have been better paid out for debts or invested in necessarys. Alex seems to think that he can get the new issue for it by loosing 1/3 but I fear he is mistaken, from what I can learn. I hope it will work out for the best in some way if not I will not fret atall for I am no money worshiper.[44] Write soon and write me a long letter all about my boy and every thing of the kind. Pray for me. May God bless you.

Your husband,
Hill

---

[42] "Ruffus" was Amanda's brother, Rufus White, who enlisted in Co. C. of the 27th Ga. on March 29, 1864. He joined his brothers George and Henry in that company.

[43] The "John" here was probably John A. Wilder, who had returned to Crawford County on a medical discharge, while "Tom" was Tom Rickerson, at home on furlough.

[44] Confederate paper money became less and less valuable. MHF is referring to a new issue of devalued Confederate money which was intended to replace the old issue.

૨ৡ

Camp Near Orange Courthouse, Va. *(Letter Number 64)*
Apr. 10th/64

Dear Amanda,

It is Sunday evening and is raining. I wrote to you last Sunday, and
have no letter from you since then to answer, but will write anyhow to
keep up the times. But news is a scarce article, except that we have rain!
rain! rain! in superabundance. We had two days of pretty weather last
week and only two. Yesterday morning it commenced raining early
and rained all day and nearly all night hard down. Our Comp. went on
pickette and returned this morning, looking considerably worsted. The
river where they pickett rose so that they had to move out some
distance. This morning it faired off and I thought we would have a
pretty day but since 12 o'clock it commenced raining again, and is
coming down to it with no prospect of ceasing soon. We built a chimney
to our tent last Monday, and we fare finely now rain or shine. It is a
great help sure. We built it large and roomy and are not so much
crowded as we thought we would be. All the Comp. have chimneys to
their tents now.

My health is fine at this time, and I am getting on finely except in
the eating line or rather the bread part of it. For the last two days we
have drawn a little flour and a little meal, but both together would not
more than make a good days rations. The cause of it is that they cannot
get it here to us fast enough on the cars just at this time from some
hindrance. It will soon be all right, no doubt. Drew and I had some
ahead and have not felt it yet but some of the boys are grunting pretty
loud on the subject.

We had what we call Brigade preaching today. Himan, Pastor of
49th Ga. preached[45] and Steward,[46] our Brigade Missionary, closed.

---

[45] "Himan" was the Rev. John James Hyman, chaplain of the 49th Ga. A very
effective chaplain according to *History of the Baptist Denomination in Georgia*,
282-283, Hyman was ordained on April 12, 1863 while already serving the 49th.

[46] "Steward" was almost certainly the Rev. Thomas H. Stewart, a Methodist.
In 1864 he was appointed as a missionary to the Army from the Georgia
Conference of the Methodist Episcopal Church, South, and was attached to
Thomas' Brigade. In 1859-1861 he had served in Crawford and other nearby
counties. See Harold Lawrence's *Methodist Preachers in Georgia, 1783-1900*
(Tignall, Ga.: The Boyd Publishing Co., Ltd., 1984) 529-530.

Steward once rode the circuit in that Country, and has preached often at Macedonia.[47] I reckon you have heard him preach. I recollect him very well. He has not been with us but a short time.

We had another Masonic meeting night before last, the first we have had since we came back from the valley, in consequence of having no room. I got a room over at Montpelior, upstairs in the house we stayed in while guarding there. It answers the purpose finely and if it would quit raining so much, we would meet regular. I will send you a song ballad to interest you some, at least. Tom Smisson is drawing it off for me. He knows it by heart and can sing it. There is much solid truth in it though often sung by rowdies.

We got a half quire of paper and half bunch of envelopes to the man from the government the other day. We drew it like clothing and will have to pay for it. But it comes much cheaper than to buy from the sutlers.[48] This is some of the paper. It cost $2.00 per quire and the envelopes $1.00 per package.

There is more clothing and shoes here for the soldiers than I have ever known before. All can draw as much as they need and many I notice have drawn[,] I think[,] more than they need, or will need on the march. I have drawn nothing nor do I expect to in a long time yet if I can keep what I have got.

I fixed my pants the other day. I wish you could see the job. I know you would brag on it. I took out the whole piece in front nearly up to the knee and put in a new piece of the patches you sent me, and they are just as good as ever. I would not know what to do without my scizzors anyhow. I get just what sewing I can do for the other boys in the Comp. and make expenses by it.

It will soon be two years now since I first left home, and nearly fourteen months since I was at home on furlough. It seems long indeed to be separated from you and my darling boy. I try to submit to it with as good grace as possible, knowing that I am doing my duty to my country, and by so doing I will have a clear conscience. I want this war to end and to be at home as bad as anybody can but I do not believe I could enjoy myself at home such times as these if I was able to do duty. Others would be fighting for their Country and my Country and home while I would be skulking my duty, and it would render me miserable. So taking all things into consideration I am happier just as it is while the war lasts. I would enjoy a furlough though to the greatest extent, but

---

[47] "Macedonia" was Macedonia Methodist Church, near the Elim settlement in Crawford County. The church closed in 1923, but a well-preserved cemetery remains.
[48] "Sutlers" were merchants who sold to soldiers.

my chance for one is a long way off yet, I fear. There are four yet in our Comp. who have not been at home atall, but I hope they will get off this summer and then my chance will come early next winter. But who knows but what the war will end by that time and then we will all get a long furlough and happy times for the future. For this let us hope and cheer up.

Write me all the news and all about my boy, write me whether he has a hat or not. If not, try to get him one made or make him a cloth one. I have seen some very nice quilted and made by the ladies. I would like for him to have a knife but there is no chance for that I reckon. Write me all you know about Doc. Pray for me. May God bless you.

Your husband,
M. Hill Fitzpatrick

ॐ

Camp Near Orange Court House, Va. *(Letter Number 65)*
Apr. 14th, 1864

Dear Amanda,

I rec. yours of 4th inst. this morning, and am more than glad to hear from you again and to learn that all were well. My health is very good at this time[,] not so bouyant as it is sometimes but much better than a great many others. It is Spring of the year now and the worst time we have on soldiers. There are many cases in our Regt. and Comp. and some of them pretty serious. Colvin is quite sick and has been for several days. They are going to send him off to the Hospital in the morning.

I feel a little sleepy today. I was at our Lodge yesterday and last night, is why I did not get your letter till this morning. I rec. at the same time one from Pat & Camilla Greene[49] of 2nd inst., and was glad to get it. I was in hopes that I would hear direct from Doc by some of you, but I suppose he is unable to get home yet. I see much uneasiness about him and am anxious to hear from him often.

---

[49] MHF's nephew and niece. They would have been around 14 and 12 years of age.

I am glad to learn that you are doing well in the shoe line and that Henry has his Uncle Jim's[50] hat. His head must be pretty large for Doc's hat to fit him. I wish I could see him with it on.

I am sorry the hawks catch your chickens so badly. I wish I could be there to kill them. But I reckon I would not do much hawk killing unless I done better than when I was at home. You must get some ammunition and kill them yourself. You can soon learn to shoot, and it might be of great advantage to you, if the Yanks should ever get that low down in Ga. I want women[,] children[,] old men and all to kill them every possible opportunity rather than let them pass through our noble old State.

I am so sorry to learn of your sad misfortune in losing your cows. I was in hopes you would do well in that line and soon have a nice stock. It seems that we were unfortunate with cows from the beginning but try again and hope for better luck next time. I am also sorry to hear that old Watch is dead. He was a good dog and I know was much company to you. Write me if you have another. You spoke of my suspenders, whether I liked them or not. I like them just well enough. I first wrote or sent word to you to make some cloth ones because I thought wool was so scarce, but I prefer the knit ones because they give way like rubber. I will be glad to get my syrup flour &c, if Alex got it in, but I fear we will be on the march before it gets here and then it will stand a good chance to go up the spout. But I will hope for the better.

I did not know that you were going to send anything by Colvin or I should not have written for any more, but I hope you only sent a little so that if it is lost it will not be a heavy loss[,] that is if you could get in any. We have some of the ham you sent me on hand yet, it has been a great help to us sure. We drawed old bacon the last time which is pretty rank sure and takes a stout stomach to conceal it. We drawed some old crackers the other day. Drew and I eat some once, and let the balance rip. We get plenty meal now, but it is a little coarse and not sifted but goes finely. The weather is fine and pleasant today and was also yesterday, which is quite a treat to us in one sense of the word at least, but of course will hasten the time of fighting, should it last long. Surplus baggage is being sent to the rear and a standing order for the commissarys to keep seven days rations on hand, all of which indicates a preparation for the coming conflict. Our sharpshooting squad drills often now. We drill now in judging or guessing the distance to objects and will commence target shooting soon. I am highly pleased with the

---

[50] This is a rare time when MHF refers to his brother James by something other than "Doc."

drilling. A great many reports are in circulation about the opening campaign but none reliable with me at least. My notion is that the campaign will not open in several weeks yet, and then Lee will attack Grant and go on to Pennsylvania.

Write me a long letter and give me all the news. I am looking for a letter from Cousin Emily. Write me all about my boy and whether he is still fond of books and how big he is and how fast he can run. Be sure to write often whether you have a letter to answer or not. I am always uneasy when I fail to get letters. May God bless you. Pray for me.

Your husband,
M. Hill Fitzpatrick

ॐ

Camp Near Orange Court House, Va. *(Letter Number 66)*
April 16th, 1864

Dear Amanda,

Wash. Piles, one of our Company, has a discharge and will start home in the morning.[51] I wrote to you day before yesterday and sent it by mail. I wrote in answer to yours of 4th inst. and should not write again so soon if it was not for the chance of sending by hand. But the oftener the better for me, and I believe or rather know it is so with you. Today is Saturday. I was at the Lodge again last night. We returned about midnight in the rain, and this morning it was still raining and there was no roll call so I slept till about 9 o'clock. Drew had breakfast ready when I got up, to which I paid my respects and felt considerably better. It rained on till near 12 o'clock and ceased, but is still cloudy. After breakfast I finished a job of sewing which I had on hand which was making a havresack, and now sit down crosslegged on our bed in the tent to write you a letter. The boys are out on Battallion drill, which duty, as I said before, I miss by being a Sharpshooter.

My health is very good now. I spoke in my last letter about Colvin being sick, and that they were going to send him off to the Hospital. He left yesterday morning. I do not know where they sent him, probably to Charlottesville or Lynchburg. We are looking for Tom Rickerson in tomorrow or the next day. I shall be glad to see him if he has fully recovered, if not, I shall regret his coming so soon. I hope he will bring

---

[51] Pvt. George Washington Piles must have been given a medical discharge.

me more letters. We drawed four days rations of old bacon yesterday which outranks Gen. Lee and three days rations of meal, one day's ration of flour which is excellent and is quite a treat to us. Drew and I have had one good mess of biscuits, which tasted like Sunday morning at home when new wheat first comes in. I love biscuits as well as ever and I reckon always will if can get them. We also drew some sugar and coffee. A quarter of a pound of the old bacon is the greatest plenty for us. It takes but little of it to do. We have only a very small piece of our ham on hand yet, but if the Smisson box has good luck, it will soon be here. Do not understand me to be grumbling in the eating line. No! Far from it. We can do finely on what we get, which is far better no doubt than many poor soldiers' families are getting at home. If there is any true charity in the Southern Confederacy, it should be bestowed upon the suffering families of our brave defenders.

I have $5.00 yet of the money you sent me but shall spend a portion of it pretty soon for tobacco. The boys keep me busy sewing, and I cannot keep up. I reckon I shall have to put up a tailor's shop when I get home. I found some old tent cloth the other day which makes excellent havresacks, and I make them and sell them at $2.00 a piece, but have to sell on a credit. I have only made one yet. It is thick and hard sewing and rather slow making money but much better than doing nothing or trying to die with the blues and homesickness. Dissatisfaction is the worst complaint a soldier can have.

Having nothing else to write I will tell you of a little scrape Tip and Mose got into about a ham. In the boxes we got over in the valley, there was a ham with the mark rubbed off. Mose said he thought it was his. We knew it was his or Tips. Mose kept it and before he left sold it. He did not cut it so I eat none of it and was glad of it. Mose said when Tip came back they would decide it. When Tip came Mose was gone. When Mose came Tip asked him about it. Mose said his wife sent him a whole ham and two pieces. Tip said his Ma sent him a ham and no other meat. They wrote home for the folks there to settle it. They did not get mad about it. Say nothing about this but whenever you send me anything[,] do like you did then. Mark it plain and write me plainly in a letter exactly what you sent.

I would answer Alex's letter if I thought he would be at home long enough to get it, but not knowing this I will wait till I hear from him. I wish I had something to send you and my boy by Mr. Piles, but have nothing atall this time. Keep in good spirits. Take good care of our boy and hope for better times. Write soon. Pray for me. May God bless you.

Your husband,
M. Hill Fitzpatrick

෨෴

Camps Near Orange Courthouse, Va. *(Letter Number 67)*
Apr. 24th, 1864

Dear Amanda,

It did me much good to rec. yours of 12th inst. sent by Tom Rickerson, and to learn that all were well. Tom came in two days ago. He is not well but is lively and in fine spirits. I wrote to Ma and Emily the day after he got here. My health is excellent and I am getting on finely. Our box came in yesterday evening and I rec. safely my shoulder of meat and flour of which I am very thankful, and glad to get. We had biscuits, lean meat and coffee for breakfast, to which I paid my respects with the greatest magnanimity. I quit drinking coffee altogether for awhile but we had such dry eating I got at it again, though I am confident I do much better without it than with it. It took me but a little while to judge the cakes you sent me, and also to find them most excellent. Now if the Yanks will let us alone for awhile, I can enjoy my eatables to the utmost, but the weather is dry and pleasant now and a move I think will come off soon but I will hope for the better and eat like rip while we stay here, and take some of it with me if we start before it gives out.

I am glad to hear that George[52] was at home. I hope he enjoyed his furlough. I used to hear from him often when Doc was with the Comp., but since he was wounded, I never hear from him.

I am so proud to hear that you have a fine garden. I took much pains in making it and fixing it up and am glad that you are now reaping the benefits of it. I am sorry that you have so much weaving to do. I earnestly hope this war will end this year, and then the women will not have so hard a task. I am glad that you are doing so well raising chickens. I should like to have about six fried with good cream gravy, &c. I do not know the 49th Ga. soldier that rec. your socks, though the Regt. is in our Brigade and encamped within a few hundred yards of

---

[52] Amanda's brother, George, a private in Doc's old company, Co. C, 27th Ga.

here. Several boys in our Comp. got some of the socks like those you knit, and wrote to the ladies who knit them. I explained in Ma's letter about the apples I sent you by Tom. Tom has told me a heap about my boy and all about the settlement which does me much good to hear. He says he would have joined the Sharpshooters if he had been here. I would like the best in the world to have him. We had Division review yesterday, which was a grand thing. Lieut. Gen. A. P. Hill reviewed the Division, attended by his staff and Maj. Gen. Wilcox and his staff. Today is Sunday, and having to go on review yesterday, we have not practiced target shooting any since I wrote to Emily. But we will pitch in again tomorrow. I reckon you have gotten your money matters straight by this time, either by funding or exchanging for the new currency. To exchange for the new currency would be best now, since it could not be funded only at a large discount. I have some business there that I want attended to but it seems to be a hard matter to get it done. I owe three debts which is all I know of and I want them paid. The buggy note[,] Joab Willis' note and Cleveland note. I shall draw $68.00 in a short time, the most of which I shall send home, for I have nearly enough owing to me to pay my expenses for two months. I shall get Isam Miller[53] to attend to it and will write him a few lines and put in this letter for you to hand or send to him. If you have any of the old currency give it to him to exchange for the new currency. Now understand me, if then you have more than enough to buy your thread or whatever you need, give it to him to pay these debts. If not keep it and use it. The Willis and Cleveland notes he can find and pay right away. The buggy note he may not find or get to pay atall, but I want him to see and find out all about it. It is all talk about their not taking Confederate money for debts. They can be made take it if the right kind of a hand will try. I will close. Write soon. Pray for me. May God bless you.

Your husband,
M. Hill Fitzpatrick

಄

---

[53] Isom E. Miller of Crawford County.

Camps Near Orange Court House, Va. *(Letter Number 68)*
Apr. 29th, 1864

Dear Amanda,

I rec. yours of 17th inst. yesterday evening and am glad to hear from you again but sorry to learn that Henry was not well. I cannot help being uneasy about him when I hear that he is sick but I earnestly hope that he is well by this time. My health is excellent and I am getting on finely at this time. The weather is pleasant, and we are living high on the contents of our box. We have biscuits for breakfast every morning and cornbread for supper or dinner. I do not know which you would call it, as we only eat twice a day and have no regular time to do that. My piece of meat is of great value. The meat we draw is very inferior, and comes in small doses.

The call for sharpshooters to fall in was rang out just as I wrote the above, and I had to quit and put out to practice target shooting. We shot two rounds apiece at the distance of 600 yards. Out of 98 shots, only five hit the board. I was one of the five and I missed the cross some distance.[54]

Well Cout it seems that I will never finish my letter, but this is the third trial and better luck probably this time. I had just fairly commenced the second time yesterday when some of the brethren of the Mystic[55] called around for me to go with them to the Lodge. I put out with them and did not return till about midnight. The consequence of which is that I feel drowsy today. I have just returned from our morning's lesson of target shooting. I did about the same as yesterday, missed the board the first shot and hit it the next. There was considerable improvement in the other boys. A good number of shots struck the board. We shot 600 yards, the same distance as yesterday.

I was glad to hear from Doc through your letter, but I fear it will be some time yet before he gets home. I am sorry to hear that George[56]

---

[54] At the Georgia Department of Archives and History there are three orders related to these drills. Each is from Capt. James A. Englehard of Maj. Gen. Cadmus Wilcox's staff and each was addressed to Lt. William Norwood of Brig. Gen. Thomas' staff. The first two detail instructions for judging distance drills, and the third describes the target practice drill. These orders, dated April 2, April 9, and April 19, 1864, reveal the careful training ordered for this "Corps of Sharp Shooters." See the Papers of James A. Englehard, AC No. 00-272, Georgia Department of Archives and History, Atlanta.

[55] Another term for Free Masons.

[56] Amanda's brother George, who had been licensed to preach by Elim Baptist Church in 1859. See Hortman, "Proceedings of Elim Baptist Church," 113.

had to return so soon, but I hope he enjoyed his furlough well. John & Clayt Simmons came to our Regt. as recruits as few days ago. John says he heard George preach while he was at home and was highly pleased with him. It is strange that he does not get the appointment of Chaplain for some Regt. Though I do not know that he has ever sought it or would accept it. John & Clayt joined Comp. B from Monroe County. John looks as lazy as ever and we now have the honor of having the laziest man in the Army in our Regt. He brought Gus Adams with him as a recruit and will get a furlough of 30 days to go home again right away.[57]

We had a mess of fish for breakfast this morning which was quite a treat to us. We also had biscuits and coffee which went fine with the fish and gravy. The weather is fine and pleasant now, and buds are rapidly putting forth, which indicates the near approach of Spring in old Va. We will look for Jack Wilder back in a day or two. John Collum makes a splendid soldier so far.[58] He is lively and seems to be satisfied which is a great advantage. Tom Rickerson is lively and I believe is about well again. The health of the Regt. is much better now than it was awhile back. We are looking for marching orders every day now and expecting for the big fight to open soon. And in the place of all quiet on the lines, as it is this fair and beautiful day, it will be roar of artilery and clash of arms. Various rumors are afloat as usual but no confidence to be put in any of them. I have but few notions about it. When the order comes to fall in, I will buckle on my armour, sieze my enfield, and put forth with energy and devotion to my bleeding country, if I am blessed with health and strength as I earnestly hope I will be. I missed a large portion of last summer's campaign, and I shall regret it much if I miss this. Somebody is always ready to say he is playing off or that he is a coward if a man fails to be in the fight. I do not fear being accused of this, but I do not want anybody to even think it of me. I wrote to you a day or two ago, and enclosed a short letter to Isam Miller. I hope you will understand it well and recollect that I want you to use all the money you need, if it takes all and not pay any debts, but if you have it to spare do not keep it by you for I have but very little if any confidence in its remaining good long, and if we can pay these debts now, there will be a heavy burden off of us when we start in the world again if kind Providence ever permits it.

---

[57] "Gus Adams" was Floyd A. Adams who enlisted in Co. B, 45th Ga. on April 20, 1864. John and Clayt Simmons have not been identified by the editors.

[58] Jack Wilder was expected back from furlough. Pvt. John E. Collum was a new recruit to Co. K from Crawford County.

I study a heap about my little boy. The boys that come from home all have something to tell me about him and I want to see him and see how much he has growed and how he looks and hear him talk and laugh and see him run and jump and ride a horse. It was natural for me to love him, and he seemed to love me so well even from the time he began to notice anything that it made me love him more if possible. I can but hope the time will soon come when I can return to you and him to remain through life. For this let us hope and cheer up. Write me a long letter in answer to this and do not be in a hurry next time, though I freely excuse you when you are wanting to mail your letter. Pray for me. May God bless you and our little soldier boy.

Your husband,
M. H. Fitzpatrick

In Line of Battle near Spotsylvania C.H., Va. *(Letter Number 69)*
May 15th, 1864

Dear Amanda,

Through the Providence of God I am permitted to write you again. I am unhurt so far and am in good health. No doubt you have heard much about the battle which has been raging here for twelve days with more or less ferocity. I will not attempt to give you anything like a detail of the fight now. We left Camps on the 4th inst. and have been at it every since and still see no end. Our Brigade has been in three times. They got into it on the evening of 5th and morning of 6th hot and heavy. Also on 12th.[59] I have not been in any of the regular fights but

---

[59] On May 4, 1864 the Army of the Potomac crossed the Rapidan River to begin Grant's great attempt to destroy Lee's Army of Northern Virginia. Although outnumbered two to one, Lee struck the Federals in the Wilderness, where the thick undergrowth would help to offset the Federal advantage. The Battle of the Wilderness erupted on May 5. Hill's Corps and Thomas' Brigade helped to stop the Federal advance the first day. Early on May 6, however, Hill's entire Corps was pushed back in disorder by Hancock's Federals. Most of the casualties in Co. K appear to have taken place on May 6. MHF and his comrades re-formed and contributed to the Confederate counterattack. On the night of May 7, Grant tried to turn Lee's right flank by marching to Spotsylvania Court House, but Lee had already sent Anderson's Corps (formerly Longstreet's, who was badly wounded on May 6) toward that crucial crossroads. Anderson won the race, throwing back the Federal advance. Both sides entrenched around the crossroads. From May 8-21 vicious fighting would ebb back and forth. May 12 was an unbelievable day, when the two armies fought from before dawn until past midnight in a ferocious struggle known as the "Bloody Angle." Few engagements in the War, if any, were more murderous. On May 15, when MHF

have been hard down skirmishing day and night. I have run some pretty narrow risks but not near like being in the regular fighting. They won't let the sharpshooters go into the regular fights but form us in the rear to stop straglers. We have whipped the yankees badly, but our loss is heavy. In our Co., John Collum and Jerry McGhee supposed to be killed. Capt. Gibson, Lieut. Walker, Jim Walker, Wm. Seymore, Bill Sanders, Greene Boman, Dan Wheeler, Castle George, Jack Mathews are Wounded. Journingham Slocumb, Bill Mathews, Bill Miller, Bob Wilder, Jasper Mathews are missing.[60]

Never has such fighting been known before. They have locked bayonets time and again and fought with the buts of their guns. The fighting first commenced some distance above here, but Grant fell back down the river and we have been at it here for several days. We are behind good breastworks awaiting the attack, or rather the Brigade is, but we Sharpshooters are holding the front all the time. Night before last, I never lay down all night, or slept a wink except nodding a little. Last night I slept all night. Tonight is my time to be on again all night. We have a skirmish often sometimes while it is as dark as pitch, but none from our Regt. of my squad has been hurt bad yet.

I rec. yours of Apr. 2nd since the fighting began and was glad to read one more letter from you. I have also rec. one from Doc and one from Lou since the fight began. It has been raining off and on for three or four days. It was hot at first and dry and I had liked to have given out. I feel much better now. I hate to write before the fight closes but I know you want to hear from me. I will write you a long letter if I live through the fight. Do not be more uneasy about me than you can help but trust in God. Pray for me. May God bless you and my boy who I think about so much.

Your husband,
M. Hill Fitzpatrick

---

wrote this letter, the two armies were shifting their lines to the east and south of Spotsylvania. MHF's appraisal of the Wilderness and Spotsylvania battles is remarkably accurate for a soldier in the ranks.

[60] Pvts. John Collum and Jerry McGhee had been captured, rather than killed. Pvt. James A. Walker was mortally wounded May 6, Pvt. William P. Seymour was wounded May 6, Pvt. Green B. Bowman was wounded May 12, Pvt. William Daniel Wheeler was wounded May 6, Pvt. J.C. George was wounded May 6, and Pvt. Andrew Jackson Mathews was mortally wounded May 6. The wounds to Capt. A.W. Gibson, Lt. Joel Walker, and Pvt. G.W.R. Saunders must not have been severe enough to be noted officially, for they are not included in Henderson's *Roster*. Corp. William J. Slocumb was wounded and captured May 6. Pvt. William A. Mathews was captured May 6, as were Pvts. William M. Miller, Joseph C. Wilder and William Jasper Mathews.

꙲

In Line of Battle Near Spotsylvania, C. H. , Va. *(Letter Number 70)*
May 19th, 1864

Dear Amanda,

I wrote you a few lines on 15th inst. I will write you a few more this
morning. We are still here at the same place. We had hot times awhile
yesterday morning. The Yankees attacked us early in the morning
while it was thick foggy. I was out on skirmish and run a narrow risk.
We saw them coming in one direction and thought it was only a line of
skirmishers. We opened fire on them hot and heavy and fought like
tigers, it being the order not to fall back until we saw the line of battle.
The line of battle came in by flank through a thick wood and was in
twenty steps of where I was before we saw them. We poured a fire into
them and retreated to our breastworks in all possible speed, while the
balls came thick and fast by us. One of our sharpshooters that was near
me is missing. I suppose he was captured. After we got back to the
breastworks, our boys opened a hot fire on them and the canon mowed
down their ranks and they stood it but a short time before they
retreated. They did not get very close. We sharpshooters took our
positions again after the fight. They left a great many guns but carried
off their dead and wounded except one dead man and one of our boys
got a watch from him. We can see where they drug off their dead, and
blood in profusion through the woods. They killed one man here at the
breastworks in our Regt. and wounded one. None hurt in our Comp.
Last night they fell back down the river about half a mile, and this
morning our Sharpshooters are at the breastworks they left, but our line
remains here at same place.[61]

Old Grant is a tough customer but Lee is an overmatch for him.
There is no telling when the fight will end. The prisoners say that
Grant says he is going to Richmond or Hell one, before he quits, and
has no idea of recrossing the river as long as he has a man left.

Well, Cout, I have stood it so far and am not hurt yet but I tell I am
tired and worn out. One half the sharpshooters stay on post at a time
now and we get a little rest. I was relieved at midnight last night and
will stay off till 12 o'clock today and then go on again and stay till

---

[61] MHF described for Amanda his viewpoint of the dawn attack by
Hancock's and Wrights' Federal Corps on the Confederate lines at Spotsylvania
on the morning of May 18, 1864. Although the Federals charged several times,
they did not succeed.

midnight tonight. My health is excellent, and we fare very well in the eating line. I feel too sleepy to write any more now. You must write to me and not wait till the fight ends before you write for there is no telling when it will end. I am confident peace will be made soon after this fight ends. As I said before I hate to write in the fix we are in now, but I know you all want to hear from me and I will try to do my duty to friends and my Country as long as I live.[62] Pray for me. May God bless you and my boy.

Your husband,
M. Hill Fitzpatrick

⁊❧

Near Hanover Junction, Va. *(Letter Number 71)*
May 23rd, 1864

Dear Amanda,

I have just rec. and read with much interest your kind letter of 9th and 11th inst. I am glad to hear from you again and to learn that all were well at home. My health is very good but I am worn out or about so. I wrote you on 15th inst. and again on 19th.

We left the place where I wrote you on 19th on the evening of 21st and had a hard days march yesterday. It was very warm and tiresome. This morning we moved a few miles farther down and stoped here in a pine grove where have been for several hours. We are neither in line of battle or in Camps and I presume will move again soon.

Grant would not fight us again in our breastworks, and move down the river towards Richmond and of course Lee had to move too. I understand some of the troops are throwing up works near here. I would not be surprised if we have another fight somewhere along here. I can hear skirmishing and occasionally a canon not far off. We had a considerable skirmish fight the evening we left up near Spotsylvania C. H. We advanced to find out if the yankees were gone. We soon came in contact with their skirmishers and a brisk engagement ensued. We

---

[62] Before the Battle of the Wilderness, Co. K had no more than fifty-two men available. Three members of Co. K died of wounds suffered at the Wilderness and Spotsylvania; six others were wounded; and seven were captured. That's a casualty rate of almost thirty-one percent. MHF lists another five men as injured who are not so noted in Henderson's *Roster*.

drove them a good long ways till we came up with too strong a force for us[,] who were well fortified. We then retreated and that night commenced our march down to this place.[63] My feet stood the march pretty well but I am poor and thin and am tired down. I wish Old Grant had fought us up there but he knew we would whip him there, and he wants to try another place. We may fall back to Richmond but I do not like that idea and hope we will whip him here.

I am truly sorry to hear of the death of Billy Miller.[64] I thought a great deal of him. I think it would have been best for him to have come to Va. Comparatively few die with sickness here, but many with the bullet. I rec. a letter from Alex and one from bro. Ben.[65] just now when I got yours. Alex is at Dalton now tasting of a true soldier's life. I could not help enjoying a laugh when I read his tricks in the eating line, &c. He now knows something about soldiering.[66] I earnestly hope Doc is at home by this time. I have a letter from him that I have not answered. You are all the one I write to except one short letter I wrote to bro. Burwell on 19th inst. I know you all suffer much uneasiness about me now but you must cheer up and hope for the best. I have been in danger often since the fight commenced but am unhurt so far.

May 24th Just as I wrote the last word of the above, orders came to fall in. We went back a short distance on the same road we came and we sharpshooters deployed and forwarded ahead of the Brigade through a thick woods. We soon ran up with the yankee skirmish line, and fought them hot and heavy, drove them in and fought the line of battle for awhile. But they got too strong for us and we fell back, expecting to find the Brigade in our rear ready to go on and whip them out. But we had inclined to the right and the Brigade to the left, so where I was I found no support atall in my rear. Several of us fell back to the railroad where started from. The fight then opened in earnest.

---

[63] Grant was indeed pulling elements of his army out of the Spotsylvania lines and heading toward Guiney's Station, and from there to the crucial crossroads of Hanover Junction. Lee's army got there first and placed itself between the North Anna River and the crossroads. Lee would be frustrated by his generals' inability to make effective strikes against the enemy, which was divided by the river and open to counterattack.

[64] Unidentified by the editors.

[65] MHF's brother Benjamin, a captain and quartermaster of the 16th Mississippi, in the Army of Tennessee.

[66] As noted, brother Alex had begun serving in Co. B, 8th Battalion Cavalry, Georgia State Guards in July 1863. There is no information in his record after January 7, 1864. He probably joined a state militia unit that was a part of Joseph E. Johnston's Army of the Tennesse, defending against Sherman's drive through North Georgia. Johnston had evacuated Dalton on May 12, so Alex's letter must have been written before that date.

They drove the Yanks a good ways but fell back about a mile last night. I am now on the skirmish line and our forces are building breastworks. There were four wounded in our Comp. Jack Wilder in the head slightly. I learn Jim Mathews in the head slight, Noah Cloud in the hand slight. Lieut. Joel Walker wounded for the second time since the fight began but I did not learn where at. None killed or missing. Several of our sharpshooters were wounded. I helped to carry one off, whose wound I fear is mortal. He was a noble young man beloved by all. We are looking for another fight at any time. I slept but little last night. It is useless to talk about how tired and sore I am.[67] I have not changed clothes or shaved since the fighting commenced. Do write often. Pray for me. May God bless you and my noble boy.

Your husband,
M. Hill Fitzpatrick

꿍

Near Hanover Junction, Va *(Letter Number 72)*
May 26th, 1864

Dear Amanda,

I finished my last letter to you of 24th inst. while on skirmish post. Soon after I finished it we were relieved and since then our Brigade has been in reserve or on the second line and we have had some good rest. I rec. yours of May 4th and Emily's of 5th enclosed together, the evening we were relieved. I was glad to get them and to learn that all were well at home. There is something a little strange that I rec. yours of 11th before I did yours of 4th, and yours of 11th was written in answer to one of mine written Apr. 17th while yours of 4th was written in answer to one of mine written Apr. 24th. But it is in the irregularity of the mail I suppose. I have slept undisturbed for two nights, and also have slept a good portion of the day time and feel considerably revived. I shaved yesterday and took off all my whiskers which helped my feelings. If I had the chance to wash the shirt and drawers I have on I would feel much better. I have a clean shirt and pair of drawers along

---

[67] About 6 p.m. on May 23, A.P. Hill used Wilcox's Division to attack Warren's Federal Corps. After an initial success by Thomas' Brigade (and the 45th Ga.), the Confederate attack failed due to lack of coordination. MHF gives a very good description of this confusing engagement, called the Battle of Jericho Mills.

but do not want to put them on unless I could wash these I have on, for they would be too heavy to carry with so much mud on them. As I said we are on the second line now but we are only about 100 yards from the first line. We have excellent breastworks and are waiting the attack of the Yanks who are in sight of us. They canonade us hot and heavy, sometimes with solid ball and sometimes with shell. They threw about a dozzen solid balls at this point yesterday evening but done no damage except wounding one horse. Some of the balls struck our works but did not go through. Heavy skirmishing is going on at this time and continues nearly all the time but it is not much sign of a fight. I almost wish they would come on us here in our works, for we would ruin them. I may be deceived but my opinion is that Grant is afraid to fight us behind works and will try to dodge around us again and get nearer Richmond.[68]

I wrote you that our Company had four wounded in the last fight. Two of them were so slight that they have returned to us. Lieut. Walker and Jim Mathews are the two that have come back. The other two[,] Jack Wilder and Noah Cloud[,] have gone to the hospital. The boys that came back say that Jack will be well in eight or ten days. Cloud's wound was in the hand and will be longer in getting well but is not dangerous. Colvin, who was slightly wounded in the _____ soon came back to us and is here now. Tip Hamock and Jeff Raines is with us yet unhurt. Tom Smisson and Lieut. Rutherford are off at the Hospital sick. We have had some hard rains for the last two days. My messmate Drew and I have a yankee tent which we stretch and it does us much good. The boys have got a good many yankee tricks off the battle fields some of which are very valuable. I have not found much yet. I got a good blanket and threw away my old one, and a good new havresack in the place of my old one, and a splendid pockette Bible, and a small looking glass, and my tent, and a cup, and some buttons. These Yankee tents are very light, and button together so that one man can carry one piece and another man the other piece. Three men can sleep under one of them very well. The one I got is right new and I would not take a pretty for it, especially if I live to go in Camps again. But now it is nothing but fight, fight, and we are in danger more or less all the time

[68] On May 26, as MHF wrote this letter, the fighting between the lines had eased along the North Anna River. MHF had a good reading of Grant's strategy. On the night of May 26, Grant and Meade began withdrawing the Army of the Potomac across the North Anna. They would then cross the Pamunkey River and head for Hanovertown, Va., far around the right of Lee's lines, to reach Richmond before Lee. By May 28th Lee would have his army in front of Grant in the area of Mechanicsville and Cold Harbor, just north and east of Richmond.

and God alone knows when it will end. I hope Doc is at home by this time. If he is tell him to write to me right away, and not wait for me to answer his letter, as I have such a poor chance to write and tell Cousin Emily that this must do for an answer to her letter too, and she must write to me again. I have no paper or ink here, and have to beg or borrow when I write. A good many of the boys have not written home atall since the fight commenced.

I am glad to hear that my boy has new breeches and that he likes them so well. I want to see him so bad. But it seems doubtful now about ever seeing him again. Men are killed and wounded around me nearly every day, and I know not how soon my time may come. But let us hope for the best. Be sure to write soon. Pray for me. May God bless you.

Your husband,
M. Hill Fitzpatrick

ॐ

Cold Harbor, Va (*Letter Number 73*)
May 4th, 1864 [69]

Dear Amanda,

I will write you a few lines again. I wrote to Emily 29th May, which was the last I have written home. I am well and unhurt yet. Soon after I finished Emily's letter we marched back the way we came in about two miles, and formed a line of battle. We were on the second line, and got some good rest. We staid there two nights, and moved farther down to our right, and took the front line. There we had some heavy skirmish fighting but none of our squad got hurt. We staid there two nights, and then moved still farther to the right to this place where we have been two days and nights on the front line. We are on the old battle ground of Cold Harbor fought on Friday evening 27th June nearly two years ago. We are not far from where I done my first fighting. Our Brigade has done no fighting since I wrote last, but much hard fighting has

---

[69] Although MHF dated this letter May 4th, 1864, the editors believe that he made a mistake and intended to write "June 4th, 1864." The heading "Cold Harbor, Va." and the text make this clear.

been done since then. Yesterday was one among the bloodiest days of this war. The sun refused to shine on the awful scenes. It was thick cloudy all day. The fighting commenced right close to us on our left and I learn extended along our whole line from here to our extreme left. Our Division is on the extreme right of our Army at this time, its right resting on the Chickahomany, and was the only part of our whole line but what was attacked yesterday. We occupy the position that McLellan did nearly two years ago, and it is a good and strong position. I am on the skirmish line with the sharpshooters at this time and have been here two days and nights. I have heard the fighting but have not seen any of it here. Reports and dispatches say that our boys killed the yankees by the thousand, and captured a great many prisoners, and that our loss was very light, and that in some places our forces drove the yanks for some distance. Our boys had good works to fight behind and I just know they poured it to them right. But before you get this you will find out more about it from the papers than I can tell you now. Old Grant tried mighty hard to get this position, but Gen. Lee was too smart for him.[70]

Colquit's Brigade is near here. I saw George, Rufus and Henry day before yesterday, also Jim Wilson and many other of our settlement boys.[71] I was with them only a few minutes. They were all well then, but were in the fight yesterday and I have not seen or heard from them since. I am anxious to go and see about them, and I hope we will be relieved tonight and perhaps I can then get the chance to go. I was surprised to see Henry here. He brought me the latest news I have from home. In vain have I looked day after day for a letter from home. I was glad to hear through him that Doc had gotten home. They had done some hard fighting before I saw them but their loss was not very heavy, and none of our settlement boys I believe had been hurt. Tell Mother I saw Jim Langford about four days ago. He was well, but I learned from him the sad news that John Langford was killed. He was killed on 5th May, up in the wilderness fight. Jimmy said he was shot through the body, and lived about three hours afterwards and was in his right mind up to his last moments, and that he died perfectly resigned to his fate. It hurt me much to hear of it. I was with Jimmy

---

[70] Because Thomas' brigade was on the extreme right of the Confederate line, it missed helping to repel the dawn attack of three Federal Corps at the Battle of Cold Harbor, on June 3, 1864. This massive assault resulted in around 7,000 Federals killed and wounded in less than an hour, with under 1,500 Confederate casualties. See E.B. Long, *The Civil War Day By Day*, 514.

[71] Colquitt's Brigade had been sent from Florida to reinforce the Army of Northern Virginia. "George, Rufus and Henry" were Amanda's brothers, all in Doc's old company.

only a few minutes. He looked well and has grown considerably since I last saw him.[72] Jim White is here somewhere but I have not seen or heard from him since the fighting commenced.[73] It is now about two o'clock in the evening. There has been canonadeing and skirmishing all day on our left but I think no regular engagement. All is quiet right here where we are, but we know not what moment they will come on us. I hope the fight will end soon. I have not changed clothes in over a month. We fare very well in the eating line. Do write to me all of you. May God bless you and my noble boy. Pray for me.

Your husband,
M. Hill Fitzpatrick

P.S. There was some heavy fighting on 3rd as well as yesterday, of which I know but little about except I learn that our forces were very successful. Things are brightening. All are hopeful.[74]

෨෪

Camp Jackson Hospital *(Letter Number 74)*
3rd Div. Ward G
Richmond, Va.
June 18th, 1864

Dear Amanda,

I am sorry to say to you that I am sick at this time, and have been for several days. I wrote to Doc on 7th inst. On 9th I was taken with Diareah, and it soon ran into bloody flux which made me very weak and almost past traveling. I staid on duty till 13th when we had orders to move. I reported to the Doctor, and he put me in an ambulance and carried me till we stoped that evening, which was not far from the old battle field of Frazier's Farm and Malvern Hill. I staid there at the Brigade Hospital in the woods till 16th when I was sent in our ambulance to this place, with many others that were sick. I am better

---

[72] John and Jim Langford were nephews of MHF, the sons of his older sister Elizabeth and her husband William H. Langford. John was a 2nd lieutenant in Co. C, 10th Ga. He was killed at the Wilderness, May 6, 1864. His brother, a private in Co. B, 14th Ga., was wounded the same day.

[73] Amanda's brother James was 2nd lieutenant, Co. C, 59th Ga.

[74] MHF seems somewhat confused in his dates. The major Federal assault at Cold Harbor took place on June 3.

now. My opperations are not bloody now, and by getting some good sleep and rest I hope to recover soon and return to the field, though I am quite weak yet. This is a very good Hospital. I get plenty to eat for a sick man at least. It is about 1 1/2 miles from Richmond, near Camp Winder Hospital. A great many of our Brigade are here sick and wounded. Lieut. Rutherford & Smisson have been here but I learn that Smisson has gone home and Rutherford has returned to duty.

Our Sharpshooters had a hard fight on the evening of 13th and lost several killed and wounded. The 45th Sharpshooters lost 1 killed, Tom Lawson of Taylor Co.[,] none wounded.[75] It is the only fight I have missed. I regret it much, but sickness cannot be helped. The Brigade was not engaged atall on 13th. I do not know where our Brigade is now. There is fighting about Petersburg and has been for a day or two but I can learn nothing very definite about it. I am anxious to hear from you. The last letter I got from home was written by Doc 24th May. I know you are uneasy about me, in consequence of not getting letters more frequent from me, but you must bear it patiently, as I have no paper, only what I can borrow from my friends from the Regt. and not a cent of money. I reckon we will draw money the first of July. I borrowed this paper from Lieut. Col. Carter[76] of our Regt. who is here sick. Edd Jordan got to our Comp. as recruit, a day or two before I left it.[77]

I will write again soon, as I have another half sheet. I have tobacco a plenty that I drew from the government or it would go much harder with me to do without money. Write to me and direct, Camp Jackson Hospital, 3rd Div. Ward (G), Richmond, Va. and if I go to my Comp. before the letter gets here it will be forwarded to me. May God bless you.

Your husband,
M. Hill Fitzpatrick

ॐ

---

[75] Pvt. Thomas J. Lawson of Co. E, 45th Ga. was killed at Riddle's Shop, Va., June 13, 1864.

[76] James W. Carter, who was first the captain of Co. C, 45th Ga., a company from Dooly County. He was promoted to major in 1862 and then to lieutenant colonel of the 45th on March 17, 1864. Shortly after he gave this paper to MHF, he was killed defending the Weldon Railroad near Petersburg on June 22, 1864.

[77] Edwin T. Jordan enlisted as a private in Co. K on June 1, 1864.

Jackson Hospital, 3rd Div., Ward G. *(Letter Number 75)*
Richmond, Va.
June 21st, 1864

Dear Amanda,

I wrote to you on 18th and having a chance to send this to Knoxville by one of our Comp. I will write again. For fear that you will not get my last I will recapitulate a little so that you can understand this if you fail to get that. I was taken sick about 9th of June with bloody flux and on 16th was sent to this hospital. I have been improving since I came here, and am much better now than when I wrote on 18th. I hope to be able in a few days more to return to my Regt. The man who belongs to my Comp. and is going to start home today, is named Greene Boman.[78] He was severely wounded in the leg on 12th of May. He is at Winder hospital near this place. He heard I was here and sent for me to come to see him yesterday. I will send you some buttons in the letter, which I have picked up in my late tramps, and which will be of some use to you. I am glad of the chance to send them, as I do not want to carry them on the marches with me.

In speaking of the heavy skirmish fight on 13th inst. in my last letter, I said the 45th Sharpshooters lost 1 killed and none wounded, but I was mistaken. There was one wounded in the foot pretty badly. I forgot him while writing. He is in this hospital and will probably get a furlough soon.

I do not know where our Brigade is now. I left it near Malvern Hill, and have not heard from it since. I hope there are some letters at the Comp. for me by this time. I am anxious to get back to the boys, but must wait till I get stronger. I take no medicine now. I am on the diet list yet, and fare much better than if I had to go to the table. I walk about and read and pass off the time the best I can. I went to the City Cemetery[79] yesterday evening. It is worth a visit. It is right on the banks of the James River, and is a beautiful scene. Among the notable characters that are burried there are the remains of President James Monroe. You must all write to me, and it will be best I reckon to direct to the Regt., as I hope to be there soon. I am anxious to hear from you

---

[78] Pvt. Green B. Bowman had served with MHF since Co. K was formed.
[79] Hollywood Cemetery.

all especially my boy. You must put some of the buttons on his clothes and tell him his Pa sent them to him. May God bless you.

Your husband,
Hill

᠄

Jackson Hospital, 3rd Div. Ward (G) *(Letter Number 76)*
Richmond, Va.
June 23rd, 1864

Dear Amanda,

I will drop you a few lines this morning, to inform you that I am about well again and shall start to my Regt. this morning. My health has improved rapidly since I came here. I reported for duty yesterday morning. I do not know where our Regt. is or how long it will take me to get to it, but I suppose it is somewhere about Petersburg. I have had a shirt and pr. of drawers, and my Coat and Pants washed by the Government, since I came here and my clothes are in very good condition now. I have the two shirts and two pr. drawers you sent me yet and shall swing to them late. I have the pants also and only 1 pr. which is all I want. My coat is wearing out, pretty badly. I shall patch it up the first chance I get and try to make it last till the first of next winter when I hope to get a furlough and go home and get my new one. I have three pair of good socks yet.

I went to the James River a short distance from here, yesterday and the day before and took a delightful swimming frolic, which was quite a treat to me. I wrote to you on 18th and 21st since I came here. I will send this by somebody going on furlough so you can get it sooner. I hope to find some letters for me at the Regt. I will write again soon as I get there if I have the chance. I hope we will draw money the lst of July.[80] I thought I would give you a description of this Hospital, but I do not know that it would interest you. It covers a large space of ground, and has 80 wards or houses in it besides some out houses. 64 of these wards contain about 30 patients each. The others are used to cook and eat in and for baggage rooms, &c. Each ward is built separate to itself, with streets running at right angles about 30 feet wide. There are about

---

[80] According to MHF's Compiled Service Record, he was paid $34 on June 23. Perhaps he was paid after writing this letter.

1800 patients in the wards and some 300 in tents near the hospital. There are about 500 nurses cooks ward matrons Doctors Clerks &c. Jeff Davis is feeding many people at this time.[81] Be sure to write soon and put the name of the Brigade on the letter also which may do some good. May God bless you and my boy.

Your husband,
M. Hill Fitzpatrick

ॐ

Line of Battle near Petersburg, Va.[82] *(Letter Number 77)*
July 3rd, 1864

Dear Amanda,

I rec. yours of June 4th and 11th several days ago, and at the same time one from Doc which I answered right away, and thought I would answer yours in a day or two, but the yanks tore up the railroad and stopped communication, and it has been useless to write. There is a man from our Brigade going to start home on furlough tomorrow, and says he will carry this for me, if he gets through himself.

My health is very good and we are here in line of battle as usual. I do not know whether you recd. any of my last letters or no, if not, you will think [it] strange, no doubt and I fear will be very uneasy about me. I do not want you to see no more trouble about me than you can possibly avoid. We have had no fight since I wrote to Doc which was on 18th June, I believe. I mean our Brigade has been in no fight since then, but there is fighting every day or two, around here. Our forces captured several hundred prisoners, and recaptured about 500 negroes that they had stolen from citizens a short time ago. I saw the negroes.

---

[81] Camp Jackson Hospital was one of eleven major Confederate hospitals in Richmond. Chimborazo Hospital was the largest in the world at that time, but Camp Jackson wasn't much smaller. All the large Confederate hospitals in Richmond were organized as MHF describes in this paragraph.

[82] On June 12, 1864, Grant pulled the Army of the Potomac out of the lines at Cold Harbor and with four of his Corps moved south and east of Richmond, crossing the James River near Windmill Point on June 14. Grant should have been able to take Petersburg on June 15, but poor coordination coupled with a strong Confederate defense saved the city. Further attacks on June 16, 17, and 18 also failed and the siege of Petersburg began. The majority of MHF's remaining letters will be from the trench lines of Petersburg.

They looked badly sure and said the Yanks gave them nothing to eat. It was a motly mess of women, children and men. I was so glad to get your letters and to hear that you were all well and doing as well as you were. The death of Sam Miller[83] surprised me much. You spoke of waiting to hear from me before you got somebody else to attend to that business. You need not have done that, of course, it makes no difference who does it but the misfortune is getting anybody to attend to it. I had concluded to quit trying.

It is very warm and dry here yet. We sharpshooters are not on duty today but will go on again this evening. The yankee line is some distance from us here, but in some places on our left, the two lines are very near each other. The yanks throw shells into Petersburg every day and have killed several women and children. Tomorrow is the day Old Grant was to take a big dinner in Richmond but I rather think he will be sadly disappointed. I have no idea that he will ever take Richmond or Petersburg, but he may trouble us for some time yet. The boys are generally well what few there are here. Tom Rickerson came in today. He has recovered from his wound.[84] Jeff Reins is at the Brigade hospital sick, but I learn is getting better. We get plenty of cornbread, bacon and coffee and some sugar. I am getting biscuit hungry.

I have heard nothing from the 27th Ga. recently, but would like to hear from them the best in the world. I am sorry to hear that Greene[85] was wounded, but glad to learn that he had got home. I am glad that you have such a nice corn patch. Like you I wish you had more of it. I wish I could be there to catch the rogue that steals your chickens, and to eat some that he does not steal. I am so proud to hear that my boy is doing so well, and is so fat and saucy. It is useless to talk about how bad I want to see him. I hope communication will be opened again soon and I will get some more letters from home. I am anxious to hear from Alex again.

Edd Jordan is in the mess with Drew and I. He is a splendid messmate and a wholesouled man.[86] I mended my coat the other day, cut off the sleeves and it does finely now. I was glad to get the paper you sent me, but I have a little money to buy some now. We drawed

---

[83] Unidentified by the editors.

[84] Rickerson was wounded at the Battle of the Wilderness. It is interesting that MHF forgot to mention that Rickerson had been wounded when he wrote to Amanda on May 15, 1864.

[85] Amanda's brother Joshua Green White, a private in Co. H, 18th Ala. He was wounded during the Battle of Chickamauga, September 19-20, 1863, and during the Atlanta Campaign, which must have been the wound MHF refers to here. See David Lee's *The White Family of Crawford County, Georgia*, 24.

[86] Edd Jordan had only recently (June 1, 1864) enlisted in Co. K.

tobbacco again the other day. I have more now than I want to toat, as I had not used more than half of the first draw. I will close. May God bless you. Pray for me. Write soon.

Your husband,
M. Hill Fitzpatrick

ᶎ❧

Skirmish Line Near Petersburg, Va. *(Letter Number 78)*
July 10th, 1864

Dear Amanda,

I have not written to you in several days, and have not heard from you in a long time. June 11th is the latest date I have from home, which is now a month ago. The yanks tore up the railroad and stoped our getting letters, but I learn the mail will pass again in a short time, and I hope it will, for I am anxious to hear from home again, and I know you all want to hear from me. I saw a man just now belonging to our Brigade, who has a discharge and will start home in the morning and promised to carry this for me. I am in fine health now and getting on first rate just at this time but I fear it will not last long. We are now about five miles sorter northeast of Petersburg. We came here on 4th inst. The right wing of our skirmish line rests on the Appomattox River and my post is on the extreme right, so I am now sitting on the banks of the river writing.[87] The Yankee skirmish line is a short distance from us in full view. By mutual agreement, we do not fire at each other, there being no use of it unless an advance is made. They are quite friendly with us. We meet them everyday nearly and exchange papers. Only one or two go at a time and they meet half way. We have traded with them some too, but that is against orders and it got to be so common that they have put very strict orders against it, and have about broken it up. But occasionally some of the boys run the blockade and trade with them yet. Our boys give them tobacco and cornbread for crackers and

---

[87] At this early point in the siege, Thomas' Brigade was north of Petersburg, along the Appomattox River, near the area of Swift Creek and Fort Clifton, a Confederate fort which anchored the "Howlett Line." The Howlett Line opposed the Federal army under Benjamin Butler massed on the Bermuda Hundred peninsula. The maps in Richard J. Sommers' *Richmond Redeemed: The Siege of Petersburg* (Garden City, N.Y.: Doubleday & Co., Inc., 1981) are especially helpful in placing Thomas' Brigade for July through October of 1864.

knives, soap, pockette books, &c. I gave one of them the other day a plug of tobacco for a pockette knife and six crackers. It was old Jeff Davis tobacco that I drawed about a month ago and I was glad to dispose of it. I swapped my old knife yesterday to one of our Sharpshooters for a neat little knife that he got from a yank. It has a crosshandle with U.S. on it. I am going to send it to Henry the first chance I get. We are close to a good spring here and our duty is very light. They do not relieve us atall now and we stay here all the time. I had much rather stay here than back at the Regt. There are two wash pots and two tubs at the spring and we can wash our clothes. I have made a general washing since I came here and once or twice a day I get a tub of water and wash myself good all over. The tide water comes up this far in the river and keeps the banks so muddy that it is not fit to go in a washing. Some of the boys catch a good many fish here. Our rations are a little light at times but we do very well on them. This morning we got half in biscuits and half in cornbread and half in bacon and half beef, which suits mighty well. We get plenty of coffee yet and some sugar.

The Regiment drew two months wages day before yesterday. I drew two months wages in Richmond when I was there and did not draw any here this time, but I have collected enough to do me some time. Jack Wilder got back to us day before yesterday. He is all right again. Tom Rickerson is not well, his hand where he was wounded is swelling up and he fears it will trouble him. One of his feet is also very sore with a kind of leprosy and he cannot wear his shoes. He does duty yet, but it is pretty tight on him. Tip Hammock is well and doing finely. Colvin is also well, I believe. Jeff Raines is at the Brigade Hospital yet sick, I do not know how he is. We have done no fighting recently. Down opposite Petersburg they are cracking away more or less all the time but no regular engagement. Of the future I can tell nothing more than you. We have been at it two months and over, and Old Grant still pecks away, but he is as far from having Richmond now as when he started. I have used nearly all of my red peppers. Send me a little in your next letter. Just pound it fine and put it in the letter, a small quantity and it will come all right. Tom Smisson had my soap, paper and envelopes in his valise, which he carried home. I could not carry it if I had it now, and I reckon he will be back after awhile. It is still warm and dry here. Our recruit Edd Jordan stands it finely. Do write often. May God bless you. Pray for me.

Your husband,
M. Hill Fitzpatrick

ॐ

Skirmish Line Near Petersburg, Va. *(Letter Number 79)*
July 18th, 1864

Dear Amanda,

The mail comes to us again now, and yesterday evening it brought me yours of 3rd inst. with the glad tidings that all were well at home and that Alex was improving all of which I am glad to hear. This is the first news I have direct from home since June 11th. I rec. a letter from Camilla Greene day before yesterday stating something about Ma and Doc being at Columbus, and you wrote that they had come back from there, and by putting it all together I find out that they made a visit to Alex there. You and Camilla both wrote like I knew all about their going, but I account for it easily by knowing that you had written letters previous telling about it, which I have not rec. yet and probably never will. And no doubt you are getting my letters in the same way.[88]

I was too fast in saying the mail brought me your letter all the way. Rufus mailed it at Petersburg, and wrote me a short letter himself, which he enclosed with yours. It was the first I knew about his going home, and I am puzzled yet to know how he got there, whether on a wounded or sick furlough. I would like to see him, but the chance is bad. I learn that his Brigade is in the rear resting somewhere near Petersburg, I suppose about 5 miles from here. I shall write to him today and try to get him to come to see me, and also write him directions about the socks and money you sent me, which I am sorry you sent as I have no use for either at this time, having three pair of socks on hand, which is one pair more than I want to toat, and having drawn money recently I have a plenty to do me now. But I know you did it with the best intentions, and I will manage it the best I can or [get] Rufus to do it, for it is very doubtful about my seeing him in a long time, or getting the things atall.[89]

I am glad to get the paper and envelope you sent me, for it is a hard matter to get it here. My health is better than it has been in a long time,

---

[88] Apparently Alex was taken to one of the Confederate hospitals in Columbus. Whether he was sick or wounded is unclear. His sketchy Compiled Service Record doesn't mention this hospitalization. This is the first hint in this collection of letters that Alex was ill or wounded. Clearly Nancy Fitzpatrick and Doc went to see Alex, and by July 3, 1864, they had returned to Crawford County. Alex must have been hospitalized sometime in June 1864.

[89] It seems MHF was surprised that Amanda's brother Rufus, a recent recruit of Co. C, 27th Ga., could have gone home on furlough so soon.

or in other words I am stout and hearty. I wrote to you about a week ago and sent the letter by one of our Brigade, which I hope you have rec. by this time. We are still here at the same place and still in line fronting the enemy. We have been here 16 days today. We are not so friendly with the yanks now. All communications, trading, &c., is stopped except an occasional exchange of papers by the officers. There is still no firing between us and I hope will not be till an advance is made.

We sharpshooters have not been relieved since we came here, and do not want to be as we have a better position than back at the Brigade. I gave you a sketch of our position in my last letter. We still continue to catch some fish and some days a great many are caught, and our rations are a little better now, so upon the whole we are living well. In addition to this, the boys have pressed a large amount of cider from half ripe apples in an orchard near by, which was quite a treat, but the apples have given out now. Soldiers are up to any emergency that presents itself.

I am so proud to hear that my boy can talk plain and that he wants to go to school to learn to write to his Pa and that he thinks so much of his Pa. I wish he had his little yankee knife that I wrote you about. I am taking good care of it for him, and hope to get a chance to send it to him before a great while.

I have heard of the death of Mrs. Ziegler. Like you, I heartily sympathize with her little children. I am anxiously looking for a letter from Doc. I want to find out all about the crop. I have never learned yet how much wheat Ma made or whether she had thrashed it out or not. Doc wrote about it in the letter Drew tore up and I did not get to read it. I hope you had the pleasure of hearing old Bro. Oxford preach again. I did not know what had become of him.[90] I do not know what to say about the war. You can learn from the papers more than I can tell you. The news from Early is highly encouraging, while that from Johnson is gloomy.[91] We are in high spirits here, having no idea of getting whipped. Write me a long letter. May God bless you. Pray for me.

Your husband,
Hill

---

[90] The editors have been unable to identify Mrs. Ziegler or "old Bro. Oxford."
[91] After driving the Federals from the Shenandoah Valley, a Confederate force under Gen. Jubal Early went on an extended raid through Maryland almost to Washington, D.C. Although Early had retreated back across the Potomac by July 14, his raid did scare the Federal Government. By "Johnson," MHF means Joseph E. Johnston, who MHF assumed was still commanding the Army of Tennessee in defense of Atlanta.

ત્ય

Skirmish Line Near Petersburg, Va. *(Letter Number 80)*
July 29th, 1864

Dear Amanda,

I have just learned that Colvin will start home this evening and in haste will drop you a few lines to send by him if I can get it to him in time. If not I shall send it by mail. I gave Tom Rickerson Henry's knife so he could be sure to send it by Colvin, knowing that my chance was bad having to be on skirmish all the time. So I hope Tom will get the knife off by him, if I do not get the letter though, he may miss it.

My health is excellent. We are still here at the same place where we have been ever since July 4th. I wrote to Emily[92] a few days ago. Nothing new here has transpired since then. I rec. your kind letter of July 14th several days ago, and waited to answer it till Colvin started home. I hope you were fortunate with your Indigo works and will have some pretty cloth. I also hope you went with Lou and had a pleasant trip. I am _____ that Alex was mending. I hope that he will recover soon. I am also glad to learn that Lou is going to stay with you all again and I hope she will remain there now.

I have been looking for a letter from her for a long time. I wrote you several letters that I have not heard from yet. In one I sent you some buttons by a furloughed soldier. I am sorry you were suffering for rain when you wrote. I am anxious to hear from the crop again. I have not seen Rufus or heard from him since he sent me your letter. I tried to get a pass to go after the things you sent, but failed. We drawed two months wages yesterday. I now have $53.00 in money and some oweing to me. I hope to be able to send you a pretty little sum of money this winter but will keep this now for fear of getting sick again. I am glad to hear that Henry has a new hat and is so well pleased with it. May God bless you. Pray for me.

Your husband,
Hill

ત્ય

---

[92] MHF's cousin, Emily Fitzpatrick.

Skirmish Line Near Petersburg, Va. *(Letter Number 81)*
Aug. 5th, 1864

Dear Amanda,

I rec. yours of July 23 a day or two ago, but as I had just written to Lou I thought I would wait a while. I was glad to hear from you again, and to hear that Alex had gotten home. I hope he will improve fast now. My health continues good and I am still doing well. We draw good rations and I catch a mess of fish nearly every day. We draw two days rations at a time[,] half in bacon and cornbread and the other in biscuit and beef. I rec. my pepper all right and am obliged to you for it. I will trouble you for some thread in your next. Just send me a little loose in the letter. It is a hard matter for me to keep thread. I have to give away so much or absolutely refuse, which I hate to do. I am so proud to hear that you got off on a visit once more and that you and Henry both enjoyed the trip so well. I hope Colvin has got home by this time and Henry has possession of his knife. I want to bring him some present or other when I come home but it will be a troublesome job to bring him a goat. I keep hoping for a letter from Doc but it seems that I will never get one. Your letter came through quick but since I got it we have had no southern mail. I fear that the mail route is interrupted again. I am so sorry to hear of the protracted drouth there. I still hope it has rained there before this time and crops will brighten up yet. Write me in your next how much wheat Ma made and whether she lost much of it by the rains or no.

The fight in front of Petersburg the other day was a brilliant victory on our side. The Yankees loss was about 7000 and ours about 800. The yanks held our works for awhile but were hurled back with heavy loss. I wrote Lou that Colquitt's Brigade was in it but I do not know for certain that it was.[93] It is a hard matter to hear the truth. We draw plenty of soap now which is a great help. I got a letter from Tom Smisson at the same time I got yours of 24th July. He is in a pretty bad

---

[93] MHF probably refers to the "Battle of the Crater" on July 30, 1864. Members of the 48th Pennsylvania Infantry dug for more than a month on a tunnel extending to behind the Confederate lines. Explosives blew a hole 170 ft. long, sixty-eighty ft. wide and thirty ft. deep. But because of inept leadership, Federal troops failed to take advantage and in fact suffered far more casualties than the Confederates, who mounted a strong counterattack.

condition.[94] I will close up. Write soon and write me a long letter. May God bless you. Pray for me.

Your husband,
M. Hill Fitzpatrick

෨෨

Skirmish Line Near Petersburg, Va. *(Letter Number 82)*
Aug. 13th, 1864

Dear Amanda,

Captain Gibson's boy will start home day after tomorrow morning, and I will write you again and send by him. It seems to be the only chance almost of passing letters between us now. And I eagerly grasp the chance when I can of sending by hand. I have been looking a long time for a letter from some of you. The last I recd. was yours of 23rd July. No letters come from Ga. recently for anybody scarcely. I hope it will get right soon and we can get the mail. My health continues good and we are still here at the same place, getting along about as usual with the exception that our beef rations have stopped which hurts pretty bad. Today is Saturday and it is getting late in the evening. I thought at first that I would wait and write in the morning, but I want to carry my letters up to the Regt. tomorrow, and concluded just now to commence this evening, for fear of not getting them there in time as the negroe does not stay on the line with the Captain. I shall send Ma two plugs of tobacco by the boy if I can get them to him. I have fixed it up and marked it. I put two brass buttons between the plugs for you. It is tobacco that I drawed and have that much more than I want. I hope Ma will get it and enjoy many a good smoke from it. I went to the 27th Ga. last Monday. Col. Simmons came down here Sunday and I saw him personally about it and he readily granted me a pass and soon Monday morning Tip Hammock and I put out. George, Henry, Jim Hammock and Jim Wilson were all well and getting on finely. Rufus was sick and

---

[94] The Smisson diary stops its daily entries on March 30, 1864. Smisson was ill for much of the last year of the War, and was eventually transferred to the Confederate Invalid Corps.

off at the Brigade Hospital.[95] I came by where he was on my way back and staid with him some time. He looked badly, but said that he was improving and thought he would be well soon.

I got the money and socks you sent me, all safe. I came back and having too many socks on hand for the session, I sold one pair for $1.00. It was a pair you sent me last year by Jeff Raines. They were beginning to wear out but I darned them and had them clean so they showed pretty well. So getting the new socks is a very good thing after all, and I am very thankful to you. I was surprised and to tell the truth, a little vexed, to see the money to be the old issue. I know if somebody had tried in time and in the right way, they could have gotten the new issue or bonds one for it. If I could have been there I would have straightened it dead sure. But enough on that news.

I am writing you a long letter in deliberate tone and feel like I am talking to you.[96] I washed my clothes soon this morning while it was cool. I wash once a week regular since we came here. We are having a long heat at this place, having been here forty days and nights. Our Regt. moved to the left about 3/4 of a mile a few days ago to take a position in another Division, but the move is considered only temporary, as they did not move us and they took the place of another Regt. that it is said will be back again soon.

The weather is very warm and dry and there is a good deal of sickness. Edd Jordan[97] is very sick, I fear dangerously sick. I think he has the typhoid fever. He is not in his right mind half his time. He is at the Brigade Hospital back in the woods about a mile from here. I went to see him yesterday. I think his wife ought to come or send somebody to see about him. He got Berry Frazier to write him a letter to her yesterday.[98]

There is no war news atall scarcely stirring here. They still shell and skirmish in front of Petersburg and there was some shelling on our left this morning. The 27th Ga. was back in reserve the day I was there and I was glad of it. Cicero Futrell[99] was off on pass the day I was there and

---

[95] "George," "Henry," and "Rufus" were Amanda's brothers serving in Co. C, 27th Ga. with Jim Wilson and Jim Hammock, Tip Hammock's brother.

[96] The original of this letter, at the Georgia Department of Archives and History, perfectly reveals the beautiful penmanship of MHF. The quality of his penmanship varied considerably, however, due to circumstances. The letters written during battle are, as a rule, much harder to read than those written in more settled conditions, such as the Petersburg siege.

[97] Edwin T. Jordan, a recent recruit in Co. K.

[98] "Berry Frazier" was 4th Sgt. Ellsberry S. Frasier of Co. K.

[99] Cicero Futrell was elected 2nd lieutenant of the 27th Ga.'s Co. C on Feb. 12, 1863.

I did not get to see him, but he and Jim Hammock was over here yesterday and I was with him a short time. He is looking well and hearty. He and Jim Wilson always remind me so much of Doc that they feel like kinfolk to me, and for what I know they or one of them may be family connection to me yet, as each has a good looking sister and Doc is still single.

We were startled a few days ago by a tremendous explosion over in Yankeedom some miles from their front. Various speculations were extant as to the cause, but no light could be gathered till day before yesterday, when a negroe boy escaping Yankee clutches got over to us, and reported that a lumber yard and an immense pile of bombshells, a large number of kegs of powder and a small boat were blown up, killing three hundred negroe soldiers and white Yankees dead. He said it was caused by a negroe soldier dropping a bombshell accidentally. I see in the yesterday's paper a report of a Yankee deserter about it which is the same as the negroes except only 75 were killed, and I will believe the negroe in preference to the Yank.[100]

This negroe boy I speak of is only about 12 or 14 years old and was taken by the Yankee raiders in Charlotte County near Danville. He says he was going to mill and they threw away his bags and took him and his horse. He dodged the Yankee pickette and came to the vidette from our Squad of Sharpshooters. He was the proudest negroe to get back I ever saw: He belongs to a widow woman and was anxious to get back to his old mistress and his Mammy. He was sent right on home.

Aug. 14th Sunday morning. I have just ate breakfast and will now finish my letter. I was speaking of the negroe boy. He told us a heap about the Yanks whom he hates with all vengeance. The Captain who captured him took him for his waiting boy. He says they would not let him call them Master, and did not whip him but slapped his jaws severely. He tried to get back several times before he succeeded. They caught him once and put him in jail. He says all that are large enough to fight they draft and put in service and that he knowed a great many that wanted to get back to their Masters.

I saw a North Carolinian a few days ago belonging to our Division who was captured on 6th of May, up in the Wilderness. He was taken to some Fort and guarded by negroes who kicked and cuffed him at their pleasure. Determined not to stand that he took the oath, joined the Yankee Army and the first opportunity deserted them and came back

---

[100] Confederates caused this explosion on August 9, in one of Grant's main supply depots, in City Point, Va. The explosion killed forty-three (Federal) soldiers, wounded 126 and damaged vast amounts of property. See E.B. Long's *The Civil War Day By Day*, 553-554.

to his old Company where he is now doing duty. He is quite intelligent and it is highly interesting to hear him narrate his travels and tell how he felt while acting Yankee. The Reg. he joined guarded commissarys and he did no fighting and had no idea of doing any. It is no uncommon occurence now for our soldiers to play that trick. It is so humiliating to be guarded by negroes and the treatment otherwise is so bad that it is hard to stand.

A recruit came to our Regt. a short time ago from Monroe County who is a highly interesting character. He served in the western army, through Arkansas and around there for nearly three years. He was a Lieut. and resigned in consequence of bad health, came to his father's in Ga., got well and joined our Regt. For about three months out there he belonged to a part of garilia's or bushwhackers, and can tell many interesting anecdotes. He now belongs to the Sharpshooters and is a splendid soldier and is also a Mason. They fought them there in Marion's plan in S. C. during the Revolutionary War, and often had rich times.[101]

We hear but little news from Atlanta now, but have high hopes that all will be right there. The dry weather in Ga. renders me more uneasy than the war now. I fear you will not make support there. I am anxious to hear again and still hope you have had rain in time to do much good. I sent you a newspaper not long ago by mail, The Magnolia,[102] but it is uncertain I expect about you getting it. You must all write and keep writing, probably some of the letters will come through. Sometimes I fear they are not written is why they don't come through, though you yourself have been very punctual. Others though are like me getting no letters.

May God bless you. Pray for me.

Your husband,
M. Hill Fitzpatrick

ॐ

---

[101] By "garilia's," MHF meant "guerrillas." He also refers to the exploits of South Carolina's legendary hero Francis Marion, the "Swamp Fox," who fought the British using "hit-and-run" or guerrilla tatics.
[102] A Richmond literary magazine.

Hospital 45th Ga. (*Letter Number 83*)
Near Petersburg, Va.
Aug. 28th, 1864

Dear Amanda,

I have been sick with fever for about two weeks. I was taken very suddenly. I was sent to our Brigade hospital first but our Reg. moved and they moved the sick too. I have had too much fever to try to write to you before this morning. My throat and mouth is very sore. I think I am salivated. I have rec. three letters from you since I have been sick, one dated July 30th and one Aug. 10th but the other I cannot tell the date. You are very careless in dating your letters. You should take more space. I got Doc's letter July 31st at the same time I got yours July 30th. I had heard of Alex's death before I got your letters telling about it.[103] I am in no fix to write. I am too weak and feverish. Mr. Jordan is here with me. We sleep together. He is improving.

You must all write to me. Don't be atall uneasy about me.

Your husband,
M. Hill Fitzpatrick

ʒ❧

45th Ga. Hospital (*Letter Number 84*)
Near Petersburg, Va.
Sept. 15th, 1864

Dear Amanda,

One of our Regt. will start home on furlough today and I will write you a few lines to send by him. I wrote to Doc a few days ago and sent it by Mr. Jordan.[104] I am sorry to say that I am no better than when I wrote to him, and I fear I am worse. I hate to write so discouraging, but if I write atall I have to tell the truth. It seems that I have gotten into a

---

[103] MHF's brother Alex died on July 28, 1864 at their mother's home in Crawford County. An obituary appeared in the September 2, 1864 issue of *The Christian Index*. His cause of death and burial place were not noted and remain unknown to the editors.
[104] Jordan apparently had been sent home on furlough to regain his health.

low state of health and it is a hard matter for me to take a rise. I have an every other day kind of dumb chill or something and severe headache and fever but not much fever either. The Dr. says it is very near fever. I take medicine on my well days but there is not much well about any of them. My appetite is good and they feed us well but nothing I eat agrees well with me. I am getting pretty weak and poor and I get gradually weaker for the last few days. Now this is about as gloomy an account of myself as I could well put up and since I have been so frank in telling you, you must not by any means let it render you uneasy, for I am not low spirited myself, and still hope that I will have the pleasure of writing you in a short time that I am improving fast. A great many are having the chills and fever now. Tom Rickerson has had them for some time and is pretty low. He is coming here today to stay. We are looking for Colvin every day now. I am anxious for him to come as I am confident almost of getting some letters by him. We heard from the prisoners of our Comp. the other day. 9 of them are at Fort Delaware. John Collum, I am certain now is not dead or was not killed when we thought he was for it takes him to make the number 9. Webb my old messmate is there.[105] I am due Emily a letter but feel so little like writing anything of interest that I will postpone it awhile. Do write soon and do not be uneasy about me. May God bless you. Pray for me.

Your husband,
Hill

ॐ

Skirmish Line near Petersburg, Va. *(Letter Number 85)*
Sept. 24th, 1864

Dear Amanda,

I rec. yours of 3rd and 12th inst. day before yesterday, and was more than glad to hear from you again, and to hear that all were well. I have

---

[105] Using Henderson's *Roster*, the editors have identified seven men from Company K who were captured at either the Wilderness or Spotsylvania and imprisoned at Fort Delaware. They were: John E. Collum, William A. Mathews, William J. Mathews, William J. McGee, William M. Miller, William J. Slocumb, and Joseph C. Wilder. Corp. E.R. Webb, who had been MHF's messmate earlier in the War, was captured at South Mountain, Md., on July 5, 1863 and imprisoned at Fort Delaware.

returned to the Sharpshooters. I came back day before yesterday evening. I have not regained my strength fully yet, but I got heartily tired of the hospital and had much rather be here than there. I am doing no duty here yet. The boys say they want me to get entirely well before I set in for good. The Doctor gave me a pint of cherry bark bitters when I left which does me much good. It is strange how our letters work sometimes. Yours of 3rd written 9 days before your last came to me on the same day of the last. I wrote to Lou three days ago and fortunately got to send it by hand. I never let a chance slip to send by hand if I can help it, but you seldom get that chance.

I do not know what fight you are talking about my being in. Our Regt. nor Brigade has been in no fight in a long time. Soon after I was taken sick, our Regt. was ordered down on the right and was under some heavy shelling in which our Comp. lost one man killed, Castle George.[106]

I suppose the report took note from that. Also since I left here the sharpshooters have had some brisk skirmishing with negroe troops that were put in our front on the Yankee skirmish line. Our boys could not stand for negroes to be so near them and pitched into them and drove them off. During the fight we lost one man killed, Matt Lawrence of Co. E from Taylor County.[107] There are all the fights that our Regt. has had anything to do with lately. We have a heavy canonadeing frolic occasionally. They opened for awhile this morning hot and heavy on both sides all along the lines. Several shells passed over us but none fell near us.

Well I suppose the booming of cannon is in hearing of you. It is getting too close to be healthy. It makes me feel bad to think of it, but I hope it will come no nearer. Of course I can tell nothing about Sherman's intentions only by guess, but it is my opinion that he will do but little more there for the present. He has already sent off 20,000 troops which reinforced the yanks in the valley, and caused them to succeed in surprising and defeating Early. I cannot learn the particulars but our loss was heavy, consisting of about two thousand prisoners and 700 killed and wounded. Among the killed are Major Gen. Rhodes and one Brigadier Gen. It seems that we are in a streak of misfortune of late, but I hope the scene will change soon and continue the other way till our independence is gained.[108]

---

[106] Pvt. George was killed at Petersburg on August 21, 1864.

[107] Pvt. Lawrence was killed by a sharpshooter near Petersburg on August 25, 1864.

[108] At the Third Battle of Winchester, Va., Federal troops under Philip Sheridan defeated greatly outnumbered Confederates under Jubal Early.

You want me to write you all about my clothes. I shall want a coat like the last one you made for me, but shall need no buttons on it as I have good brass buttons on this coat to put on it. Now I think it would be best for me to draw all my clothes here, especially now since thread has got to be such a high price and so hard to get, but if you will insist on making them I shall need one pair pants, two shirts and two pr. drawers. I want you to send none of them to me yet, for I hope to get a furlough this winter and carry my old ones home which will do some of you some good and get my new ones if you will make them but I have much rather lighten your labors that much. You spoke of having some of Alex's clothes. Just keep them, till I come home or write for them. The Coat would suit me very well now to wear under this coat, but there is no chance to get it right away, and I shall draw one in a few days. So do not try to send it to me. The shirts and drawers that are drawn here are but little account, but the coats and pants are very good and undoubtedly much cheaper than can be made at home if the coats were only long tailed. I do not like to wear the shorttails alone.

I am so proud to hear that Henry is well and fat, but tell him there is no chance for me to bring him a saddle but I will try to bring him some presents. I am sorry he has such a hard case with his puppy, which seems to be a little overmatch for him. But I reckon he has got him under his control by this time. I am sorry you did not get to send the syrrup by Colvin. It would have been a great treat to me. If Doc could see Edd Jordan before he starts back no doubt he would bring me some. We draw very good rations now. We get some good yankee beef and some bacon and good flour. Drew is down here with me and I am just fixed to get on finely.[109] We have warm rainy weather now. It has been raining nearly all day today. I expect it will turn off cold but we have a good warm place fixed up to sleep in. A good many of the boys have had the chills but they are all missing them now, I believe. I hope you are having good fall seasons in Ga. which will make you good Fall Gardens and help the pee and potatoe crop out, and compensate in part for the short corn crop.

Confederate Maj. Gen. Robert E. Rodes was killed, as was Confederate Brig. Gen. Archibald C. Godwin. See the *Historical Times Illustrated Encyclopedia of the Civil War*, Patricia Faust, editor (New York: HarperPerennial, 1991) 313.

[109] On September 16, 1864, Confederate cavalry under Wade Hampton captured some 2,400 head of cattle and 300 prisoners in what is known as the "Beefsteak Raid." MHF's old friend Jim Drew must have joined the sharpshooters.

Write soon and write me a long letter. May God bless you. Pray for me.

Your husband,
M. Hill Fitzpatrick

᠌᠌᠌᠌᠌᠌᠌᠌᠌᠌᠌᠌᠌᠌᠌᠌᠌᠌᠌᠌᠌᠌᠌᠌᠌᠌᠌᠌᠌᠌᠌᠌᠌᠌᠌᠌᠌᠌᠌

Near Petersburg, Va. *(Letter Number 86)*
Oct. 4th/64

Dear Amanda,

Having the chance to send this by hand to Fort Valley, I will drop you a few lines. My health is excellent at this time and I am getting along very well in my new position.[110] I wrote to Lou on 28th Sept. I believe, or a day or two ago at least. We have heard but little of the fight since then. There is no fighting going on now. They fought last Thursday, Friday & Saturday. The Yanks still hold a small portion of our works on each wing, which it will be hard to recapture now and I do not think will be tried anymore. Our loss is said to be very light. The enemy's loss is reported to be heavy. A great many prisoners have passed near here enroute for Richmond. From the best information I can get, the prisoners amount to about 2500, and the ground was literally strewn with dead and wounded at many places so the reports say. Colquit's Brigade was in the fight, I have learned none of the casualties yet. I am anxious to learn and will write as soon as I find out.[111]

It was Oct. 2nd I wrote to Lou instead of 28th Sept. Well I reckon you all think I write often enough unless I had something of interest to write. It is rainy warm weather now. The boys have about all got rid of the chills now. There are no cases in Co. K now and their health is better than usual, which is a little surprising for they stay in the swamp

---

[110] MHF's Compiled Service Record shows he was appointed sergeant major on October 1, 1864. He was now part of the regimental staff.

[111] On September 29, Grant's Federals attacked both ends of the Confederates' Petersburg and Richmond defenses simultaneously. North of the James River, on the Richmond front, the Federals took Fort Harrison and nearby works. The other prong of the attack struck west of Petersburg in an attempt to take the vital South Side Railroad. Fighting began September 29 and continued for four days in the Battle of Peebles' Farm, Va. See E.B. Long's *The Civil War Day By Day*, 589.

right on the river all the time. We have been fortunate in keeping out of the fights recently but I reckon they will bring us into the next one of Grant's movements.

The spirits of the army are reviving now, though they have never been at a low ebb. We have checked Grant in all his grand movements on Richmond[,] inflicted severe loss on him, and we have high hopes that with the aid of Forest in the rear that Hood will be enabled to drive Sherman from Ga. soil. I look for trouble from Sherman's raids as it seems there is a large gap left open for him but I will hope for the best.

I do my own cooking and washing here the same as when I was with the Comp. I cannot afford to hire it done at enormous rates charged and do not mind doing it myself. I drawed a Confederate shirt yesterday, the first I have ever drawn. My two checked shirts both wore in holes in the back and I took the tail of one and put in the back of the other, which brought me down to one shirt till I got that one yesterday. I have not had the chance of drawing a Jackette yet but they say some will be issued soon, when I will get one, and a pair of pants too, to wear when it is cold for these are getting thin. I can have my clothes hauled on a march now which will help me along considerably. I and Jim Drew together have used about all the thread you sent me. Send me about as much more in your next and I think that will do me.

I wish I could be there to see Henry eat syrrup now and to help him too. From what I can learn Jordan[112] will not be able to come back at the expiration of his furlough and I will miss my syrrup. He said he was going to bring a big jar full for our mess and I know I would get some if I am away from the mess now.

I will close up. You must cheer up now and hope for better and brighter times close at hand and write me a long letter.

Your husband,
M. Hill Fitzpatrick

---

[112] Pvt. Edwin T. Jordan of Co. K.

?❧

45th Ga. Regt. Near Petersburg, Va. *(Letter Number 87)*
Oct. 10, 1864

Dear Amanda,

I wrote to you on 4th inst. and thought sure that by this time I would have a letter from some of you to answer, but am disappointed. It is a month ago today since I wrote to Doc and sent by Jordan, and I have looked eagerly for an answer. I am anxious to learn whether he succeeded or not in getting on the retired list, and to hear from him generally.

My health is excellent and I am getting on finely with my Sergeant Majorship, though I am quite green in many things yet. I had more real enjoyment with the Sharpshooters than here, but here I am thrown in better company and have a better chance of mental improvement, and I make it a rule to be satisfied in any position and under all circumstances when it is the best that can be done. When we are in Rome we must do as Rome does to a certain extent at least. Being severed from my mess was the worst obstacle in my coming here. When I wrote you last I was messing to myself. I got tired of that[,] the way things are fixed here, and am now messing with Lieut. Walker and Rutherford.[113] They each have a negroe and the negroes stay here and do the cooking here. They stay on the line some half a mile from here and when convenient or when it is so they can leave they come out here to eat, when not, their meals are carried to them by the negroes or some one passing. They very readily took me in to mess with them. I do not know yet what the charge will be but not a great deal if anything. I still do my own washing. Fifty cents per garment is charged for washing here and I will pay no such prices as long as I can do it myself.

All is quiet on the lines now except the usual canonadeing and skirmish firing, but since I wrote you last, there has been some hard fighting on the north side of the James River opposite Richmond, in which our forces were highly successful. They drove the Yanks about four miles, killing, wounding and capturing a great many. The fight was on 8th inst. Our loss is reported light, but I have not learned the

---

[113] Joel Walker and Williams Rutherford. Apparently the two lieutenants were staying with Co. K in the lines of entrenchments while MHF was staying at the regimental headquarters half a mile in the rear of the lines.

amount yet. I do not know whether the 27th Ga. was engaged or not, but they were over there and in all probability were in the fight.[114] I have never been able to learn the casualties of that Regt. in the fights before the last, which took place over a week ago, and am in the dark yet about whether George and Henry came out safely or not. The war news from all around Mossuria,[115] Ga., Western Va., Valley of Va. and Tennessee are all highly encouraging at this time. The news from Ga. is not official, only rumor but we hope it's true. The rumor is that Rome is recaptured with 3000 prisoners, also that Marietta has been recaptured and our forces are pitching into Sherman's rear generally. I think the dark clouds that have been hanging over will soon be dispersed by a bright ray of light now seen glimmering at a distance, which will grow larger and brighter till the last speck of cloud is dispelled and the sun of Liberty will blaze forth in its meridian.[116]

I sent you a Yankee Paper yesterday, The Philadelphia Enquirer.[117] I did not read it and do not know what was in it, but I know a late yankee paper would be gladly rec. by you all for the curiosity of the thing if nothing else. They get papers from the yanks here nearly every day but I hardly ever read them. They tell so many and such outrageous lies that I soon get vexed and cast them aside. I have another one given to me this morning which I will send you. It is not a political paper and no account anyway, but it is a yankee trick and some of you can kill time by looking at it awhile. It is torn but I will send the pieces torn off so you can get the reading matter together. It is as cold as blixim or something of the kind here now. We had a big white frost this morning. I have the best place to sleep that I have had since the war has been in possession of my services. Andrew Wright[118]

---

[114] MHF was probably referring to an attempt on October 7, 1864 to push the Federals back from some of their positions north of the James River. Attacking on the Darbytown and New Market roads, the Confederates engaged the Federals at Johnston's Farm and Four-Mile Creek. After initial successes, the Confederate attacks were repulsed. See E.B. Long's *The Civil War Day By Day*, 580-581.

[115] Missouri.

[116] During October 1864, various Confederate forces were aggressively on the move. Sterling Price led a bold effort in Missouri, Hood's Army of the Tennessee had returned to North Georgia and was striking at Sherman's supply line, John S. Mosby was leading his raiders effectively in western Virginia, Early was still active in the Shenandoah Valley and Nathan Bedford Forrest's cavalry was playing havoc in Western Tennessee. Price and Early would be routed before the month was out, Forrest would join Hood for the ill-fated invasion of Tennessee and Mosby's efforts would have very little effect on the War's outcome.

[117] *Inquirer.*

[118] A private in Co. K who had served since the company was mustered into service on March 4, 1862.

(who is regimental butcher) and I sleep together in a little room about 6 x 10 feet in the vacant house we are occupying, The room has a glass window and one door, and we have a block for a chair and straw on the floor for a bed, and nails drove in the walls to hang havresacks, hats, coats, towels etc., on, so we are all right for the present. I would like to winter here, and from the prospects we may do it.

We drew two months wages of money the other day. I was about out when we drawed it. I spent a good deal of money when I was sick. Every thing is unreasonably high here and it takes a months wages to buy almost anything. We also drew more tobacco the other day which is a great help. We draw plenty of beef now and tolerably plenty of good flour and some coffee, rice and occasionally bacon.

We had a rich beef or cow scrape just before I left the sharpshooters which I do not think I told you about. About an hour by sun one bright beautiful morning, a fine fat young cow was seen crossing the yankee pickette line, and making direct for our line, with a high head and quick step looking as wild as a buck. She halted in front of our outposts or videttes but two of our boys anxious to obtain some fat yankee beef succeeded by getting around her in forcing her to cross. They then yelled at her and on she came to our line in full tilt. Several of the boys gathered their guns, determined not to let her pass unmolested, myself among the rest. Just before she got up to our line the sharp crack of a rifle rang through the air, but as she was running, the ball missed her and the noise only made her more wild and quickened her pace. Bang! Bang! Crack! Crack! went another and another rifle but on she went or came; crossing our line and going to the rear. I shot at her about 150 yds. in full speed, the ball passing just over her shoulders and entering the ground beyond, making the dust rise but getting no beef. By this time several of the Sharpshooters from each Regt. were after her. Crack! Crack! went the sharp ring of the rifles till I think about the 20th shot she fell headlong to the ground. She was immediately butchered and divided among all the sharpshooters from the Brigade, each man getting a large hunk of tender fat beef. Now the mournful part of the tune had not come. Up to that time it was all excitement and fine fun for us. The Col. commanding the Regt. in our rear, thinking sure we were attacked, had his men to Arms _____ yet in the trenches _____ wait patiently the approaching conflict as he thought. As no Yanks came he sent down to know the cause of the alarm. Learning the cause he sent for all that fired to appear before him immediately. I being Sergt. had to carry the squad up and myself with them. There were 6 of us from our Regt. being arraigned in his august presence, he called on me for full detail, which I gave, closing with a plea of defence, as we did it under excitement, etc. He gave us a long lecture, telling us he did not mind our getting the cow but the fuss we made. He sent us back and that night sent us word that he would acquit us but we must do so no more. The boys said they would not unless another cow came over.

Jordan's time is out but I do not look for him much as I hear he is not well yet by far. Write soon and write me a long letter and tell me all about my boy whether he wears britches every day or _____&c. May God bless you. Pray for me.

Your husband,
Hill

೫೪

Hd. Qrs. 45th Ga. Near Petersburg, Va. *(Letter Number 88)*
Oct. 16ᵗʰ, 1864

Dear Amanda,

Having a chance to send by hand I will drop you a few lines. I wrote to Doc three days ago and sent by hand. There are three of our Regt. going to start home all on the retired list. My health is excellent at this time and I am getting on finely. I have a good amount of walking to do which just gives me a good appetite, an article which I am very seldom in need of whether I walk much or not. Today is Sunday. I rose early this morning and went to a spring about 150 yds. distant which spouts through a trough and took a good wash[,] returned, and assisted in making out the morning reports[,] eat breakfast and then went down on the line to the four Companies nearest to us and got the reports from them, returned and am now sitting in our little room. I wrote you about writing you a letter, which I will finish and then go to the remaining six Companies and get their reports, come back and eat dinner and probably go to town to evening preaching. This will give you a small idea of my daily avocation, though it varies to a great extent some days.[119] We have beautiful weather now, cool or rather cold at night,

---

[119] MHF's new assignment required paperwork essential to a smoothly running regiment. While the adjutant was in charge of these duties, clearly MHF served as his assistant. Confederate infantry regiments had ten companies, designated: A, B, C, D, E, F, G, H, I, and K. "J" was skipped because in 19ᵗʰ Century handwriting a capital "J" closely resembled a capital "I."

and fair and pleasant in the day time. We have had several killing frosts which has about killed the chills with it, though a few cases are on hand yet. Jeff Raines has been visited recently by them but they have stopped on him now. Tom Rickerson had a big old shaking one yesterday. He is staying here at the Hospital now. Our hospital & Head Quarters are all here together now. Tom is in a low state of health, but is cheerful and able to walk about. Col. Simmons got in night before last. He is in fine health.[120] I got a letter from Mrs. Edd Jordan the other day. It will be some time yet before Jordan will be able to return even if he has good luck. One of Co. F, Marcus Jackson of our Regt. was taking the powder out of a shell two days ago and it exploded and killed him. It tore him up wretchedly. He lived about 5 hours. They had another fight on the North side of the James on 13th inst. The yanks attacked our works and were repulsed with heavy loss. Our loss reported very light.

I very unexpectedly got my piece of soap just now that I thought Tom Smisson carried home with him. One of our Comp., Henry Knight[121] deposited his knapsack in Richmond and when Tom went home he exchanged his valise for the knapsack. Knight sent for his knapsack yesterday, and got the valise in its stead with my soap in it. I had also in the valise a portfolio which I fear has gone up the spout as it was not in the valise when it got here. Get Doc to ask Tom what he done with it and if he carried it home with him tell Doc to get it and you can take care of it for me.

All is quiet on the lines this morning but there was heavy shelling last night, and a few shells were thrown into Petersburg yesterday evening, for the first in some time. I was in town myself at the time, and one shell fell near me but did not explode. The citizens do not seem to care for it atall scarcely. The ladies were promenadeing the streets at the time and did not even quicken their pace.

I sent Henry in this letter a piece of an old newspaper that I got hold of yesterday. The pictures will probably amuse him for awhile. Tell him his Pa wants to see him bad enough with his britches on, and cutting sticks with his knife. I am looking every day for a letter from

---

[120] At this point the field officers of the 45th Georgia would have been Col. Thomas Simmons, Lt. Col. William S. Wallace, and Maj. Charles A. Conn. The regimental staff would have consisted of Adj. Robert U. Hardeman, surgeon James J. Winn, MHF as sergeant major, and assistant surgeon Willliam C. Goodwin.

[121] Robert Henry Knight was 1st sergeant of Co. K and Smisson was 2nd lieutenant.

you. Write soon. Just then the mail came and brought me Emily's of 4th & yours of 5th inst. which I am glad to get and will answer soon.

Your husband,
Hill

ॐ

45th Ga. Near Petersburg, Va. *(Letter Number 89)*
Oct. 23rd, 1864

Dear Amanda,

I rec. yours of 5th inst. last Sunday a week ago today and feel ashamed for not answering it before now. I wrote to Emily about the middle of the week and have had so much running about to do that I kept putting it off. I went to see my old Comrades, the Sharpshooters one day. They are still at the same place and getting on finely. And I went to get my shoes fixed another day. I got them half soled and the eye-seams which had bursted sewed up and they do finely now. The Brigade has one man detailed from each Reg. to mend shoes and it costs us nothing now and is a great help. And yesterday, I and Drew took a general wash on both our shoes and clothes, so with the dodging about that I have to do, with the extra added to it I have been pretty busy.

My health was never better in my life and I am getting on finely. I am well pleased with my mess and we draw plenty to eat. I wrote you about drawing a coat or jackette rather. I drew a pr. of pants this week and have a good nice suit now. I wanted to get some pants the color of my coat but could get none to fit. These are a blue color but not like the yankee blue. I have drawed two shirts. They are thin and sleazy but beat no shirts out of all hollow. My drawers you sent me last winter are very good yet. Now you just fix up the clothing matter to suit yourself. You know I make it a rule not to meddle with women affairs, but I want you to make me some drawers anyhow, for the government drawers are pretty sorry sure and soon rip up. In making soldiers' clothing, all of you should recollect that we have some neighbors here called lice and be sure to fell (I believe that is what they call it) all the seams. Or in other words, sew it down tight everywhere so they will have no hiding place. Doc can explain it. You need not make me any shirts or you can make them if you have the cloth and take these and cut them up when I get home just as you like any way does me that is the least trouble and most satisfaction to you. If you have the cloth to spare you can make me a vest, if not it makes no difference atall. I begin to need my overcoat like rip now, but I know of no chance to get it. If Jordan should come shortly he could bring it but his coming is extremely uncertain. Do not send anything by Rufus for his Reg.[122] is 25 miles from here now.

I got a letter from Ma & Lou just now which I was glad to get and will answer soon. I am glad to hear of so many good meetings there. I hope much good has been done. I am glad you have a prospect of getting _____ soon. I hope your corn will do well. I sent you a few postage stamps in my last letter to you and will send more this time. I send you all some papers occasionally which I hope you rec. safely. I am sorry to learn from Ma's & Lou's letter that they cannot hear from bro. Ben now. I feel a great anxiety about him, but hope for the better.[123]

I am always so glad to hear that Henry is well and hearty. I suppose he can controll his puppy pretty well now. I would be so glad to see them frolicing together. Write me if Henry can go to his Grand Ma's by himself now, and all about him. All quiet on our lines. Early has been defeated again in the valley.[124] This is bad but we must put up with it. Tom Rickerson is still quite sick. I hope he will get a furlough. The rest of the Co. is in fine health. Write soon. May God bless you.

Your husband,
Hill

2&

---

[122] Co. C, 27th Ga.
[123] MHF's older brother Benjamin Fitzpatrick was a captain and quartermaster of the 31st Miss. Infantry Regiment. By this point he was also quartermaster of Featherston's Brigade in the Army of Tennessee.
[124] On October 19, 1864, Confederates under Jubal Early attacked two Federal army corps encamped at Cedar Creek or Belle Grove, Va. Early's forces were defeated and Federal dominance in the Shenandoah Valley was secured.

45th Ga. Near Petersburg, Va. *(Letter Number 90)*
Nov. 3rd/64

Dear Amanda,

Two of our Regiment are going to start home on retired papers this evening and I will write and send by them. My health continues good and I am getting on finely. I see that I will have to grumble again about getting letters. It has been twelve days since I got a letter from home, and I know it is not because you have none from me to answer for my last letter spoke of Lou & you each having one from me unanswered. If you only knew what a great pleasure it is to me to get a letter you would not postpone a moment in writing. However, the mail may be to blame (at least it is a convenient thing to lay the blame on) so I will look and wait patiently, as possible. Though I get quite childish at times and imagine a great many things the matter.

I wrote Lou last Sunday and wrote about the late fighting. We captured more prisoners than I wrote her. In all, about fifteen hundred. Two nights after the main fighting Gen. Mahone completely surprised and captured 230 prisoners without the loss of a man. They were all on skirmish. He made a clean sweep for half a mile. Our whole loss it is said will not exceed 500 in killed, wounded and prisoners, while that of the enemy was immense. This is a great victory for us for which we should be very thankful.[125] I do not know for certain but from what I can learn Colquit's Brigade was not in the last engagement. They are still on the North side of the James and was near the fighting if not engaged. All is quiet now except the usual canonadeing and sharpshooting. For two days we have had no skirmishing on our line here. The Yanks agreed to quit if our boys were willing and they readily consented and again are at liberty to walk near the line. The most of them are busily engaged preparing for winter, which is fast approaching here. Instead of building huts as formerly, they dig a hole in the ground about 6 feet deep and 10 ft. square, put over the top a layer of large logs. On that a layer of boughs and leaves, and cover the whole with dirt which they pile on till it is shaped like a potatoe hill.

---

[125] Probably the engagement at Boydton Plank Road, Va., on October 27. Federals tried again to strike the South Side Railroad, near Burgess' Mill, about twelve miles southwest of Petersburg. They were defeated by Confederate infantry and cavalry. The Federal losses were much less than MHF thought: 166 killed, 1,028 wounded and 564 missing, out of 17,000 engaged, according to E.B. Long's *The Civil War Day By Day*, 589.

They then fix a chimney and are not only very comfortable but protected from the enemy's shells.

The Yanks are also building quarters, so from the prospect we are in for the winter. I fear that furloughs will come very slim this winter, but I hope to be able at some time during the winter to put one through, but _____ to uncertainty you had better send my tricks to me if you get the chance, but if no chance, all right.

Tom Rickerson gets no better. He ought to have a furlough and I hope he will get one soon. Frazier is getting well fast.[126] No other sick in our Comp. and but little sick in the Regt. It is raining today. It commenced yesterday evening. It is a cold disagreeable rain. It is reported here that Sherman has evacuated Atlanta, but not generally believed. The Conscription of negroes in the South is freely discussed now. It is a serious and momentous question. I am not competent to decide which is the best for us. I had much rather gain our independence without it but if necessary I say put them in and make them fight. But I hope it will not be necessary. I have long been in favor of making them wagoners and putting them in shops to do government work. All details between the ages of 18 to 45 are revoked and bombproofs[127] are daily coming into us with musket and blanket. This is a good thing and a great help. Write soon and write me a long letter and tell me all about my boy and things generally. May God bless you. Pray for me.

Your husband,
M. Hill Fitzpatrick

P.S.[128] Just as I closed the mail came and brought me yours of Oct. 19th which I am more than glad to get and to learn that all were well. I will take back my grumbling now. I have the thread safe and am under great obligations to you for it. I was out or nearly so. I am sorry to hear of so much sickness there. I hope the cold weather will abate it. I hope you have rec. the stamps I sent you. I will send you some more when you want them. Write me freely about everything you need and I will do all in my power to supply it. I can get many things here easier than you can get them there. I will send you some pens as soon as I can

---

[126] Sgt. Ellsberry Frazier of Co. K.

[127] "Bombproof" was a Civil War term for a bunker. Here MHF refers to men who had previously held safe rear echelon jobs as "bombproofs."

[128] This postscript was found loose in the collection of MHF letters at the Georgia Department of Archives and History. The date and text seem to fit either this letter or the following letter.

get them, or anything else that you need that I can get. I hope ere long you will realize your dream of my arrival at home. Cheer up and let us hope that better times are in store for us at no distant day. I am glad to learn that my boy is well and fat. Kiss him for me.

Hill

ॐ

Hd. Qtrs. 45th Ga. Near Petersburg, Va. *(Letter Number 91)*
Nov. 10th/64

Dear Amanda,

I will drop you a few lines this morning and send by one of our Regiment that is going home on furlough. My health is excellent and I am getting on finely. I wrote to Doc three days ago and told him to tell you about my clothes. Since then I have drawn another good pair of drawers from the government and am fixed all right in that line too now. They are the best drawers that we have rec. in a long time. The most of the drawers we get are almost worthless.

Tom Rickerson's furlough has not come back yet but will probably be in in a day or two and will write and send by him. I traded for a pair of shoes the other day that I will send to you by him. I think you can wear them though they may be too large for you. I have got to draw the fellow a pair from the government to pay for them. I drew a pair for him day before yesterday, but they did not suit him and I kept them myself.

There has been some more heavy skirmish fighting in front of Petersburg, the result of which I have not learned yet. They pitched in last night hot and heavy for about 30 minutes. Day before yesterday was the great election day.[129] The Yanks all got drunk that day and hooped and _____ around to a great extent. Our lines are so near in some places that our boys can smell the whiskey and generally tell when a fight is going to take place by their getting whiskey. I think it

---

[129] November 8 was national election day. President Lincoln was reelected with 212 Electoral College votes to twenty-one each for George McClellan and George H. Pendleton.

time for them to quit when they have to make their men drunk to get them to fight and this has been the case during this campaign.

I learn from a letter received by one of Comp. K that Cousin Eliza is married but did not give the name of the man. I reckon I will learn all about it shortly.[130] All of our Brigade is here close together now and are going into winter quarters a short distance in the rear and pickette on the river. One Regiment is moving today out here near our quarters. I hope we will not have to move any more this winter unless forced to move and we all move home. We have warm cloudy weather now with only occasional showers. I do not have to walk near so much now. Any report is sent to the General's Quarters by the mail carrier and when the Regiment gets moved up here I will have still less to do but there is generally something on hand to attend to. I am going to town as soon as I finish my letter to get some paper, pens &c.

Write me a long letter and write me all the particulars about how you are getting along and everything you can think of about my boy. I think of you and him day and night and wonder if you are comfortable and not suffering for the necessities of life and long to be with you again. I hope the yankees will go to cutting each other's throats over the election and will let us alone. Remember me in your prayers. May God bless you.

Your husband,
M. Hill Fitzpatrick

゜

Hd. Qr. 45th Ga. Near Petersburg, Va. *(Letter Number 92)*
Nov. 11th, 1864

Dear Amanda,

I wrote to you yesterday and sent by one of the Regiment. Tom Rickerson's furlough came in yesterday evening and he will start home this evening. So I will write again and send by him. I wrote in my letter yesterday about the shoes that I had for you. I will send them by

---

[130] Eliza Fitzpatrick, MHF's first cousin, married Washington McKenzie in Crawford County on October 30, 1864, according to William R. Henry's *Marriage Records of Crawford County, Georgia*, 99. She was listed in the 1860 Census as a twenty-five-year old schoolteacher.

Tom. They are second handed and have been worn but are newly half soled and good calf skin and if you can wear them will last you a long while. I will send you two yankee papers and two steel pens, also a few buttons and some little pieces of lace that I had left about putting the strip[e] on my coat. I also have four cartridges that I will slip in my shoes that you can do as you please with. You must go to see Tom as soon as he is home. He is in a low state of health but I hope will soon recover when he gets home. He is a particular friend of mine, and is highly worthy of the friendship of all.

The weather has faired off clear and pleasant. The boys overall are busy as bees now preparing their winter quarters. The skirmish fighting I wrote of yesterday amounted to nothing. They have a frolic occasionally just to keep up the times they say. They are protected so well with works on both sides that it is a rare thing that anybody is hurt. They have portholes to shoot through and unless a ball happens to hit in the hole where some fellow is shooting, it does no harm. John Owens,[131] Bob's son was here yesterday. He belongs to an Artillery Company stationed over there opposite Petersburg. He says our boys and the yanks quit shooting the other day and commenced throwing rocks and clods of dirt at each other and had a regular fight of it that way for some time. By this you can give some idea how near each they are. In some places, they probably are in ten paces of each other and but short distance from the main line at that. They have a deep ditch to go in to the picket posts and a long ditch out when it is necessary to go in and out from the main line.

There are already many rumors about in regard to the election, but I cannot see how they can find out this soon. It is rumored this morning that Lincoln carried every state, but that McClellan has received a large vote in each state. No doubt Lincoln is elected, and I think it best for us but in this matter there is no telling. We will at least take it for best, and make the best we can of it. Jeff Davis recommends the calling out of Forty Thousand ablebodied negroes for teamsters _____ _____ which I heartily support. But the _____. This is requested by many but I do not think Congress will do it. I shall go back to my old messmate, Jim Drew, as soon as they get fixed up here. He will be close by, and I prefer messing with him. There are too many in my present mess to suit me and the expenses is too heavy to suit me, also. I shall sleep here at my same place.

---

[131] According to the Census of 1860, John Owens of Crawford County would have been sixteen or seventeen by this time. The editors have been unable to identify his artillery unit.

We have drawn no money in some time here - we are nearly six months overdue us now. The Payrolls are all made out and sent up and we are looking for the money everyday. I was in hopes we would draw before Tom got his furlough so I could send some by him. Go to see Tom sure and he can tell you all about how we are fixed up here and how we are getting along. Maybe I may get there before he gets back but this is extremely doubtful. Write soon. Pray for me. May God bless you.

Your husband,
M. Hill Fitzpatrick

ℰ❧

Camp 45th Ga. Reg. Near Petersburg, Va. *(Letter Number 93)*
Dec. 8, 1864

Dear Amanda,

I received yours of Nov. 24th yesterday and two from you previous to that time of Nov. 11th and 15th. I did not answer them because I thought it useless almost as it was so uncertain about your getting the answers and I suppose it is equally as uncertain about your getting this but I will wait no longer but risk it. It had been some time since I had received a letter from home till yesterday and I was surprised and truly glad to get one from you and also at the same time one from Doc of Nov. 20th giving me a description of the false alarm that occurred in Crawford the day before he wrote, which is really laughable.

I am so sorry to learn from your letter that you were unwell. I feel quite uneasy about you but hope that you are well long ere this time.

Edd Jordan has not come yet. I expect they pressed him in Macon and I feel a little uneasy about my overcoat but I know he will take care of it if he can.[132] I am glad you sent no other clothes but the overcoat as they would only be in my way and I do not need them but would have been proud of the patches if you could have gotten them through to me.

---

[132] Pvt. Edwin T. Jordan had been at home in Crawford County on sick furlough. He must have been returning to Virginia when he was stopped in Macon.

Your letter is the latest that I have heard of that did come through. I suppose it got to Augusta before Sherman cut the railroad. I feel in great hopes now that no yankees will invade our county. I have eagerly gathered all the news from Ga I could to find out Sherman's course. We get nothing scarcely but rumors but from all I can learn he is making his course east of Macon, and I hope, as I said before, that he will pass our section unmolested.[133] But I will feel great concern till I hear direct from you again. I have written home only twice since I heard of Sherman's move. The first letter I wrote to Ma and sent by mail. The other I wrote to Doc and sent by one of the Regiment going home on retired papers. My health is excellent and I am getting on finely. We are still here at the same place and every thing is moving along as usual except some orders last night to keep the men in camp and be ready to move. We have heard nothing more yet and it is generally thought there will be no move soon. But we may have to go at any time.

A list of the casualties of the Ga. Malita[134] at some fight, I forget where now, was seen by Col. Simmons and several others here in a Petersburg paper a day or two ago and they say Frank White's name was among the wounded and that he was shot through both knees. I did not get to see the paper myself. I am truly sorry to hear of this and fear that Frank will have a hard time.[135]

I have no doubt from what Doc says you all had stiring times for a while when you heard the yanks were coming. I am glad it turned out no worse. It's strange they could not tell Reb from Yank and that 17 should be reported 1000. I should like to have had a canteen of the whiskey that was poured out.

We had a change of the monotony of camp life last Sunday. An old gentleman named R. O. Davidson delivered an address on the invention of a bird of Art. He says he made an artificial bird to go by steam through the air that can carry a man to guide it and a number of shells which the man can drop on the Yankees as he passes over them which will soon kill and scare them all away. He first applied to the

---

[133] MHF was correct. Sherman did not go through Crawford County.

[134] Militia.

[135] Amanda's brother Frank White originally served in Co. E, 6th Ga. Infantry, but was discharged due to disability on August 20, 1861. In 1864, he enlisted in and was elected 2nd lieutenant of Co. A, 8th Regiment, 3rd Brigade of the Georgia Militia. After the Atlanta campaign, when Hood's army was invading Tennessee, the Georgia Militia tried to slow Sherman's "March to the Sea." Frank White was mortally wounded at the Battle of Griswoldville on November 22, 1864. He died at his father's Crawford County home on December 17, 1864, according to David Lee's *The White Family of Crawford County, Georgia*, 21-22.

Government for aid but was refused and he now appeals to private contributions. At the close of his address the boys contributed $116.00 to assist him in forwarding his designs. He proposes to make five hundred of these birds to follow one behind the other, he taking the lead and to drop bomb shell on yanks wherever found. Quite an idea if he can only succeed and who knows but what he will. Of course it is ridiculed to a great extent, also the idea of steam cars, telegraphic wires and all other great inventions, laughed at at first. He says he will be ready for active operations by the middle of February next.[136]

They have built a rude log church in our camp and we have preaching regular and prayer meeting nearly every night. We started a Bible class last Sunday which is quite interesting and I hope will do much good. They are also speaking of getting up a Literary School for the purpose of learning all who desire it to read and write. This will do much good if properly conducted.

We have beautiful and pleasant weather and it is unusually warm for the season. The morning papers have come in since I commenced writing which states that a forward movement is daily expected from Grant. But this is no more than we expected and are prepared to give him a warm reception if he advances which is a little doubtful to say the least.

I am glad Tom Rickerson got home safe but sorry that Doc did not know about his things so he could have brought them along.

I am always glad to hear that my boy is well and hearty. I was well pleased with his speech and wish I could hear him speak it. I had hoped to get home sometime before a great while but old Sherman's raid has bursted it up for the present at least but I still hope things will work around so that I can get off yet sometime this winter. I shall anxiously look for letters from home now and I cannot help feeling considerable uneasiness about your health.

We draw flour again now instead of meal. Drew and I eat but little meat and save it to exchange for something more palatable. Our bread

---

[136] R.O. Davidson served in the 11th Miss. Inf., then as a clerk in the Treasury Department in Richmond. (See "Roster of the Prairie Guards," *Confederate Veteran* XXXIII:1 [1925] 50-51.) The Feb. 27, 1862 notes of the Senate of the First Confederate Congress describe "... a memorial from R.O. Davidson concerning a machine which he had deemed would be of great service if introduced into the military department of the Confederate States." (See *Southern Historical Society Papers,* [1923] 44:64-65.) A Charleston News and Courier article, reprinted in the *Southern Historical Society Papers,* (1900) 28:303-304, describes an unnamed "Professor" who solicited funds from Lee's soldiers in the winter of 1864-65, for the building of an "Artis Avis," Latin for "bird of art." The professor was not named but the story reads much like MHF's account.

rations are better than they have been but pretty short yet. We swapped some meat for flour a few days ago and have plenty of flour ahead now and we have more meat on hand which we are going to exchange for syrup the first chance we get. We still get some sugar and coffee. We have just had dinner. We had batter cakes for dinner and sugar and vinegar to eat with the batter cakes which was a rarity. I made up the batter in a tray with a spoon and put some rice in it that was left over from breakfast and it went fine sure.

I have been all day writing this letter off and on. I have to quit to attend to something every few minutes. I will close up. Write me soon and write me a long letter. I have a letter from Lou of Nov. 16th unanswered yet and Doc's of Nov. 20th, which I received yesterday. Tell them I will answer them soon if nothing prevents. Remember me in your prayers. May God bless you and my darling boy.

Your husband,
M. Hill Fitzpatrick

Letters
1865

Stuart Hospital, Richmond Va
March 27th 1865

Dear Amanda, You no doubt are surprised at the Caption of this letter, I will explain. About 10 or twelve days ago I was taken quite sick with severe cold and fever, and had one of the hardest chills on 19th inst I ever had in my life, On 20th our Regt received marching orders and the Surgeon sent me here, I had no more chill and am nearly well now, I shall return to my Regt tomorrow, I do not know where they are but suppose they are not far from Petersburg, This is an excellent Hospital, and I have fared very well I drew 4 months wages of money today the first I have drawn since my return from home, I hope to find letters from home for me when I get back to the Regt, I long to hear from you all again, I wrote to Doc just before I was taken sick, and sent by mail, I am to send this by a Lt going to Augusta, The war news is highly encouraging, and our troops are in the best of spirits, Johnson has checked Sherman in his wild career, twice, and Lee captured a few days ago, a considerable portion of the Yankee work in front of Petersburg with a large number of prisoners, I have not seen the official report yet, but have seen several wounded that were in the fight, I see from the papers that Colquitt's Brigade has been engaged again recently, I see a list of the Casualties of the officers of 27th Ga which was pretty heavy, I hope George Henry & Rufus came out safely but am anxious to learn straight from them It is hard to me not hearing from home, but I will

First page of letter written from Stuart Hospital,
Richmond, Virginia, on March 27, 1865.
Photo: Jack Deacon, Decatur, Georgia.

Camp 45th Ga. near Petersburg, Va. *(Letter Number 94)*
Jan. 1, 1865

Dear Amanda,

I wrote to Lou last night, but having the chance, to send by Capt. Gibson tomorrow I will write again tonight.

I rec. yours of 16th Nov., sent by Tom Rickerson, a few days ago and wrote to Doc right away and to Lou last night as I have just said. I never let a good chance to send by hand pass without sending one especially now when there is but little other chance to get them through. I was truly glad to hear from you again and to learn that you and my boy were well and getting on as well as could be expected. I am in fine health and getting along pretty well.

Bread rations are very short now, and we failed to get any atall today. The excuse is that they cannot get it on the cars to us. I hope it will be remedied soon. Edd Jordan has pretty plenty of money and by buying some we manage to do pretty well.[1] Yesterday we drew crackers but only little more than half enough of them. Tomorrow we are to get the big New Years' diner, and it will be welcomed heartily I assure you.

Today is or was Sunday, and was a clear, beautiful, cold day. I mean beautiful to look upon not to feel. It snowed yesterday evening and last night, and the ground was covered with snow today, but not deep. I wrote to Doc what to tell you about my overcoat but for fear you or he rather, will not get the letter I will recapitulate. Jordan says he left the coat at his house in a box and I want you to get it home and keep it, and not try to send it to me anymore this winter. I have drawn a good new blanket which I use as a wrapper and do not need my overcoat now.

From a conversation between Capt. Gibson and Col. Simmons last night, I now think there is some chance for me to get home yet this winter, but it is so uncertain that you need count but little on it. I need some socks now which is all I do need in the clothing line but I see but little chance, if any, to get them from home.

Our preacher has gone home on furlough but prayer meeting every night is still kept up and sometimes in the day. The meeting has been going on for three weeks now, and a good many have joined. Five

---

[1] Pvt. Edwin Jordan must have returned to Co. K between the writing of the previous letter and this one.

joined since our Chaplain left. We have gotten up a Bible class that is quite interesting. We met and had a lesson this evening.[2]

I ought to scould you good for writing such awful short letters, but if you will do better next time I will let you off, but you must do better or I will grumble like rip. Write me all the little tricks generally, and especially about my boy. You have never said whether you got the shoes I sent you by Tom Rickerson or not, but I know what Tom says. I suppose you got them. I care nothing about this though, but am just stimulating you to write longer letters.

We have drawn no money yet, and have no idea when I will get any, but that hurts but little. The spirits of some of our troops is rather dull but, generally speaking all are in good heart yet. We have some croakers here but not so many as you have there at home. I hate to hear them talk, but it is natural for some. I have no distant dream of ever giving up. Yankees may kill me but will never subjugate me.

Write soon. Pray for me. May God bless you.

Your husband,
M. Hill Fitzpatrick

            ?❧

Camp 45th Ga., near Petersburg, Va. *(Letter Number 95)*
Jan. 7th, 1864[3]

Dear Amanda,

I received yours of Dec. 12th a few days ago,, and soon after that yours of Dec. 2nd both of which I was glad to get, although they came

---

[2] The Army of Northern Virginia experienced a powerful awakening of religious practice and belief during the winter of 1864-65. The desperate nature of the Confederate cause and the settled conditions of the siege lines helped make this possible. Devout Christians like MHF were greatly strengthened by the work of chaplains, visiting preachers, and especially by their fellow Christians in the ranks who led Bible classes such as the one he notes here. See Bell Irvin Wiley, *The Life of Johnny Reb, The Common Soldier of the Confederacy* (Baton Rouge: Louisiana State University Press, 1988 [reprint, 1943], 182-184); and Gardiner H. Shattuck, Jr., *A Shield and a Hiding Place: The Religious Life of the Civil War Armies* (Macon: Mercer University Press, 1987).

[3] MHF made the same mistake many of us do in January when we continue to use the old year in writing letters and checks. The context makes clear that the correct date was 1865.

in at a late date, in consequence of mail developments. I was glad to learn that you had rec. the tricks I sent you by Tom Rickerson, and I take back what I said about the shoes in my last. I am always so proud to hear of my boy being well and hearty and so smart to do things, and want to save something for his Pa, when he gets home. I am truly sorry that he was disappointed in not seeing me, but if he lives he will suffer many disappointments through life.

No doubt it was a severe disappointment to you too, but I hope you will not take it to heart any more than you can help but try to be resigned and cheerful under all your trials. I long to get home but if I cannot I will take it easy and do the best I can. It is useless to write on the subject, consequently I say but little about it. I will be sure to come as soon as possible but the chance is slim, dull and uncertain, and there is much wire pulling, in which I do not participate. Our boy must be of considerable size by this time. He is nearly four years old now. I want to see him with his jeans suit on with pockets in his britches, and a hat on, and see him run and jump. The later part of next year he will be old enough to start to school, or by the next year after that, anyway. I want you to start him as soon as you can when he gets old enough and keep him going whether there is any chance to pay for it or not.

My health is very good except a case of camp itch that I have had but hope that I am clear of it now. I caught it by sleeping with a fellow two nights. I have been working on it this week. I washed and rubbed once a day with sulphur and greece for three' days and on the fourth day which was today, washed off clean and changed clothes, and hope it is now gone up the spout.

Joe Walker and Henry Gibson will start home tomorrow or early the next morning and I will send this by them.[4] I want to be sure to have it ready is why I am writing tonight. Tonight is Saturday night. I went to prayer meeting before I commenced to write. I am writing in Col. Simmons room. He has a candle burning nearly every night and I do nearly all of my letter writing in here now after night. Since Mr. Jordan came back, we all three sleep in our hut now and have a comfortable place. Our rations keep about the same. We get plenty of meat, but little a plenty bread. By buying some we make out very well. We have drawn no money yet nor do I know when we will draw any but I suppose sometime soon.[5]

The war news is exciting from all quarters except here. We have no changes here of any importance. Things look dull and these are times to

---

[4] 1st Lt. Joel Walker and Pvt. Henry Gibson of Co. K.
[5] The three messmates were Edd Jordan, Jim Drew, and MHF.

try men's souls, but I have no doubt all will work out right, yet. There seems to be a general despondency, at this time throughout the Confederacy. I am truly sorry to see this and sometimes I wish I could instill my feelings on this subject in every man, woman and child in the Southern Confederacy. It is natural for some to grumble all the time while many others hearing so much grumbling and despondent chatt have not the spirit to rise above this, but fall in under the influence and conclude that we are gone up. And we have had some reverses and bad Generalship, with a prospect of a continuance of the war which makes some good men croak and have the blues, and study over it till they conclude that we are about gone up, and they have their influence. But a large number are yet left who have resolved to die rather than submit to Yankee Rule, and never; never give it up. If croakers would but consider a moment the consequence of subjugation they would certainly talk different. Pen cannot describe nor tongue tell the degradation and suffering of our people if we ever submit.

The picture is too horrible to contemplate and like Francis Marion of the Revolutionary War, I say never shall she, clanking in her chains, point to me and say it was your cowardice that brought me to this. They may overrun us but never subjugate us. We will rise again and again and fight them till they will gladly let us alone. After passing the present crisis that is on us, I have no doubt things will brighten soon and we will prove ourselves worthy of freedom by learning the true value of it, in these dark times.

I could write forty pages on the subject and then not tell half what I feel, but I have said enough for this time, at least, and as it is getting late, I will close up for tonight and if I do not get this off tomorrow, maybe I will muster up something else by tomorrow night to fill the other side. I long for the mails to open regularly again so that I can hear from you often. Yours sent by Tom R. is the latest I have from home and I am getting anxious to hear again. Write soon and write me a long letter. May God bless you. Pray for me.

Your husband,
M. Hill Fitzpatrick

P.S. Jan. 8th Well Cout if you can see any sense in this letter or understand it you can beat me. I wrote last night on two half sheets as I thought, and folded them up and put them in the envelope, but I wrote on three half sheets and only put two in the envelope, and tonight opened it to write the promised Postscript and could not tell how it was as I could find no beginning to it. But after awhile I found the other half sheet and will send you the whole concern to hunt over. Fortunately Walker and Gibson did not start today or you would have had a strange letter. They will start early in the morning. I forgot to tell you about our New Years dinner. We got it on 4th inst. I believe. It was nearly a failure. I got a little piece of turkey and two small pieces of meat and about four good mouthfuls of lightbread. It was too large an undertaking to try to give the whole army such a dinner. We have cold weather and some snow but not much yet. We had prayer meeting today and again tonight which I attended before I came in here to finish your letter. Thus another Sunday has passed in the war. I drew a good pair of shoes today. The Regt. got a large lot of shoes today. The last pair I drawed did me but little good. I ruined them when we took the tramp through the snow. Do write soon.

Hill

Well Cout I will write another slip and put in my letter.[6] I have just got yours of 1ˢᵗ inst. which you sent by Rufus.[7] I am glad to hear from you again and to hear that all were well. I rec. the thread which I am proud of, though not needing it right now. I have not rec. Lou's letter yet, but am anxious to get it and hear from the wedding.[8] I am glad you are supplied with shoes and if I had known it would not have traded for them old things for you, however take them as you may need them yet before the war ends and they are the best I could do for you away here in the war. I am sorry you are making me a coat and heartily wish you had used the cloth for Henry and yourself. Do not make me any more. I want you to have it for I can draw here and you have a hard task to cloth yourself and family without me. I am so sorry you lost one of your hogs but hope you have found it before this time. I hope you will do well with those you have. I am glad you got the _____ pens. I will continue to send you some when I can get them. Cheer up and do the best you can and hope for better times. Hill

ʒ◟

---

[6] This postscript was found loose in the collection of original letters. Judging from the text, it might have originally been placed in an envelope with the above letter.

[7] Amanda's brother Rufus White, who had been on furlough.

[8] Possibly the wedding of MHF's cousin Eliza Fitzpatrick to Washington McKenzie on October 10, 1864.

Editors' Note: Shortly after the preceding letter, Marion Hill Fitzpatrick received his second furlough. "Furloughs of Indulgence" were usually granted for thirty days. Family tradition related by Mansel Hammock holds that while on furlough, MHF was begged by relatives not to return to the Army, because the Confederacy seemed doomed. Many soldiers did stay home, but MHF is said to have replied: "I would rather for my bones to bleach in Old Virginia than to be called a deserter in Georgia." The following letter was written as MHF began to make his way back to Virginia.

Macon, Ga. (*Letter Number 96*)
Dec. 13th, 1865[9]

Dear Amanda,

I will drop you a few lines tonight. I got here early this evening and got my transportation to Augusta, then found Gus Murchison[10] and left my baggage with him and strolled over town. I bought you an Almanac which I will send you in the letter. I found out that Ward my buggy man is yet here and went to see him but he was not at home. Gus will attend to it for me, and take up the note if it is all right and wait till I can pay him. I told him though if he got the note to let Pap[11] have it and I can pay Pap. I had rather he had it. Tell Doc Gus has got his watch yet but it is locked up in a fellow's trunk who is off at this time with the key. Gus had bargained it away for $160.00. I told him not to take that for it and he says he will not but will keep it for Doc. He paid $20.00 to have it repaired.

Nothing would do Gus but what I must go with him to the Theatre tonight, he paying all expenses. It was a poor thing and I did not enjoy it atall. From all I can learn, there is a bad chance to get through to my Command and if I get through I will have to walk over a hundred miles. It is useless for me to try to carry all them socks and I have left them here with Gus, who will send them out to you and you can

---

[9] The original reads Dec. 13th, 1865, which is clearly wrong. Judging from the content of this letter and the next two, the proper date must have been February 13, 1865.

[10] Murchison enlisted as a private in Company D, 13th Georgia Infantry, on May 13, 1862 and was wounded in 1863. His wound disabled him for the remainder of the War. His family was active in Elim Baptist.

[11] A nickname for William B. White, Sr., Amanda's father.

distribute them. I will try to carry Jordan's. It is late. I am here with Gus in his room and will leave early in the morning.

Cheer up and may God bless you and my darling boy.

Your husband,
M. Hill Fitzpatrick

꣠

Milledgeville, Ga. *(Letter Number 97)*
Feb. 14th, 1865

Dear Amanda

I will drop you a few lines again. I wrote you a short letter late last night. After which I lay down and slept soundly till this morning and took the cars at 8 o'clock for this place, but 16 miles from here four or five boxes run off the track and one box broke up pretty badly. I was restless and impatient, and it was drizzling rain and cold and I thought it would probably be 24 hours or longer before the cars could be gotten back and I and a few others put out afoot for this place, and just as we got to the Depot, 2 miles from here the cars rolled up. I was completely sold, and am tired and I think fully cured of my restlessness now. I came on with an old citizen of this place who had a negroe with him who I hired to toat my two havresacks for me, and when I got here to his house I asked him to let me stay all night, to which he assented and gave me a big drink of wine and would have me to eat with him, although I told him I had plenty with me and says he never charges a soldier.

It has been raining all day slowly and is still at it. It is nearly night now. I have dried myself and things, and feel quite comfortable, but Cout, my heart is heavy. I think of you and Henry all the time, and often want to get off to myself and take a big cry, to relieve the burden from my heart. Poor little Henry, he followed me up to his Grandma's that morning and I told him good-by again, and he halloed goodby Pa after I had got in the buggy and started. It nearly broke my heart. May God protect him and you is my humble prayer.

Cout, I want you and all of you to pray for me. I am a poor backslidden Creature, if a Christian atall, but I want to do better. From what I can gather I think I can flank Augusta by going by

Washington[12] and walking 60 miles across in South Carolina. I think I shall try it, but I will find out all about it before I get there.[13] Be sure all of you to send me letters by Jim Hammock if you don't write sooner.[14] I dread it, it will be so long before I hear from home again. Cout, if possible, you feel dearer to me than ever. You have done all you could for me. I can never repay you, but God will bless you for it. Cheer up Cout, I earnestly hope that we may yet meet again and spend many happy days together. I will try to write a time or two before I get to the Regt. I love to write to you. May God's richest blessings rest on all of you. I hate to quit writing, I feel like I was talking to you, but it is simply I must be more of a man, so good-bye.

Your husband,
M. Hill Fitzpatrick

ꝗ

7 Miles from Washington, Ga. *(Letter Number 98)*
Feb. 17th, 1865

Dear Amanda,

I will drop you a few lines tonight. I am well and jogging along finely. I wrote you night before last. We staid that night a short distance from the road, and the next morning started early and went 3 miles out of our way which was vexatious. We staid last night at Edd Jordan's Aunt's 2 miles from Mayfield and fared sumtously getting a good warm supper, bed and breakfast. This morning we took the cars and went down to Camack on the Augusta road, then turned up to Washington, and are footing it again. We got to Washington about 1/2 hour by sun, and got in here by hard work some time after dark. We will have 35 miles now to walk to Abbeyville, S. C., then take the cars to Alston, then foot it again to Winnborough; then take the cars to Va. The last

---

[12] Washington, Ga.
[13] MHF was afraid he would be stopped by Confederate officers in Augusta and prevented from returning to Virginia and the 45th Georgia.
[14] Jim Hammock was the brother of MHF's good friend Tip Hammock. Jim served with Doc in Co. C, 27th Ga. He was shot in the hand at the Battle of Seven Pines, and had two fingers amputated, but served until the end of the War.

gap is 19 miles. My feet is getting better now but I was awful tired last night sure.

There is an Order for all Lee's men to go through Augusta but we flanked orders and all. I met several men from my Regiment today going home. One of them said John Spillers was on the road home.[15] I wear my cotton socks and would do badly without them. It is a fine thing I did not try to bring those socks for the boys, for it has taken my best to get along without them. My rations have not given out yet. It would be a poor do without them. I shall have enough to last several days yet. They have fixed down a good bed on the floor for us but we do our own eating. A fellow from 61st Ga. is my traveling companion.

Tell Henry his Pa could not do without his cup hardly and thinks of him every day and wants to see him bad. Cheer up Cout, and be lively. I will write again soon if I get the chance. May God bless you all. Pray for me.

Your husband,
Hill

♒

Camp Near Petersburg, Va. *(Letter Number 99)*
March 4th, 1865

Dear Amanda,

One of the Regt. will start home on retired papers tomorrow morning and I gladly accept the chance to send you a letter. I am happy to say to you that I arrived safely here night before last at 10 1/2 o'clock, after a tramp of 18 days from the time I left home.

I am well and in high spirits, again. I found the Regt. at the same place, in fine health generally and also in fine spirits, much better I am glad to say than when I left. The eating line is about the same as when I left. Meat is tolerably plentiful, but bread rates scarce. The boys have drawn money and they buy meal occasionally, at from 1 1/2 to 2 dollars per lb., which is from 90 to 120 dollars per bushel.

---

[15] Spillers was a private in Co. K and in the original group of recruits who traveled with MHF to Virginia. A February 28, 1865 roll for Co. K shows Spillers absent on a furlough of indulgence.

I wrote you several letters while on my way here which I hope you received. The last I wrote was a P S to one I had written for several days, while at Charlotte, N. C. I did not get along much faster on the cars than I did on the gravel train as we called it or taking it afoot, and lacked much of faring so well in the eating line.[16]

It is rainy cloudy weather now and quite warm for the season. It was pretty dark when I got to Petersburg but happened not to be raining. I knew all the road well but got a slip down sprawling in the mud which was all the difficulty I had. The boys were asleep but Mr. Jordan waked up as I went into our hut, and pulled off my baggage and soon joined them in the land of dreams. Yesterday morning I was crowed and welcomed by nearly all the Regiment and asked a thousand questions, and glad was I to be with them again. Well, after breakfast, I got my hair shingled nicely, got shaved and took a big wash, put on clean clothes, washed my dirty ones and felt considerably better. I did not report for duty yesterday, and did not know what they would do with me for being absent without leave so long, but early this morning the Col. sent for me and told me that I must act as Adjutant till our Adjt. returned from home, and that he wanted me to get the books straight once more, as they had not been right since I left. Well, I pitched in and had a busy time for about two hours at my same old business which I found in a tangled condition.[17] I am the only one of the Regt. that came through or in all probability that will get here in some time, they being all stopped at Augusta which I am glad I flanked although I had such a long walk. In all together, I walked 180 miles or more since I left home. I walked 10 miles after I left Charlotte, N. C. They were tearing up the railroad track making it wider, so they could run the S. C. cars on it.[18] I found several letters here for me which I read with interest, although I had seen you all since they were written. I found one also from George W.[19] which I will answer soon. It was written about the time yours was that you received from him while I was at home.

I hardly know what to write on the war news. Various opinions are afloat, in regard to the future movements. One thing certain, Peters-

---

[16] The Charlotte letter wasn't received by Amanda or has been lost over the years.

[17] MHF was at least two weeks late returning from his furlough, if he left Virginia shortly after Letter Number 95 was written on January 7-8, 1865.

[18] MHF's trip, as best the editors can tell, was from Knoxville, Ga., to Macon (buggy); then to Milledgeville (train); then to Washington, Ga. (train); then to Abbeville, S.C. (foot); then to Charlotte (foot and train); then to Virginia (train). It took him eighteen days. The Colton's 1858 Map of the United States carried by MHF during the War survives in remarkably good condition.

[19] Amanda's brother George White, a private in Co. C, 27th Ga.

burg and Richmond are not evacuated yet and I see but little if any sign of their evacuation. We received orders last night to be ready to march at a moment's warning but it is about 12 o'clock now and we hear nothing more from it. It is nothing unusual to get such orders, and I hope these will pass quietly away for this time at least for I do not feel like taking another tramp so soon.

General Lee is Commander in Chief, and Johnson has been restored to the Command of the Army of Tennessee, which are both good things. The Law to arm the negroes has not passed Congress yet. It is causing much debate. Sherman's whereabouts is not known exactly but he left the railroad below Chester, S. C. and it is thought is making his way to Wilmington, and will form a junction with Grant. If so we will whip him sure. With Johnson and Beauregard to assist us I feel confident that we will be able to manage Mr. Grant and Sherman too. Now is the time for all to rally around the standard of our Country and let us route Sherman and I firmly believe that peace will soon follow. How can a man lag from duty at these times I cannot see for my life.

The celebrated African Missionary Mr. Stone preached for us yesterday and last night, gave us a lecture on the people and the Country of Africa which was highly interesting. It was very different from the ideas I had formed of the Country and inhabitants.[20]

Some few letters come through by mail yet, and I want you all to keep writing and send by hand when you can, and by mail when you cannot. You cannot imagine how bad I want to hear from you and Henry again and from all of you. I want to hear what Henry has to say about me now, and all about him. Write me all about how you are getting along and all the news generally. They are exchanging prisoners rapidly now, and I am glad of it.[21] Capt. Gibson has been promoted to Major, and Lt. Rutherford to Captain since I left, and several other promotions in the Regt.[22] I hope we will get to remain

---

[20] The Rev. Richard Henry Stone was a Baptist missionary in Africa from 1858 to 1863, and from 1865 to 1869. He was accompanied by his wife, Susan Broadus Stone, a cousin of John Broadus, first president of the Southern Baptist Theological Seminary. During the War, Stone was a chaplain in the Army of Northern Virginia. After his missionary days, he was an educator in Virginia and Kentucky. He died in 1915. (On Rev. Stone's life see George Braxton Taylor's *Virginia Baptist Ministers, Sixth Series, 1914-1934, with Supplement* [Lynchburg, Va., : J.P. Bell Company, Inc., 1935] 23-24.)

[21] From Co. K, the following privates who had been captured in May 1864 at either the Battle of the Wilderness or at the Battle of Spotsylvania were exchanged in early March 1865: John E. Collum, William J. Mathews, William J. McGee, William Miller, William J. Slocumb and Joseph C. Wilder.

[22] Henry Gibson was elected major of the 45th on December 2, 1864, and Williams Rutherford was elected captain of Co. K in February 1865.

peaceably here for some time yet. The old pickette firing is kept up to some extent yet. It greeted my ears as soon as I got off the cars at Petersburg and sounded quite natural to me. I study about home a great deal, but really have no time to have the blues. I hope to hear from you soon. I will write again soon. Old Abe is to be inaugurated today and we are listening to hear a salute from their big guns. May God bless you all. Pray for me.

Your husband,
M. Hill Fitzpatrick

ॐ

Stuart Hospital (*Letter Number 100*)
Richmond, Va.
March 27th, 1865

Dear Amanda,

You no doubt are surprised at the caption of this letter. I will explain. About 10 or twelve days ago I was taken quite sick with severe cold and fever, and had one of the hardest chills on 19th inst. I ever had in my life. On 20th our Regt. received marching orders and the Surgeon sent me here. I had no more chills and am nearly well now. I shall return to my Regt. tomorrow. I do not know where they are but suppose they are not far from Petersburg. This is an excellent Hospital and I have fared very well. I drew 4 months wages of money today, the first I have drawn since my return from home. I hope to find letters from home for me when I get back to the Regt. I long to hear from you all again. I wrote to Doc, just before I was taken sick and sent by mail. I aim to send this by a Lt. going to Augusta.[23]

The war news is highly encouraging, and our troops are in the best of spirits. Johnson has checked Sherman in his wild career, twice, and Lee captured a few days ago a considerable portion of the Yankee

---

[23] MHF was admitted to Stuart Hospital in Richmond on March 21, 1865 and returned to duty on March 28. According to his Compiled Service Record the diagnosis was "Febris Interm Tertiana," or a fever which returns every third day.

works in front of Petersburg with a large number of prisoners.[24] I have not seen the official report yet, but have seen several wounded that were in the fight. I see from the papers that Colquitt's Brigade has been engaged again recently. I see a list of the casualties of the officers of 27th Ga., which was pretty heavy. I hope George, Henry & Rufus came out safely, but am anxious to learn straight from them.[25] It is hard to me not hearing from home, but I will try to be resigned to it, the best I can. Tip Hammock joined the church just before I left the Regt. He joined the Primitive Baptist. I never witnessed such intense religious feelings in my life as there was in our Regt.

One of Comp. (K) is here on guard at the President's house.[26] I went to see him this morning and while there saw one of Wash. Oxford's brothers who is on guard at the same place. He is a fine looking young man. Tell Henry I saw a pretty little bit of a black pony the other day, hitched to a pretty little wagon, and a man and a little boy like him riding in the wagon. I thought of him and how glad he would be to have them. Tell him I have not had the chance to get him a knife yet, but I hope he has found his before this time.

Yesterday was Sunday. I went to church at a large fine Presbyterian Church, where they had an organ and splendid music and singing, also a good sermon.[27] I do not want you to be the least uneasy about me. I am well except my strength which I am rapidly regaining. Andrew Wright came in just before I left. He staid at home on the account of his child which was sick he said.

I will write again to some of you when I get back to the Regt. We must not stop writing, but write and hope on. No doubt Spring is upon you by this time with all its beauties, but Stern Winter still reigns supreme here. The negroe troops have been called out. I have seen two

---

[24] By "Johnson," MHF meant Confederate Gen. Joseph E. Johnston, who had been given command of what was left of the Army of Tennessee. Johnston attacked Sherman twice in North Carolina, on March 16, 1865 at Averasborough, and March 19 and 21 at Bentonville, but his force was too small to do more than delay Sherman's advance. The reference to Lee capturing "a considerable portion of the Yankee works..." could mean the Confederate attack on Fort Stedman at Petersburg on March 25, 1865. After initial success the Confederates could not hold the position and retreated.

[25] Colquitt's Brigade was in North Carolina. George, Henry and Rufus White would all survive the War, surrendering in North Carolina.

[26] The member of Co. K assigned to President Jefferson Davis' guard was Pvt. James Augustus Moore.

[27] MHF probably attended Second Presbyterian Church, which was served by the Rev. Moses Drury Hoge as pastor. According to Dr. Fred Anderson of the Virginia Baptist Historical Society, Second Presbyterian had a pipe organ installed in 1859.

companies.[28] I hope it will work well. I will close up. Tell Henry I have his cup yet, and that I want to see him mighty bad. May God bless you all. Pray for me.

Your husband,
M. Hill Fitzpatrick

ᘏ

Line of battle 2 1/2 Miles south Petersburg, Va. *(Letter Number 101)*
March 28th, 1865

Dear Amanda,

I have just received yours of Feb. 18th 24th and 28th all of which I am truly glad to get and to learn that all were well at home.

Many sad changes have taken place since you heard from me last. I wrote to you a day or two ago but as I have the chance to send this by a negroe, going home, I will go back to the first and explain as you will be apt to get this first.

Well about the 16th of this month I was taken quite sick with chills and fever and on the 19th had a severe chill that lasted me 1 1/2 hours, on the 20th we received marching orders and I was sent to the Hospital in Richmond. I got there on the 21st. I had no more chills or fever, and soon got well. I left this morning and got here to the Regt. this evening.

While I was gone the Regt. got into a severe fight. It was on 25th and like to have all got killed and captured.[29] Edd Jordan, Jim Drew, Lt. Walker, Tip Hammock, Tom Rickerson, Loucious George, Henry

---

[28] On March 13, 1865, the Confederate Congress finally sent President Davis a measure for enlisting black men into the Confederate Army. Davis signed it into law immediately. Black companies were raised and training began, but these troops never saw combat (see E.B. Long, *The Civil War Day By Day*, 651).

[29] Very early on March 25, 1865, Gen. John B. Gordon led a well-planned Confederate attack at Fort Stedman. Although Gordon's men took the fort, they could not hold it. About 9 a.m. troops of the Federal Sixth Corps advanced against the picket line in front of the entrenchments held by Thomas' and other brigades. The Federal attack dislodged the Confederates from their picket lines, including a key position on McIlwaine's Hill. Thomas' men tried without success to regain McIlwaines' Hill, even though all four regiments (14th Ga., 35th Ga., 45th Ga., and 49th Ga.) were eventually involved. It was in this struggle, called the Battle of Jones' Farm, that Co. K was so badly cut up. See J.F.J. Caldwell's *The History of A Brigade of South Carolinians, First Known as "Gregg's" and Subsequently as "McGowan's" Brigade*, (Dayton, Ohio: Morningside Press, 1992) 264-265, and Maj. W.S. Dunlop's *Lee's Shaprshooters; or, To the Forefront of Battle*, (Dayton, Ohio: Morningside Press, 1988) 248-249.

Saunders, Bill Seymore, Henry Pope, Henry Gibson, Frank Knight, and a fellow named Minis, a recruit from Ala. were all captured, from Co. K.[30] Henry Knight and Noah Cloud were both severely wounded. Knight had his left leg amputated. The loss of the Regt. is 6 killed, 25 wounded, 118 captured. None were killed in Comp. K that they know of. Lt. Col. Conn was killed and Major Gibson captured.[31]

From what I can gather about the fight is this. Above here in front of Petersburg our forces attacked the yanks taking a number of prisoners and a good portion of their works. To retaliate they attacked our pickette line, in front of this place capturing many but never got to our main line, and in trying to reestablish our pickette line our Regt. got so badly cut up and failed to do it that day which was 25th. Yesterday they reestablished the line with little loss. All is quiet now again but it is sad and heart sickening to look at our Regt. now. It seems that Providence ordained that I should miss it, or else I might now have been captured or killed.

I am well all to my strength, which I have not fully regained yet. I cannot guess what present you received. You must tell me in your next. I am so glad that Henry is well and hearty and has not forgotten me. I truly sympathize with you in your loneliness after I left you. I hope you are in fine spirits by this time and doing well with your garden and all your things. I feel sad and lonesome now, all my mess is gone, and I am alone again, but I can get along about that. The weather is pleasant now but it is uncertain about its continuing so long.

I am so glad you wrote to me. My getting your letters proves that letters will go through by mail, and I will continue to write and I want you to do the same. I will close up for this evening and as the negroe may not start in a day or two, I may write some more.

May God bless you all. Pray for me. Write soon.

Your husband,
M. Hill Fitzpatrick

---

[30] All the captured men were friends of MHF and have been mentioned before in these letters, except for "Minis," Elijah Minix. He enlisted in Co. K on Sept. 19, 1864.

[31] "Henry Knight" was 1st Sgt. Robert Henry Knight. He and Pvt. Noah Cloud were wounded on March 25, 1865. Lt. Col. Charles Augustus Conn was from Baldwin County, Ga., and had first been captain of Co. G, 45th Ga. Several of Conn's Civil War letters have been published in the *Georgia Historical Quarterly*, Vol. XLVI, No. 2, 169-195 and Vol. LV, No. 3, 437-441. "Major Gibson" was the former captain of Co. K, Aurelius W. Gibson.

March 29th

P.S. I will drop you a few more lines this evening. Major Gibson's boy Watt will start in the morning. I failed to say to you that our forces did not hold the works above Petersburg and (our) pickette line here I learn is not (quite) it the same old place with (a) little (loss)_________. I will (send) you _______ you ______ ____ ______ and _______ _______ pockette book. I (have) (got) me a new one. I drawed $100.00 in Richmond. I am trying to write (with) a sorry pen (sitting) on the ground and don't (know) if you can read it. Be sure to write (soon). I will write again soon.

Hill

(After "our forces did not hold the works above Petersburg" this P.S. is very difficult to read. By using a negative photograph, the editors arrived at the above version. The words in parenthesis are probably correct. The underlines mark illegible words. This postscript is the most difficult text to read in the Fitzpatrick collection.)

June 8th, 1865
Jackson Hospital, Richmond, Va.

Mrs. Fitzpatrick
Dear Madam,

As you in all probability have not heard of the death of your husband and as I was a witness to his death I consider it my duty to write to you allthough I am a stranger to you. But your husband and myself have share the same dangers under the same army for the past four years, allthough I did not get acquainted with him until he was wounded. Him and myself was wounded the same day the second of April[32] and were brought to Richmond that night layed in the cars that night and Richmond was evacuated the next day and we fell into enemy hands, but that morning before the Yankees got into Richmond we wer carried back on the other side of the river to Manchester wher the ladies dressed our wounds[33] and had us moved to a house and all the attention was paid that could be given both by the ladies and private physicians of Manchester, but it availed nothing in regards to your husband. He died on the 6th of April, but I am happy to say he died happy and I certainly think that he is now better off. A few minutes before he breathed his last he sang Jesus can make a dying bed as soft as downy pillows are[34] & he said he would of liked to of seen you before he died. He said that the Lord's will be done and for you to meet him in heaven. He died as I wish to die and as I believe all persons wish to. Though you probably will think he didn't have proper attention but I can assure you he did. There wer ladies with him all the

---

[32] On April 2, 1865, Gen. Grant ordered a general advance of the Army of the Potomac that caused the collapse of the Confederate lines at Petersburg. Family tradition (from Mansel Hammock) states MHF was struck in the hip with shrapnel when he rushed to the top of earthworks to replace the flag of the 45th Ga. after it had been shot down.

[33] Pvt. Field's obituary in the January 1914 issue of the *Confederate Veteran* magazine reads: "... he (Fields) got some one to put him on the train, where he lay all night suffering agony and begging for water, the train having been run back into a cut near Manchester. Next day the ladies took charge of the wounded and moved them to an old outhouse, where a temporary hospital was arranged."

[34] This verse forms the first two lines of the fourth stanza of a hymn by Isaac Watts, "Jesus can make a dying bed/ Feel soft as downy pillows are." It was first published in Watts' *Hymns and Spiritual Songs*, London, 1707. This long meter hymn—known by its first line of "Why should we start and fear to die?"—was included in Benjamin Lloyd's 1841 Primitive Baptist hymnal and B.F. White's 1844 Sacred Harp hymnal. Dr. William J. Reynolds of Southwestern Baptist Theological Seminary identified this hymn for the editors.

tim and surgeons but his wright thy was shatered all to pieces an recovery was impossible as it was so high up that it could not be taken off.

He is buried in Manchester. The ladies had him buried nicely. Mrs. Clopton[35] of Manchester has all of his clothes and other things. If you wish so address Mrs. Judge Clopton, Manchester, Chesterfield County, Va. I will send this letter by one of his company that is here. For any other information that you may wish as regards him, address as yet Mrs. Clopton. My prayers are that God will sustain you in your troubles an loss. You must excuse this writing as I am feeble yet myself and as I am still in bed can not get out but my wound is doing very well now and I soon hope that I shall be able to get home. So I remain your sorrowing friend.

William Fields
Co. I, 48th Va. Infantry

My address will be Abington, Washington County, Va. I hope to hear from you soon.

꒰ঌ

---

[35] Maria Clopton is described in local history accounts as having rescued wounded Confederate soldiers on the morning of April 3, 1865, hours after Richmond and its suburbs had fallen. Mrs. Clopton, widow of Virginia Judge John Bacon Clopton, learned that wounded Confederates had been left on a rail car in Manchester, across the James River. She arranged for them to be brought to her daughter's home nearby, even as neighbors were fleeing and Federal troops were marching through the city. Earlier in the War, she had established her own hospital in Richmond to care for the Confederate wounded. Her daughter, Sarah Clopton Pulliam, lived at 1007 McDonough Street in Manchester. MHF probably died there. Known as the "Archer-Pulliam House," it was demolished some time after 1940. See Benjamin B. Weisiger, III's, *Old Manchester & Its Environs* (Richmond: William Byrd Press, 1993).

Manchester
Sept. 5th, 1865[36]

Mrs. M.H. Fitzpatrick,

Dear Madam,

Your husband requested me to write you a few lines before he died. I would have written (then) but it was impossible (for) (me) to do so as there was no mails running. he was mortally wounded in front of Petersburg on the second of April ______ and died (on the) fourth—he left his sword with me for you so you can get it by sending for it. I would _____ it by the gentleman that _____ but he is a wounded soldier and cannot take it. answer this badly writen note. I will have more time to give you the perticulars in my next.

Yours respectfully,
Bella Knight[37]

---

[36] A copy of this letter can be found near the end of the microfilm of the Marion Hill Fitzpatrick Collection of Letters in the Georgia Department of Archives and History. This is the first publication of this letter. It is difficult to read. The words in parenthesis are probably correct.

[37] "Bella Knight," who noted on the reverse of her letter that she was "Miss Bella Knight, Manchester," must have helped Maria Clopton care for MHF and the other Confederate wounded. Research suggests she was Isabella Knight, who married William Moody in Chesterfield County, Va., on Nov. 9, 1869. In the 1870 Census she and William were living in the Jefferson Ward of Richmond. By the 1880 Census Isabella Knight Moody was living in Manchester, age thirty-seven, with two children: Jessie and Fannie.

Epilogue

The cost of the Civil War can begin to be seen in the number of deaths felt closely by Amanda White Fitzpatrick. She lost her husband, two brothers, a brother-in-law, a cousin by marriage, and numerous Crawford County friends. Her husband died just three days before Robert E. Lee surrendered the Army of Northern Virginia. More poignant still, Amanda was pregnant at Hill Fitzpatrick's death. They had conceived the child during his second and last furlough. Amanda gave birth to a daughter on November 7, 1865. She was given her father's name exactly—Marion Hill Fitzpatrick.

Amanda moved back to the Crawford County farm of her father, William Benjamin White, Sr., after the war. She lived there some years with son Henry and daughter Marion. In 1873, she married John T. Rigdon, and would have two more sons by him. She died on August 7, 1907, at age 59. An obituary attributes her death to tuberculosis, which followed a stroke. She is buried in the Rigdon plot of a cemetery in Culloden, Georgia.

Marion Hill Fitzpatrck's "Ma," Nancy Hill Fitzpatrick, moved to Texas after the war and divided her time between the homes of her daughters Sarah Fitzpatrick Law and Elizabeth Fitzpatrick Commander. We have a single letter she wrote back to Amanda, dated March 12, 1874. She included a postscript to Henry. "It does your old grandma so much good to get a letter from her little Henry," she wrote. "It makes me think so much of your dear father." Nancy Hill Fitzpatrick died in Texas on May 14, 1875.

James G. "Doc" Fitzpatrick served a term as tax assessor of Crawford County after the war, but eventually moved to Terrell County, Georgia. He married and had children, and lived until 1911. His and Hill's older brother Ben, a Confederate veteran of the 31st Mississippi, ended up as a cotton factor in Mobile. He and his wife had four sons. He died in Mobile in 1905, at the age of eighty-nine, prompting an editorial in the *Mobile Register* that lauded his business integrity and civic works.

Louisa "Lou" Greene, Hill's beloved niece, married James L. Jackson soon after the war. They had five children. Lou died of pneumonia in 1883.

The two children of Hill and Amanda Fitzpatrick would live long, productive lives. Henry Fitzpatrick married Etta Vaughan in 1884, and with her had five children who survived to adulthood. He operated a dry goods store in Culloden. In 1901 he wrote his uncle, Ben Fitzpatrick, inquiring about the family history. Ben, in his mid-eightes, sent back a detailed account that we have drawn on for this volume. Henry Fitzpatrick died in 1934 at age seventy-three.

Marion Hill Fitzpatrick married Felix Hammock in 1887. He was the nephew of the Tip Hammock who served with her father in Company K of the 45th Georgia. Marion and Felix Hammock had five children who lived to adulthood. "Nannie," as she was called by her grandchildren, died on December 6, 1955. She was ninety years old, and had lived past the birth of numerous great-grand-children, including the two editors of this volume.

One key mystery abides about her father: his place of burial. Like other family members before us, we made a good faith effort to find out. Our conclusion, like theirs, is that he most likely was buried in an unmarked grave in Richmond's Maury-Mt. Olivet Cemetery, very close to the home where Maria Clopton, Bella Knight, and a handful of other women nursed him and other Confederates wounded at Petersburg.

It would be satisfying to know for sure, and to mark the place appropriately. But we can hardly complain.

We have the letters.

Since the hardback appeared in 1998, we have heard from more than a few readers who had information to share about Marion Hill Fitzpatrick and his world. Some of those who contacted us are descendants of soldiers or others mentioned in the letters. We hope the paperback edition will find many more readers, including some who want to get in touch with the editors. They should feel to write Jeffrey C. Lowe at 140 Hunters Glen, Fayetteville, Georgia, 30215, or Sam Hodges at 408 E. Tremont Ave., Charlotte, North Carolina, 28203.

Bibliography

Primary Sources:

The Christian Index, Vol. XLIII, No. 14, April 18, 1864 and Vol. XLIII, No. 33, September 2, 1864, microfilm, Special Collections, Mercer University Main Library, Macon, Georgia.

Crawford County Deed Book D and Deed Book E, Crawford County Courthouse, Knoxville, Georgia.

Crawford County Grantor Index, 1830-1840, Crawford County Courthouse, Knoxville, Georgia.

Crawford County Probate Court: "A list of the appraisement of the goods and chattels of Alexander Fitzpatrick, July 2, 1850, Crawford County Courthouse, Knoxville, Georgia.

Crawford County Tax Digests 1845 and 1858, Crawford County Courthouse, Knoxville, Georgia.

The papers of James A. Englehard, AC No. 00-272, Georgia Department of Archives and History, Atlanta.

Collection of the letters of Marion Hill Fitzpatrick, Microfilm Drawer 227, Box 10, Georgia Department of Archives and History, Atlanta.

The Diary of Benjamin Thomas Smisson, unpublished manuscript made available to the editors by Alfred Jordan, Memphis, Tn.

The Diary of Daniel S. Redding, Captain, Co. D, 45th Georgia Infantry, and a 1905 letter to Captain Redding from Thomas J. Simmons, Colonel of the 45th Georgia, in Civil War Miscellany-Personal Papers, microfilm, Georgia Department of Archives and History, Atlanta, Georgia.

1860 Federal Census of Crawford County, Georgia, microfilm, United States Archives.

1860 Federal Census of Macon County, Georgia, microfilm, United States Archives.

1870 Federal Census of Sumter County, Georgia, Microfilm, United States Archives.

1880 Federal Census of Fulton County, Georgia, Microfilm, United States Archives.

Secondary Sources, unpublished

Compiled Service Records on microfilm at the United States Archives for: Benjamin Fitzpatrick, James G. Fitzpatrick, Marion Hill Fitzpatrick, Francis Fitzpatrick, and Henry C. Greene.

Compiled Service Records for Georgia State Confederate Soldiers on microfilm at the Georgia Department of Archives and History, Atlanta, for: Alexander Fitzpatrick and William B. White, Sr.

Daughters of the American Revolution application for Katie Elizebeth Fitzpatrick, National Society of the Daughters of the American Revolution, 1947.

Green, Thomas M.: "Small Slaveholders in Crawford County, Georgia, 1822-1861," honors paper presented to the Department of History, Harvard College, Cambridge, Massachusetts, 1978.

Hodges, Amanda Leigh: "Letters to Amanda," paper presented to an undergraduate history class at Agnes Scott College, Decatur, Georgia, 1997.

Lee, David: "The White Family of Crawford County, Georgia," manuscript made available to the editors by Mr. Lee.

Massey, Sue Kosciuszko: "Marion Hill Fitzpatrick: the Life of A Confederate Soldier," paper presented to an undergraduate history class at the University of Virginia, Charlottesville, Virginia, 1993.

Miller, Ann L.: "Historic Structure Report, Phase II" report prepared for the National Trust for Historic Preservation, Montpelier, Montpelier Station, Virginia, July, 1990.

Periodicals

Bryan, T. Conn, editor, "Letters of Two Confederate Officers: William Thomas Conn and Charles Augustus Conn," *The Georgia Historical Quarterly*, Vol. XLVI: 2 (1962): 169-195.

Bryan, T. Conn, editor, "Conn-Brantley Letters," *The Georgia Historical Quarterly*, Vol. LV: 3 (1973): 437-441.

Hortman, Tina: "Elim Baptist Church Proceedings" *Central Georgia Genealogical Society Quarterly*, (1989): 113-114.

Howell, Tina, contributor: "Obituaries in the Macon Telegraph and News," *Central Georgia Cenealogical Society Quarterly*, Vol. 7:3: 93.

Pulliam, David L.: "The Clopton House" *Richmond News*, Saturday news Supplement, February 16, 1901, from the files of the research library of the Virginia Historical Society, Richmond, Virginia.

Steger, Charles A.: "The Texas Road," *East Texas Family Records Quarterly*, Fall, (1981): 1-4.

Confederate Veteran , January 1914 issue (Vol. XXIV, No. 1), January 1925 issue (Vol. XXXIII, No. 1.): 50-51.

Southern Historical Society Papers, "A Confederate Airship," 28 (1900): 303-305; "Minutes of the First Confederate Congress, First Session, Feb. 27, 1862," Vol. 44 (1923): 64-65.

Published Books

Alexander, General Edward Porter. *Military Memiors of A Confederate*. New York: Da Capo Press, 1993, [originally published: Charles Scribner's Sons, New York, 1907].

Bankston, Emmie Carnes, *History of Roberta and Crawford County, Georgia*. Macon, Georgia: Omni Press, 1976.

Caldwell, J.F.J. *The History of A Brigade of South Carolinians, First Known as "Gregg's" and Subsequently as "McGowans" Brigade*. Dayton: Moringside Press, 1992 (reprint).

Campbell, Davine Vining. *1840 Census of Macon County, Georgia*, Warner Robins, Georgia: Central Georgia Genealogical Society, 1988.

Chapla, John D. *48th Virginia Infantry*. Lynchburg, Virginia: H.E. Howard, 1989.

Childs, Essie Jone. *They Tarried in Taylor (A Georgia County)*. Warner Robins, Georgia: Central Georgia Genealogical Society, 1992.

Coleman, Kenneth, ed. *A History of Georgia*. Second Edition. Athens, Georgia: University of Georgia Press, 1996.

Cunningham, H.H. *Doctors in Gray, The Confederate Medical Service*. Baton Rouge: Louisania State University Press, 1993.

Dowdey, Clifford. *Lee's Last Campaign: The Story of Lee & His Men against Grant – 1864*. Bison Books. Lincoln: Univ. of Nebraska Press, 1993.

Dowdey, Clifford. *The Seven Days, The Emergence of Lee*. Bison Books. Lincoln: University of Nebraska Press, 1993.

Dowdey, Clifford. *The History of the Confederacy, 1832-1865*. New York: Barnes & Noble Books, 1992.

Dunlop W.S. *Lee's Sharpshooters; or, To the Forefront of Battle*. Dayton, Ohio: Morningside Press, 1992.

Faust, Patricia L., ed. *Historical Times Illustrated Encyclopedia of the Civil War*. New York: HarperPerennial, 1991.

Freeman, Douglas S. *Lee's Lieutenants, A Study in Command*, Three Volumes. New York: Charles Scribner's Sons, 1942, 1943, 1944.

Freeman, Douglas S. *R.E. Lee, A Biography*, 4 volumes. New York: Charles Scribner's Sons, 1948.

Furgurson, Ernest B. *Chancellorsville 1863, The Souls of the Brave*. New York: Alfred A. Knopf, 1992.

Gallagher, Gary W., ed. *Fighting for the Confederacy, The Personal Recollections of General Edward Porter Alexander*. Chapel Hill: The University of North Carolina Press, 1989.

Gallagher, Gary W. *The Confederate War*. Cambridge: Harvard University Press, 1997.

Hammock, Mansel, ed. *Letters to Amanda from Sergeant Major Marion Hill Fitzpatrick Company K, 45th Georgia Regiment, Thomas' Brigade, Wilcox's Division, Hill's Corps, CSA to his wife Amanda Olive White Fitzpatrick*. Culloden, Georgia, 1975.

Hays, Louise Frederick. *History of Macon County, Georgia*. Atlanta, Georgia: Stein Publishing, 1933.

Henderson, Lillian: *Roster of the Confederate Soldiers of Georgia*. 5 Volumes. Hapeville, Georgia: Logino & Porter, Inc., 1955-1962.

Henry, William R. *Marriage Records of Crawford County, Georgia, 1823-1899*. Warner Robins, Georgia: Central Georgia Genealogical Society, 1989.

Henry, William R. *1860 Census for Macon County*, Georgia, Warner Robins, Georgia.: Central Georgia Genealogical Society, Inc., 1985.

Hennessy, John J. *Return to Bull Run, The Campaign and Battle of Second Manassas*. New York: Simon & Schuster , 1993.

Katcher, Robert. *The Army of Robert E. Lee*. London: Arms and Armour Press, 1994, 1996.

Katcher, Robert. *The Civil War Source Book*. London: Arms and Armour Press, 1992.

Lawrence, Harold. *Methodist Preachers in Georgia, 1783-1900*. Tignall, Georgia: Boyd Publishing, 1984.

Long, E.B. and Long, Barbara. *The Civil War Day By Day, An Almanac, 1861-1865*. Garden City, New York: Doubleday, 1971.

Lutz, Francis Earle. *Chesterfield, An Old Virginia County*. Richmond, Virginia: William Byrd Press, 1954.

Melton, Ella Christie, and Augusta Griggs Raines. *History of Terrell County, Georgia*. Roswell, Georgia: W.H. Wolf, 1980.

McCrea, Henry Vaughan. *Red Dirt and Isinglass, A Wartime Biography of A Confederate Soldier*. Private printing, 1992.

Otto, Rhea Cumming. *1850 Census of Crawford County Georgia*. Warner Robins, Ga: Central Georgia Genealogical Society, Inc., 1986.

Rice, Bradley R. and Jackson, Harvey H. *Georgia*. Northridge California: Windsor Publications, 1988.

Rigdon, Raymond, ed. *Letters to Amanda from Sergeant Major Marion Hill Fitzpatrick, Company K, 45ᵗʰ Georgia Regiment, Thomas' Brigade, Wilcox's Division, Hill's Corps, CSA to His Wife Amanda Olive Elizabeth White Fitzpatrick, Revised Edition.* Nashville: Champion Resources, 1982. (Private printing.)

Rosier, William Henry and Fred Lamar Pearson, Jr. *The Grand Lodge of Georgia, Free and Accepted Masons, 1786-1980.* Macon, Georgia: Grand Lodge of Georgia, Free and Accepted Masons, 1983.

Sears, Stephen W. *Chancellorsville.* New York: Houghton Mifflin, Co., 1996.

Sears, Stephen W. *To the Gates of Richmond: The Peninsula Campaign.* New York: Houghton Mifflin, 1992.

Shattuck, Gardiner H., Jr. *A Shield and a Hiding Place: The Religious Life of Civil War Armies.* Macon: Mercer University Press, 1987.

Smedlund, William S. *Camp Fires of Georgia's Troops, 1861-1865.* Kennesaw, Georgia: Kennesaw Mountain Press, 1994.

Sommers, Richard J. *Richmond Redeemed: The Siege at Petersburg.* Garden City, New York: Doubleday & Co., Inc., 1981.

Stackpole, Edward J. *Chancellorsville, Lee's Greatest Battle.* Harrisburg: The Stackpole Company, 1958.

Steger, Charles A. *Law's Chapel, A History & Records, 1853-1976.* Atlanta, Texas: Charles A. Steger for the 1976 homecoming of Law's Chapel United Methodist Church, 1976.

Steger, Charles A., compiler, Margaret R. Nevin editor. *William and Jane Law and Some of Their Descendants.* Decorah, Iowa: Anundsen Publishing, 1985.

Taylor, George Braxton. *Virginia Baptist Ministers, Sixth Series, 1914-1934, with Supplement.* Lynchburg, Virginia: J.P. Bell Co., Inc., 1935.

Wade, Roland E. *The Langford Legacy.* Waco, Texas: Texican Press, 1986.

Weisiger, III, Benjamin B. *Old Manchester & Its Environs.* Richmond: William Byrd Press, 1993.

Wiley, Bell Irvin. *The Life of Johnny Reb, The Common Soldier of the Confederacy.* Baton Rouge: Louisiana State University Press, 1988.

Wiley Bell Irvin and Hirst D. Milhollen. *Embattled Confederates: An Illustrated History of Southerners at War.* New York: Harper & Row, 1964.

Wynn, A. Evans. *Southern Lineages, Records of Thirteen Families.* Atlanta, Georgia: published by the author, printed by Walter W. Brown Publishing Co., 1940.

History of the Baptist Denomination in Georgia, with Biographical Compendium and Portrait Gallery of Baptist Ministers and Other Georgia Baptists. Atlanta, Georgia: Jas. P. Harrison & Co., 1881.

Index

The following index does not attempt to list every reference to Marion Hill Fitzpatrick or his wife, Amanda. Such references were too numerous to list.

*Letters to Amanda: The Civil War Letters of Marion
  Hill Fitzpatrick, Army of Northern Virginia*
ed. Jeffrey C. Lowe and Sam Hodges

Book Design: Marc A. Jolley
Text Font: Book Antiqua 10/12
Book Jacket Design by Mary Frances Burt
Printed by BookCrafters on 50# Booktext Natural
  offset, smyth sewn, and covered in Roxite Linen
Printed in the United States